ENGLISH RECUSANT LITERATURE
1558–1640

Selected and Edited by
D. M. ROGERS

Volume 326

TOMAS DE VILLACASTIN
A Manuall of Devout Meditations
1618

TOMAS DE VILLACASTIN
A Manuall of Devout Meditations
1618

The Scolar Press
1976

ISBN 0 85967 342 1

Published and printed in Great Britain by
The Scolar Press Limited, 59-61 East Parade,
Ilkley, Yorkshire and
39 Great Russell Street,
London WC1

NOTE

Reproduced (original size) from a copy in the Bodleian Library, by permission of the Curators.

References: Allison and Rogers 848; STC 16877.

A
MANVALL
OF DEVOVT
MEDITATIONS AND
EXERCISES,

Inſtructing how to pray
mentally .

*Drawne for the moſt part , out of
the ſpirituall Exerciſes of
B. F. Ignatius .*

DEVIDED INTO THREE BOOKES.

Written in Spaniſh by the R . F.
Thomas de Villa-caſtin of the
Society of IESVS.

AND

Tranſlated into Engliſh by a Father of
the ſame SOCIETY.

Permiſſu Superiorum , Anno 1618.

TO THE
RELIGIOVS
BROTHERS,
OF THE SOCIETY
OF IESVS.

In the English Nouiship at
LIEGE.

R ELIGIOVS
BROTHERS,
I send you heer
a Manual of spiri-
tuall Exercises, set forth some
yeares ago, in the Spanish
tongue, by *Fa. Thomas de Villa-*
castin of your Society, now
* 2   translated

trâflated into Englifh: which doubtleſſe will produce fpecial vertues in you, who haue the fame fpirit, wherewith it was written. And this hath moued me to prefent the fame to you, in whom I hoped my fmall labours heerein fhould be moſt aboundantly recompenſed, by the increaſe of your fpirituall comfort and profit.

I was furthermore induced heereunto, becauſe I deemed no Booke more fit to be prefented vnto you then this, being deriued, as it feemeth, from the very fountayne of Bleſſed *F. Ignatius* his Spirituall Exerciſes. And I could not doubt, but you the

Sonnes

Sonnes of so worthy a Father
would receaue with great affection and tendernes an Or-
phane of so worthy a Parent.

Another reason was, for
that I hauing receaued so many, and continuall benefits
from your Society (to whom
I am euer more then most obliged) and neuer yet finding
opportunity to shew my selfe
gratefull answerable to my
desires : I thought this least
occasion not to be neglected,
in offering so small a present
vnto you, in signe at least, of
gratefull memory towardes
your Holy Order.

In this Manuall ; you
may behold and contemplate
most perfectly, the liuely ver-

*3   tues

tues of our Sauiour, & of his
Blessed Mother, propounded
vnto you for your dayly ex-
crcise of Meditation . Heere
may you learne to follow, &
trace out the footsteps of true
Pouerty, Humility, Charity,
Obedience, & the like. Heere
may you tast spiritually of the
most pleasant fruite, which
from these deuout and pious
meditations is gathered. In a
word heere may you exercise
your selues in all the heroicall acts of Vertue which our
Lord & Maister Christ Iesus,
the most exact and perfect
patterne of all Perfection, left
vnto vs for example.

I will not be tedious
thereby to detayne you from
the

DEDICATORY.

the triall of what I haue promised by meditating the Mysteries that ensue. It shall suffice me, that you willbe pleased to take in good part this
my least labour, and now &
then in these and other your
deuotions to remember

Your humble and
deuout seruant

I. W.

* 4 　　THE

THE
PREFACE OF THE
AVTHOR TO THE
Christian Reader.

*O N E of the principal
Reasens which mo-
ued me to write this
Manuall of pious
Considerations, for the help of
such as vse to pray mentally, is
the great desire I know many Religious, & other setular Persons,
seruants of God, haue of some
briefe Treatise, whereby they
might with profit spend their time
in prayer. Wherefore I haue
thought*

thought good briefly to set downe
the summe of that, which many
graue Authors, and Maisters of
spirituall life, haue more largely
and profitably handled : Whose
doctrine (especially those of our
own Order)i haue endeauored to
follow, vsing for my cheife guide
heerin the spirituall Exercises of
our glorious Father B. Ignatius,
to adorne this my little Manual,
desiring to haue that portable
in our bosome, which ought euer
to be fixed in our soule & hart,
saying with he Spouse : Fasci-
culus myrrhæ dilectus meus
mihi, inter vbera mea com-
morabitur : A undle of myrrh
my beloued vnto me, betwixt
my brests he shall abide.

The Aduertisments placed
* 5   in

THE PREFACE.

in the beginning, do particulerly
shew how to treat and conuerse
with the diuine Maiesty, togeather with the vse of the Meditations & Considerations set down
in the three Books following. The
first whereof shallbe of the last
things of man. The second, and
third, of the Life, Passion, Death
and Resurrection of Christ, placing in euery Meditation foure
points, ech one of them sufficient
for the Exercise of one or more
houres, about three seueral things
which euery Point shall contayne,
to wit, Consideration, Examination, and Application to the fruit
which out of that full measure
of perfection, which Christ exercised in the whole course of his
life, may be gathered.

In

OF THE AVTHOR.

In the end of the third Booke, I adioyne also seuerall Meditations, directing vs both how to prepare our selues before, and how to giue thankes after the holy Communion; that time being far more fit for Meditation, then for vocall prayers. Thus much I propose briefly and plainly to the pious Reader : for whatsoeuer sauoureth of curiosity, cooleth deuotion, and hindreth Prayer, in which Truth not Eloquence is to be sought.

But because nothing of this is to be obtayned without the grace of God, I most humbly beseech him to graunt vntovs such plenty therof, that his most holy life and death may be vntovs a perfect patterne, rule, and guide

of

THE PREFACE.

of all our thoughts, words, and deeds. That (like true fouldiers of his fpiritual warfare) following our Captaine Chrift Iefus, we may be partakers heere in this world of his grace, and in heauen of his Glory. Amen.

A

A MANVALL
OF SPIRITVALL
EXERCISES.

For the help of such as desire
to vse mentall Prayer.

The Introduction.

 E that desireth to in-
crease and go forward
in spirituall life, let
him know, that the
certaine and vndoub-
ted way to the same,
is the interiour and mutuall communication with Almighty God, performed in the holy vse and exercise
of Prayer: because in prayer vertues
are obtayned, conserued, and augmented. Prayer (as the Apostle S.

A   Iames

Iames fayth) afcending vnto heauen,
before the tribunall feat of Almighty
God bringeth vnto men euery good
and perfect gift, caufing fuch a league
and vnion betweene God and them,
that it maketh them apt to receaue infinite graces and benefits from his diuine Maiefty.

Daniel by prayer conuerted the
fierce and hungry Lyons into meeke
lambs. Prayer made the fire to loofe
his force, being not able to burne the
three Children in the middeft of the
flaming fornace of Babylon. Prayer
ftayed the courfe, & altered the vni-
forme motion of the heauens, giuing
power vnto the voice of man to ftop
and detaine the Sunne and Moone,
and that for fo many houres as was
neceffary for obtayning the victory
againft his enemies. Iacob through
the vertue and efficacy of prayer,
preuayled againft the Angell. Yea
Prayer tyed the hands and infinite
power(if fo we may fay) of the Lord
of Angells : for by the prayers of
Moyfes Almighty God feemed to be
as it were difabled to chaftice & ftrike
offending

offending people, when he sayd vnto his seruant: Suffer me that my fury may be angry against them; as if he should say : detaine me not with thy prayers. Prayer finally obtayneth pardon for whatsoeuer offences : the Publican getteth remission of his sins, and the Prodigall child returneth againe into fauour and friendship with his Father .

Prayer therefore being so profitable and necessary vnto spirituall life, and contayning withall so many and so great helps and excellencyes, as we haue seene, obtayning by the diuine vertue & power therof whatsoeuer it will in heauen and earth ; it is necessary that no day passe (especially with a Religious person who desireth perfection) without prayer, but that he spend therin one or more houres.

Some peraduenture will heere say, that although he grant this exercise to be both expedient and necessary, yet not for him who knoweth not how to pray, nor discourse therin : because considerations do not oc-
A 2   curre

curre wherewith to dilate and extend
his difcourfes; and fo his fkeine of
threed being cut off and prefently
ended , therewith the guſt and defire
he had to perfeuer in this holy exercife , is alfo ended , and he wearied :
for that as it feemeth vnto him , he
profiteth not at all , and thus he leaueth it quite off .

  To whome I anfwere (and it
is very much to be noted) that if
fuch a one fhould vnderſtand, that
Prayer doth rather confiſt in affects
and defires of the Will, then in difcourfes and fpeculations of the Vnderſtanding ; he would not find fuch
difficulty , nor yet be difcouraged, &
difcomforted fo much , nor would
intermit and leaue off his prayer fo
foone : and much leſſe , if he knew ,
that (as the directors and Maiſters of
fpirituall life do obſerue) great heed
is to be taken, that the fpeculation of
the Vnderſtanding , be not vfed in
exceffe, becaufe it doth greatly hinder
the deuotion, prayer, & affect of the
Will, efpecially when we intertaine
our felues with fubtill and curious
                              confide-

confiderations .

Whence it commeth to paffe (as experience teacheth) that many tymes ignorant and vnlearned perfons, pray better and are more deuout , then thofe who haue much more learning , and their prayer alfo often fucceedeth better , becaufe they do not bufy nor diftract themfelus with curiofityes, but forthwith endeauour by prayer and the firft occurring confiderations , to moue and excite the Will to Affections . And to them fuch humble and ordinary confiderations, caufe more deuotion and moue them more , working in them greater effects, then high and curious do in the learned .

Let vs bring an example , feeing we haue fuch plenty of them in holy Scripture, where the holy Ghoft with very plaine and common comparifons , doth declare vnto vs moft high and fubtill thinges . As in thofe words of the 54. Pfalme , where the Royall Prophet fayeth : Who will giue me wings, as a doue, and I will fly, and reft? And S. Ambrofe afketh

A 3   the

the queſtion : Wherefore the holy
Prophet deſiring to fly, and to aſcend
aloft, required the wings of a doue,
and not of other birds, notwithſtanding there be others more ſwift then
the doue ? And he thus anſwereth,
becauſe he knew wel that to fly vp to
the height of perfection, and to pray
well, are fitter the winges of a doue,
that is to ſay, the ſimple and right of
hart, then thoſe of ſharpe and ſubtill
Vnderſtanding.

Hence it followeth, that if our
Lord do ſhew vnto thee this fauour,
that with a plaine and ordinary conſideration (wherof there be many in
this Manuall, as if by the only conſideration how God became man,
was borne, layd in a manger, and
dyed vpon the Croſſe for thee) thou
art inflamed with his loue, and with
deſire of humbling and mortifying
thy ſelfe. and in this thou imployeſt
the whole houre, thou haſt thē made
a far better prayer and much more
profitable, then if thou haddſt performed it with many diſcourſes, and
with high and very learned conſiderations

rations and conceites : for that thou
haſt imployed and detayned thy ſelfe
in the very beſt, and moſt ſubſtantial
part of Prayer, and in that which is
the end and fruite of the ſame.

Neither doth the perfection of
Prayer conſiſt in hauing certaine ſenſible guſtes and conſolations, nor in
hauing great and vnwonted contemplation, for this is not in our owne
power, nor yet in performing the
ſayd acts with ſuch ſenſible feeling;
But in this the fruit conſiſteth, that
thou ariſe from Prayer very humble,
patient, obedient, indifferent, and
mortified. And ſeeing that this is alwayes in our owne power (the grace
of God preſuppoſed) know, that if
thou wilt thy ſelfe, thou mayſt euer
make a good and fruitefull prayer,
which is a thing of very great comfort, for thoſe who giue themſelues
to this holy exerciſe.

Wherfore it ſeemeth vnto me,
that hauing layd ſo good a foundation in this Introduction, and ſowed
in ſo good an earth (as are the harts
of ſuch as deſire Perfection) ſo im-

A 4   porant

portant feed , we may well hope to
gather (with the Diuine affiftance)
not only , Fruite of thirty, but alfo
of threefcore and an hundred fold.
Efpecially obferuing the enfuing Ad-
uertifements (it being a matter of
no fmall moment , to performe our
prayer in the beft manner) which
therefore muft be read with leafure ,
not once , but many tymes , and that
with attention & confideration, leaft
we walke as blind men in the way of
this holy exercife .

    Thefe Aduertifments inftruct
how we ought to prepare our felues,
how to enter , continue, fpeake, and
treat with Almighty God in Prayer;
they fhew the fruit and profit which
thence is to be gathered , of which
though fome(to the eyes of worldly
iudgment) feeme not to be of fuch
importance, yet are they fuch in regard of the end which is pretended ,
for as much as they difpofe to the attayning of great matters : without
the which we can very hardly be recollected and deuout And nothing
is to be efteemed as little, but of great
               moment

moment, when it is done with intent
and desire therby the more to please
and serue our great God. Wherupon
the Holy Ghost sayth: that he who
feareth God, neglecteth nothing, neither in little, nor in much: because
that euery little helpeth and furthe-
reth that which is great, & the great
cannot be construed without the
little.

The I. Advertisement.

How we ought to prepare the
matter for Prayer.

IN the Euening, before we go to
bed, let vs euer read one or more
points of the Meditations contayned in this booke, wherof the day
next following we are to make our
Prayer. And the better to put away
fowle and vncleane imaginations,
which in the night more then at other
times the Diuell vseth to raise in the
phansy, let vs fall a sleep, thinking
vpon the aforesayd exercise. And in
the morning as soone as we awake,
let vs offer vnto God al our thoughts,

A 5 words,

wordes, & deeds of the day to come.
This done, we may presently call to
mind, the points of the exercise
which we read ouer night, endeauouring to imprint in our memory
the verityes of our holy Fayth : for if
the Vnderstanding be occupied in o-
ther extrauagant imaginations, they
will be an occasion of distraction,
sloth, and irckfomnes in prayer, yea
and a cause fometymes the fooner to
leaue it off.

    S. Bonauenture and S. Iohn
Climacus, efteeme this aduife very
important : and it may well be that
from them our B. Father Ignatius
had the fame, whom we know both
to haue vfed it himfelfe, and to haue
commended it vnto vs his children
very ferioufly. For we read of him,
that not only in his beginning, but
alfo euen after he was become an old
man, he did read & prepare his prayer ouer night, and went to reft with
this care of well performing the fame
in the morning. No man therefore is
to thinke, that this thing only is to
ferue for Nouices & yong beginners.
And

And generally this holy man, our B. Father was wont to say, that vpon the obseruation of these & like aduises (which he calleth Additions, & we Aduertisements) dependeth in great part the good successe of prayer; and that we reap the desired fruit & profit thereby. And we who be his children, do proue very ordinarily, that when we go well prepared, and do exactly obserue these aduises, our prayer succeedeth well; and that it falleth out contrary when we are re-misse and negligent therein.

The II. Advertisement.

How we ought to prepare our selues to speake vnto God, in mentall Prayer.

A Little while before we enter into Prayer, let vs consider what we go about to do, and with whom we are to speake and ne-gotiate. For it is the counsaile of the holy ghost, which sayeth, That before prayer we prepare our soule : & to go without preparation, is as it

A 6   were

were to tempt God, pretending to obtayne the end and fruit of prayer without vfing the meanes ordayned to attayne the fame. This is alfo S. Thomas and S. Bonauentures doctrine, who do greatly commend vnto vs, that we difpofe and prepare our felues for Prayer by ordinary means, not expecting miracles frō Almighty God without neceffity : much like as if one fhould fay , I wiil not eate, for God can preferue mv life without meate , for this were to temp't God, whofe will is that we conferue our temporall life which he hath giuē vs by proportionable means for that end, which is , at accuftomed tymes to take our conuenient repaft.

In like manner it is the will of God , that we pray well , and with great attention, but he graunteth this ordinarily vnto vs , by the conuenient meanes of due preparation , as a thing very neceffary , for the efchewing of the forefayd inconueniences in our cōmunication with him in Prayer. For if experience teach, that thofe who go to fpeake with a King, to obtayne

taine some temporall fauour , they
first forethinke and consider , with
what reuerence and ceremonies they
are to enter, how they are to stand in
his Rovall presence, what they are to
say, and with what respect and exteriour comportement they are to
carry themselues : With how much
more reason then ought he , who
is to negotiate , and present himselfe before the King of Kings , and
Lord of Lords, to handle a businesse
of such consequence and importance
as is the saluation of his soule : How
meete (I say) is it that he enter , and
be present before such a Maiesty,
withall the care and reuerence afore
mentioned, yea & with much more
if it were possible . For so much difference there is betweene King and
King , Lord and Lord, businesse and
businesse , as betweene Heauen and
earth , Creator and creature, God
and man.

THE

THE III. ADVERTISEMENT.
Of the Place conuenient for Prayer.

VV HEN we will talke and communicate with any friend of ours concerning matters of importance, and wherin we receiue much contentement, we commonly take him aside, or walke with him into the fields, or we shut our selues vp in some chamber, wher no body may interrupt or hinder vs: After the same manner it is most expedient for him that desireth to pray well, and to conuerse and negotiate with Almighty God concerning his saluation (which is of more weight and consequence, then any thing ypon earth) to seeke a place most retyred and quiet, where no body may disturbe or hinder him.

A Religious man, if he may make his Prayer in the Quire, or Church, it is better (being in the presence of the most B. Sacrament) but if this may not be, his Cell or Chamber wilbe best. A secular person

ſon in his Oratory, and if he haue
none, let him procure to ſhut himſelfe into ſome retyred place, ſhutting
the windows and doors of his chamber, for ſo Chriſt our Lord counſai-
leth, ſaying : When thou ſhalt pray,
enter into thy chamber, and hauing
ſhut the doore, pray to thy Father in
ſecret : for with this ſecreſy and quietnes the ſenſes are more recollected,
and the ſoule more liuely and attent.
Of this we haue example in S. Antony, Arſenius, Macarius, Pacomius
and other Saints, in whoſe hiſtoryes
we read, that they betooke theſelues
into deſert and ſolitary places, that
ſo they might be the more retyred.

And we ſee that our Lord himſelfe (the Saint of all Saints) did practiſe the ſame ; for when he was to
begin the preaching of his Ghoſpell,
he retyred himſelfe into the deſert,
remayning fourty dayes and fourty
nights in Prayer : and other tyms he
went very often to ſpend the night
into the mountaynes and gardens,
where retyring himſelf for the time,
and leauing his Diſciples, he ſet him-

ſelfe

selfe all alone to pray ; not for that
his most sacred Humanity stood in a-
ny need of a retyred place to pray in
(wherein nothing could be an impe-
diment vnto him in that holy Exercise) but only to shew and instruct vs
what necessitywe haue of a retired &
quiet place to pray with attention &
recollection of mind. And certaine it
is that if darknesse did not help much
vnto recollection , S . Antony the
Abbot would not haue complayned
of the Sunne, that when it did rise, it
depriued him with his beames and
brightnes, of the quiet of contemplation . And although it be true,
that to make choice altogether of a
solitary life , is not fit for all, but rather for very few ; yet to seeke a solitary , retyred, and quiet place to conuerse alone for somedayes with God,
and euery day for the ordinary tyme
of Prayer (wherof we now treate)
appertayneth vnto euery one.

But let vs put the case , that we
cannot haue any retyred place , nor
any such opportunity as we speake
of, yet were not this a sufficient cause
to

to say, that we could not, or had
not any such quiet place wherin to
pray, as hath been sayd : for he that
is desirous to pray, and to adore
God present in euery place, may do
it in any place. For not only Adam
in paradise, but Ioseph in the prison,
Iob vpon the dunghill, Daniel a-
mong the Lyons, and Ionas prayed
& blessed God in the VVhales belly.
And we read of the holy Virgin S.
Agnes, that the fowle and vncleane
place whereinto she was thrust, became vnto her a house of Prayer. And
if this be true, as indeed it is, it followeth that we may pray, honour,
and praise God in any place whatsoeuer.

The IIII. Advertisement.

VVhat time is best for mentall Prayer.

NEXT after a retired and secret
place, a conuenient and fit time
is to be procured for Prayer:
and the best time is (as S. Bonauen-
ture noteth) after midnight till the
breake of day ; & out of all this time,
we

we may choose the houres of meditation, wherin the most easy is the first
houre in the morning To which effect it will be needfull that we lead an
ordered life, going to bed at such an
houre, that hauing slept so much as is
necessary, we may rise in due time:
for so we find that when God would
visit his Saints & discouer vnto them
his sacred misteries, he vsed ordinarily
to make choice of the night; so he
did vnto Samuel disclosing vnto him
meruailous secrets in the temple And
to the most glorious Virgin sending
vnto her his embassage from heauen
by his Angel. So to S Ioseph, admo-
nishing him to fly into Ægipt And to
the three Kinges, aduising them that
they should not returne vnto Herod.

These, and the like reuelations
Almighty God doth vse to reueale by
night, as his Prophet saith, which is
an euident signe that this time is
most apt for the couersation with God
& to contemplate celestial things, for
then with the darcknesse and silence
of the night, with the repose and quiet
of all creatures, the mind is more re-
collect

collect and attent. And so confesseth
Dauid, that at midnight and in the
morning he rose to pray, and to blesse
Almighty God. But notwithstanding
this time be most conuenient for
mentall praier, yet if then we cannot
doe it, we may take any houre of the
morning or euening; and if in that
also we be hindered, then the neerer
vnto the morning or euening the better, and so much more profitable
wilbe our recollection: for the neerer
the morning, the more our spirits
haue vigour and force, the head is
better disposed, and the body refre-
shed: and in the euening, the refecti-
on taken at noone doth lesse hinder,
and so we shall find our selues more
able and ready to pray, and more apt
to endure and perseuer therin.

THE V. ADVERTISEMENT.

Of the presence of God, helping to Atten-
tion and Reuerence in Prayer.

H AVING chosen the time and
place where we are to pray;
first of all we are to make the
signe

figne of the Croffe , and ioyning our
hands togeather ftand and paufe fot
the fpace of a Pater Nofter , then lifting vp our hart , and the powers of
our foule to heauen we are to behold,
and as it were to place our felues in
the prefence of the liuing God,
being vndoubtedly there by effence,
prefence , and power : confidering
that we are not all alone , but before
that great and infinite maiefty of Almighty God, then , and there , looking vpon vs according as the great
Prophet Elias did when he faid : our
Lord liueth , the God of Ifrael , in
whofe fight I ftand . And herewith
quickning our faith , let vs make to
this our Lord and God (three in perfon and one in effence , whome innumerable Angels doe adore) a great
and profound reuerence , bending
before him the knees of our hart , and
body vnto the ground , once , twice ,
and thrice , adoring and worfhipping
the three diuine perfons , firft the Father , then the Sonne , laftly the holy
Ghoft .

　　And this humiliation wherwith
　　　　　　　　　　　　　　　we

we begin our Prayer, is not only to
be exteriour and with the body, but
also interiour and with the mind, entring into our selues, and considering
that we haue not any thing of our selues, either in Being, Substance, or
value, nor any thing but innumerable
sinnes, for which we deserue euerlasting paine and torment. And this
may be an effectuall meanes to pray
well, for by this humiliation the iust
become more iust, and the holy more
hóly. Wherof giue testimony Abraham, Tobias, Daniel, and other
Saints, of whome the holy Scripture
relateth, that they began their praiers
by humbling themselues. And by this
sinners obtaine mercie, and become
iust. Manasses king of Israel (a great
sinner) and the publican in the Gos-
pell, by humbling himself in his Prayer, went thence iustified. And so shal
we, without doubt, if we humble our
selues in like manner, as we ought to
do.

THE

THE VI. ADVERTISMENT.

How, and with what compoſition of body we ought to pray.

THE compoſition of body in Prayer, is to be waighed, and vſed according to the health, diſpoſition, and forces thereof: now kneeling if we be in good health and able, now proſtrate vpon the ground, ſometimes ſtanding, eſpecially if drowſinesdo moleſt and trouble vs: ſometimes ſitting with humility, if our indiſpoſitions require it: yet ſo, that the humble måner of our ſitting, declare the deſire we haue not to reſt, but to pray. For if the body ſhould be in paine and torment, we cannot haue the repoſe and quiet of mind which is required for this holy exerciſe: although ſometimes it wilbe good to mortifie and puniſh the body therin alſo, not graunting all that it aſketh: eſpecially if therby we finde our ſelues remiſſe, negligent, and diſtracted.

We haue many examples in the

the holy Scripture of the exteriour
reuerence which the holy Saints vfed
in praier. Of that great feruant of
God Moyfes, it faid, that to pray vnto God in the mount Synai, he did
proftrate himfelf vpon the ground.
And of Daniel, that he praied bowing
both knees vnto the ground. This
māner of reuerence did our Lord Iefus Chrift himfelfe vfe, in the longe
praier made vnto his eternall Father
in the garden, where kneeling downe
he proftrated himfelfe vpon the gro-
und, and it is credible that he did the
fame other times, as when he went to
pray in the mountaines.

This example, the Apoftles
and other holy Saints haue followed.
And amongft the reft it is recorded
of S. Iames the yonger, that through
continuall kneeling both by day and
night, his knees became as hard as
thofe of a Camell : teaching vs thereby the great efteem we ought to haue
of exteriour reuerence in Prayer, as
a thing fingularly helping interiour
deuotion, grea ly glorifying God, &
of meruailous edification vnto our
Neigh-

Neighbours. Let vs therefore euer
procure to glorify him, and edify
our Neighbours when we pray.

THE VII. ADVERTISEMENT.

How we ought to conuerſe and ſpeake with God in Prayer.

THE manner to conuerſe with
Almighty God in mental Prayer, muſt be not with exteriour,
but interiour words : not long, or
for all the time our Prayer endureth,
but briefe and in few words, according as our Bleſſed Sauiour teacheth
vs in the Ghoſpell, ſaying : When
you pray ſpeake not much. And S.
Auguſtine expounding this place of
the Ghoſpell noteth, that it is one
thing to ſpeake much, and diſcourſe
with the Vnderdanſting, and another
thing to ſtay long in the act of loue,
and affections of the Will. Wherefore the former is that which is to be
auoyded in Prayer, for that is only
to ſpeake and prattle much: wheras
the buſines or nature of Prayer, conſiſteth not in many words, neither is
it

it the way to negotiate with Almighty God, to vſe much Rhetorike, a-
bundance of diſcourſes, and curious
conceits, but rather by ſighes, teares,
and compunction of hart For although we ſay nothing with our lips,
we may cry neuertheles with our hart
as Moyſes did, vnto whom our Lord
ſayd : Why cryeſt thou vnto me ?
Wheras the Holy man ſaid not a
word, but only prayed with ſo great
feruour and efficacy in his hart, as
if he had cryed out aloud vnto God.

    We therefore in this manner
ought alſo to make our prayer and
cry vnto Almighty God, and if peraduenture, heere with we find our
ſelues diſtracted, being not able without diſcourſe to proſecute our Prayer
with that quiet and repoſe we deſire,
but rather find our ſelues aſſaulted
with diuers thoughts & diſtractions,
it will be good to make vſe of a remedy which the R. Father M. Iohn
Auila giueth in one of his ſpirituall
Epiſtles, ſaying : That we muſt caſt
our ſelues at the feet of Chriſt, being
ſorry for the fault, and cauſe giuen
                    B   of

of that diftraction: And fo complayning and lamenting, in humble and
louing manner, we may fay vocally
thefe, or the like words.

How is it poffible, O my God,
that thou wilt permit, that I fo bafe a
creature, and fo vile a worme, ftand
in prefence of thee my Creatour &
Maker with fo little reuerence, attention and deuotion, and fo much di-
ftracted! Do not permit fo vnworthy
a thing, I befeech thee. Then turne
to thy foule, and fay vnto her: O
my foule, reflect vpon thy felfe, look
what thou doft and with whom thou
fpeakeft. Confider, that perhaps
this may be the laft houre that thou
haft to pray in, and that this may be
the laft day of thy life.

This done, let vs returne to
our Prayer againe and interiour communication with God, as hath beene
fayd, and if neuertheles we cannot
caft off and be rid of thefe diftractiós,
as being perhaps the iuft & deferued
chaftizement of Almighty God, for
the great and manifold finnes of our
life paft, and prefent negligences,
we

we may say vnto him.

O my God, I do accept with a
very good will, and do reioyce to
receiue from thy hands this Crosse of
aridity & drynesse, this distraction,
discomfort, and spirituall solitude of
being thus forsaken of thee, and left
to my selfe. And we may be assured
this patience and humility, and this
conformity with the will of Almighty God, to be a very good Prayer,
and more acceptable vnto his diuine
Maiesty, then the Prayer would be
which we desired to make. for sanctity and holynes of life doth not con-
sist in hauing the gift of Prayer, but
in doing the will of Almighty God.
And if his diuine Maiesty do please
to conduct vs by this way, yet euen
therein we shall not faile to become
holy and perfect, as well as in the o-
ther.

THE

THE VIII. ADVERTISEMENT.

VVith what force, and attention we ought to pray.

TO the end that our Prayer be performed with recollection & attention, it importeth very much, not to take it in hand as a businesse of little, or small moment, not rashly but aduisedly, not sleepily & drowsily, nor with a slow and cull hart, but with a liuely, attent, and vndaunted courage: for otherwise we should not be voyd of fault, & might iustly feare the malediction and curse of the Prophet Ieremy, who saith: Cursed be he that doth the worke of our Lord fraudulently. And it is manifest that this worke of God mentioned by the Prophet, is Prayer.

Neither yet is such and so great intention and force to be vsed in Prayer, as if by force of armes, as we may say) we would seeme to get & conserue attention and deuotion For so in lieu of pleasing & sweet milke, we should wring out bloud, as the

wisedome

wisedome of God signifyeth in the
Prouerbes. And so this labour and
paine would serue to no other end,
but to breake and weary the head,
and ouerthrow our health: causing
in vs a certaine feare and horrour of
this holy exercise, the which also we
should then be forced to intermit &
leaue off in the mid-way, for want of
forces to continue, as they vse to be
wanting vnto the way-faring man,
when he maketh ouermuch hast in
the beginning of his iourney.

Wherfore to eschew these two
extremes, such a moderation is to be
vsed, that neither by ouermuch striuing for attention the head be wearyed, nor yet by ouermuch carelesnesse
and negligence our thoughts be permitted to wander without restraint:
for one of the things which are wont
to trouble and hinder vs very much
in Prayer, are these importunate &
vnseasonable thoughts which occurr
as well through our owne frailty as
also by the suggestion, subtilty, and
malice of the Diuell, labouring to
hinder our prayers and attention.

B 3   Wherefore

Wherefore the remedies which we are to vſe for the ouercoming of them with the grace of God may be theſe that follow .

Firſt , not to behold , regard , ſearch into, or figʰt againſt euery one of them in particuler , but rather turning our mynd from them , to caſt them away , yea and makirg no account of them , to proſecute and goon without ſtay in our meditatiõ already begun .

The ſecond and moſt principal remedy, muſt be the true loue of Almighty God , for therby is obtayned a ſweet repoſe, and deuout attention in Prayer . Heereby with eaſe all vaine and fruitleſſe thoughts are expelled and baniſhed out of the mind , both in , and out of Prayer For as truth it ſelfe ſaith , Where thy treaſure is, there is thy hart alſo; that is to ſay , wherſoeuer our loue and affection is , and the thing we much eſteeme, there is our thought: ſo experience it ſelfe teacheth , that whatſoeuer we loue or deſire much , that we continually thinke on without labour

labour or difficulty: yea and without any endeauour of ours, euen of themselues our thoughts will euer be running vpon that which our hart loueth and desireth.

Let vs procure therefore, with all our endeauour, to increase & go forward in the loue of God; for by how much the more we shall loue him, so much the more easily shall we thinke of him, and without labour or difficulty be vnited with him. And thus with a quiet & sweet repose we may find our desired attention and deuotion in Prayer.

The IX. Advertisement.

How in Prayer we are to passe from one point to another.

WHEN Almighty God shal moue our Will with any affection, through the cōsideration of any one poynt in that mistery wheron we meditate, we are not to passe vnto another, but therin if we can, to spend the whole houre or time of our Prayer, and so interrupting

B 4

rupting the difcourfe of our Vnderftanding, it is good to make a paufe
and ftay in fome affection and defire
of the Will, vntill we haue fatisfyed
our felfe therein, and imprinted it very well in our mind : becaufe for the
fpending of an houre or more in
Prayer, many points are not neceffary, nor variety of difcourfes and
confiderations, neither is it needfull
by and by to paffe from one confideration to another, or from one point
to another; but finding one which of
it felfe affoardeth fufficient matter to
worke ypon, abide fometyme therin, weighing and pondering it with
leafure & attention, vntill our Wil
be moued to fome affection of moment, or admiration of fuch or fuch a
benefit, or with fome fpeciall defire
of feruing our Lord, vvho hath laboured fo much to beftovv that benefit vpon vs. And vpon this we are
to infift, as long as it fhall endure,
though it be the vvhole time of our
Prayer.

　　This is a very important aduife,
and for fuch is left by our B. F. Ignatius

tius in his booke of Exercises, where
he sayth : That hauing found the
feeling and deuotion we desire, we
are to rest and stay there without anxiety or care to passe any further, vntill we be satisfyed. For this is the
end which we pretend and ayme at ;
this the fruit we are to reap therin ; &
finally this is the marke and scope,
whereunto we are to direct all the
meditations, considerations, and
discourses of our Vnderstanding.

Neither is it necessary that because we haue prouided two or three
points, therfore all must needs be run
ouer in our Meditation : for the nū-
ber & variety of points are set down
least matter of discourse be wanting,
and that if we should be dry and litle
moued with the consideration of a-
ny one point or mystery whereon we
meditate, we may passe to another.

And if, notwithstanding this, it
chance that we find our Will not to
be moued, all the tyme being spent
with passing from one consideration
to another, let vs not therfore afflict
and disquiet our selues : seeing the

B 5 will

will of Almighty God heerin is ful-
filled, which is the principall end we
are to pretend in Prayer, and not
our owne guſt and conſolation.

The X. Advertisement.

*How profitable a thing it is to repeat
one, and the ſelie ſame thing
ence, or oftener.*

IT is a matter of ſpeciall moment,
in the conſideration of the diuine
myſteries which in this booke we
haue briefly ſet downe, not to paſſe
euer any of them in haſt or ſleightly,
as hath beene ſayd, but by leaſure,
ſtaying in one & the ſame point, therby to ponder it throughly. For one
Myſtery thus well conſidered, will
profit vs more then many ſuperfici-
ally paſſed ouer.

Of this our Lord and Sauiour
Ieſus hath giuen vs example, who in
his Prayer in the garden, taught this
manner of prayer and perſeuerance
in one, and the ſame thing. For not
content to haue prayed once vnto his
Eternall Father, he repeated the
　　　　　　　　　　　ſame

same the second , and third tyme :
yea and the holy Euangelist addeth
that towards the end , longer then
before .

And for this, our B. F. Ignatius
in his booke of Spirituall Exercises ,
doth make so great account of the re-
petitions , which after euery Exercise
once, or twice he ordaineth to be
made : for that which at the first is
not found, may be afterwards found
by repetition of the same. And so our
Lord himselfe affirmeth : He that
seeketh findeth, & to him that knoc-
keth, it shalbe opened . So it hapned
vnto that woman of Chanaan , who
for her perseuerance in renewing oft
her petition vnto our Sauiour, obtayned of his Diuine Maiesty the desired health for her daughter. So also
it will happen with vs in Prayer, that
returning thereunto once, or more
often if need require, and for seuerall
dayes renewing and perseuering in
the same consideration , we come to
discouer more vnknown grounds, (or
to say better) more heauenly mysteries not knowne to vs before . Much
B 6   like

like as entring into a darke chamber
at the beginning we see little or nothing, but staying there a while we
come to see that, which we could not
see before.

THE XI. ADVERTISEMENT.

How we are to begin our Prayer.

IT is fit (generally speaking of all
those who giue themselues to the
practise of this holy Exercise) that
in the beginning and entrance therof
they alwayes make for the space of an
Aue Maria, the Prayer commonly
called Preparatory, which is as it
were a Preparation to begin Prayer,
saying thus :

I beseech thee O Lord, to direct
this houre, or tyme of Prayer, to thy
greater glory; bestowing vpon me
such plenty of thy grace, as shall be
necessary to performe it : and I humbly offer vp vnto thy Diuine Maiesty
whatsoeuer I shall thinke, say, or do,
according to thy holy will, and as it
shall be most pleasing vnto thee.

THE

THE XII. ADVERTISEMENT.

*How the Powers of our soule are to
be exercised in Prayer.*

MENTALL Prayer, whereof
heere we treate, is the worke
of the three Powers of the
soule: to wit, of the Memory, Vnderstanding, and Will . Noting by
the way , that in euery Mysterie and
point we take in hand, of all the Meditations of the books following, we
are to exercise these three powers in
Prayer , in manner following.

First vvith the Memory, we are
to call to mind Almighty God our
Lord, vvith whome wee speake,
setting before our eyes the point or
Mysterie on vvhich we are to meditate, beleeuing with a liuely faith the
truth therof .

Secondly vvith the Vnderstanding, vve are to discourse and consider those things vvhich best may help
to moue the Will , pondering and as
it were chewing them againe and a-
gaine by leasure , to the end we may
find

find our selues moued with the vertue and fruite included therein . For
that vvhich is not vvell chevved , is
neither bitter nor svveet : and so nei-
therSinne,nor Death,nor Iudgment,
nor Hell it selfe, is bitter or loathsome
vnto the sinner, because he doth not
ruminate and chevv these things,but
svvallovveth them vvhole , running
them ouer rashly vvithout any ma-
ture consideration at all, and little to
his profit .

　　　Hence it is also,that vve take no
gust , nor haue any feeling in the Mysteries of the Incarnation, Passion ,
and Resurrection of Christ : because
we do not throughly ruminate and
chew them . Let vs therefore bruize
and chew with our Vnderstanding
this graine of mustard-seed , sear-
ching out the precious and diuine
vertue which therein is hidden, that
is to say,within this holy and diuine
Mysterie : and we shall see by experience,that it doth not only heat and
bite vs, but also prouoke and cause
in vs teares of deuotion .

　　　Thirdly, with the Will we are

to draw out of that consideration sundry affections, some belonging to our selues, and others to Almighty God: for example, Detestation of our selus in regard of our offences against God, Sorrow for our sinnes, the Loue of God and his diuine Precepts, the giuing of thanks for benefits and fauours receiued, Desires of true and solide vertues, & of imitating Christ Iesus our Lord in those which he exercised in his most holy life : to witt, in Charity, Mercy, Humility, Patience, Meeknes, and Pouerty, and so in all the rest : Neglect & Contempt of all that the world esteemeth and loueth, seeing the small account this our highest Lord made of them in his life and death : great longing and feruent desires to suffer and shed our bloud for his diuine honour, pondering with attention and leasure in euery Mystery, some one of these vertues, vntill we imprint and settle in our Will an earnest desire to obtayne it.

And these be the acts which we are to exercise with the power of our
                                                    Will,

Will, in the consideratiō of the life &
Passion of Iesus Christ our Sauiour,
thereby to come to the true imitation
of his most perfect vertues, And this
third of our Will is the principall, &
that wherin we ought to make most
stay, as a thing whereof most reckoning is to be made in Prayer; this
being alwayes in our power to performe, how dry soeuer we be, or full
of desolation. All these, and the like
affections & desires of true and solid
vertues, we must put in practise, so
that we may profit our selus in some
of them by one Meditation, and in
some by another, according as the
matter of meditation shall require.

The XIII. Advertisement.

*The fruit which is to be gathered
out of Prayer.*

IT is a thing of especiall moment,
and which maketh much to the
purpose, that before we begin our
Prayer, we foresee & know the fruit
which we ought to gather thereof.
For it is to be presupposed, that we
go

go to feeke remedy for our fpirituall
neceflityes, to obtaine victory of our
paffions, and peruerfe inclinations,
to procure forrow for our finnes, to
roote out vices, to plant vertues, to
fubdue al difficultyes which may oc-
curre in the way of vertue, weighing
firft with our felues, and very ferioufly, what is the greateft fpirituall ne-
ceflity we haue, what is that which
hindereth moft our progreffe in vertue, and that which affaulteth moft
our foule And thisis that we ought
particulerly to forethinke & haue in
a readineffe, therein to infift, and to
obtaine that our defire in Prayer.
As if we find our felues to want the
vertue of patience, thither to direct
our confiderations, for the attayning
of a true defire to fuffer and endure
for the loue of God things painefull,
and contrary to our liking. If our
cheifeft want be Charity, then to
make firme purpofes, to fhew our
felues affable, curteous, and fweet
vnto our neighbours, not to contri-
ftate, or do them any harme, but rather all the good we can &c.

For

For it were a great folly & de-
ceit for one when he goeth to pray,
to lay hand vpon that which first of-
fereth it selfe, and not that whereof
he hath most need. For we see the
sicke person going to the Apotheca-
ries shop, doth not so, but maketh
choice of that which is most to the
purpose for the curing of his infirmity. So vve see that blind man in the
Ghospell to haue done, who went to
our Sauiour, crying and beseeching
him to haue mercy on him, whome
when our Lord asked, what he would
haue him to do vnto him, he forthwith represented vnto him his greatest necessity, and that wherin he receaued most affliction, which was
the vvant of sight, and of this therfore he craueth remedy. So that vve
see, he did not demaund any other
thing, vvherof he had also need for
he did not say, Lord, bestovv a garment on me, for I am poore : giue me
necessaryes to maintaine me, for I am
in need : these things he did not beg,
but all the rest omitted, he imploreth
remedy for his greatest necessity.

After

After this manner we fee the holy Prophet Dauid to haue done, for he directed his Praiers to obtaine that which he defired, and had most need of, and fo he faith in one of his pfalmes: One thing I haue afked of our Lord, this wil I feeke for, and procure vntill I obtaine it. Euen fo we ought to do in our Praiers to Almighty God, infifting & perfeuering therin, vntil we obtaine. And hauing once preuailed againft that vice, paffion, or bad inclinatiõ which did most afflict and moleft vs, then are we to fal in hand with another, and thus in time we fhal fubdue and cut off the heads of them all with the fharpe and piercing fword of Praier.

But here it feemeth vnto me that fome will doubt and fay: How is it poffible for me to apply this point of Praier, & myfterie which I meditate, and wherin the charity of Chrift and his loue towards me doth most appeare, and wherin his greatneffe and goodneffe is most apparent, to the neceffitie I haue of humility patience, purity, and other vertues? Alfo

hovv

how (when thinking on the glorious
misteries of Christ) can I haue sorrow
for my sinnes, and in his dolorous
and painfull passage, ioy, and spirituall contentmēt? Wherto I answere
two things: the first, that it cannot
be denied, but that some mysteries
are more to the purpose then others,
to gather the fruit of some vertues
more then they be for others Let vs
put an example: In the birth of the
child Iesus, who doubteth but that
the humility & pouerty which Christ
there did practise and experience in
his owne person, doe shine most bright, and are most eminent in that
mistery? In the crowning with thornes, the contempt of worldly honour: In the whipping at the piller,
the mortification of the flesh? and in
the misterie of the Crosse, the humility, patience, and obedience which
Christ exercised, suffering himselfe
to be nailed therunto?

  The second thing is, and that
of much importance to be knowne,
that vpon whatsoeuer point or mistery we meditate, we may apply it to
                                    the

the vertue we haue moſt need of, and
is moſt for our purpoſe; for that the
conſideration of euery one of them is
a certaine diuine Manna, which taſt-
eth to euery one according to his deſire. If we wil that it taſt of humility,
then of humility the conſideration of
ſinnes, of hell, & of death will ſauour
and taſt. If of patience, and the loue
of God, hereof the Paſhon & Reſurrection of Chriſt wil taſt, being euery
where full of motiues for the one,
& incitements to the other If of po-
uertie and mortification of the fleſh,
and ſo of all the reſt, the moſt holy
life of our Lord Ieſus will affoard vs
matter for our ſpirituall guſt in ech
one abundantly. But let vs ſee the
practiſe of this, declaring it by ſome
few examples.

Put the caſe we meditate vpon
ſome part of the Paſſion, and Paines
of our Sauiour, & would draw ther-
out deſire and affection of ioy and
ſpirituall gladnes: Conſider to this
end and reflect vpon the exceeding
great glory and praiſe which through
theſe paines and ignominies did ariſe
                                vnto

vnto God both in heauen and earth, and the infinite good of grace and glory, which by meanes of the sufferings and labours of Christ, were purchased for mankind: and heerat we may reioyce, therin fulfilling the counsaile of the Apostle: Reioice in our Lord alwaies.

If we meditate vpon the glorious Resurrection of Christ our Lord, and desire to haue sorrow for our sinnes; Consider that this our Lord doth therfore rise againe, to bestow on vs the life of grace, deliuering vs from the death of sinne; and by the beauty of the glorious life which he promiseth in this spirituall Resurrection, we may gather the loathsomnesse and deformity of the death of sinne, from which, by his death, he deliuered vs. And thus we may mooue our selus to abhor & detest a thirg so vgly as sinne is, and to loue and imbrace the beautie and seemlinesse of grace.

If meditating on the Ascension of our Sauiour, we desire to reape the fruit of patience, let vs see how well
the

the eternall Father rewarded his most
B. Sonne , for the paines he suffered
for his loue , that we may likewise
haue patience in ours .

Finally if thinking vpon the
most holy life of Christ, we wouldbe
moued to the contempt of the world:
behold the litle reckoning he made
of the honours and vaine estimation
therof , & that the glory which ought
to be esteemed, is the Eternal, which
Christ our Lord hath and doth communicate vnto his .

But now , all this supposed
which hath bin said, that which here-
in maketh most for our purpose, is ,
the light and direction of the holy
Ghost , who in what misterie soeuer
we shall meditate , will best suggest
and graunt vnto vs the feeling of the
vertue we most pretend, and which it
behoueth vs most to seeke for, and
to obtaine at his holy hands .

THE

The XIIII. Advertisement.

Of Iaculatorie Praiers to be made both in, and out of Meditation.

IT is a very good remedy to exercise and ftir vp the foule that praieth, as well in time of diftraction and drineffe in meditation, as to conferue deuotion in the reft of the day, to walke alwaies as in the prefence of Almighty God, and no leffe for fuch as haue not health to pray or mediate, to vfe fome fhort praiers, or iaculatorv afpiratios, which are as if one fhould caft a dart or fhoot an arrow offeruent affection vnto heauen: Crauing of Almighty God in few words his diuine loue, his grace, or fome vertue wherof he ftandeth moft in need: & as it were reprefenting and laying before his maiefty, his owne weakneffe, afking humbly remedy therof, or victory ouer fome vice, from which he moft defireth to be freed. The practife of thefe fhort praiers, is as followeth.

O my

O my God , that I could alwayes loue thee !

O that I could perfectly obey thee!

O that I could alwayes serue thee!

O that I neuer had offended thee !

O that I could see my self free from this, or that inperfection !

O that I could obtaine this,or that excellent vertue !

Giue me, o Lord, puritie of soule , humility of hart , pouerty of spirit.

Pardon my sinnes, O my Redeemer , for they are many, and haue mercy on me .

O King of heauen, and beauty of Angels, how late is it that I come to knowe thee !

O Lord that I knew thee, & knew my selfe !

Permit not, o Lord , that euer I be separated from thee.

Graunt me , O my Strength, my God , my Spouse, that I may entierly loue thee .

Giue me , O Lord, grace alwayes to perseuere in vertue, and to do worthy pennance for my sinnes .

This manner of Praier is breise ,

C   and

and eafy for all , and from whence is
gathered much fpirituall profit being
done with affection , and deuotion :
as holy King Dauid did , who hath
left the fame written, and iterated
many times in his Pfalmes.

Of this example, thofe holy Mon-
kes of Ægipt made their benefit, of
whome S. Bafil and Caffian affirme,
that whileft they laboured with their
handes, they did alfo pray moft part
of the day . Wherfore if we alfo doe
accuftome our felues to this holy
exercife , we fhal performe that continual Prayer,which our Sauiour requireth in the Ghofpell, where he
faith by S. Luke : It behoueth vs
alwaies to pray ,and not to be weary.
For what better Prayer may there be,
then to be alwaies defiring the greater
honour of Almighty God , and alwayes conforming our Will with his
wil, hauing no other willnor nil then
the wil or nil of Almighty God. This
is (as S. Paul faith) to begin to be
Citizens of the Saints , and the do-
mefticall people of God . This is to
be as were thofe happy men whome
                                    S. Iohn

S. Iohn did fee, and faith of them :
They had the name of God written
in their forehead, which is, the continual memory & prefence of God. For
their côuerfation now is not in earth
but in heauen . And to the end that
ours alfo may be fo, and in fuch meafure as in this life we can performe ,
let vs make vfe of thefe Iaculatory
Praiers , and afpirations , in our meditations, and in other times of the
day, yea and in the middeft of our
occupations and bufines .

Neither is it to be vnderftood ,
that all thofe before fet downe are
only to be vfed , but whatfoeuer o-
thers like vnto them, yea & fuch are
wont to be better & of more efficacy
which moued by God we conceiue
and frame by our felues , although
with words leffe proper, and not fo
well ordered . And be affured that by
this compendious and fhort way,
both eafy and profitable, in time vve
may attayne vnto great fanctity of
life .

C 2   THE

The XV. Advertisement.

*Of the Speach, or Colloquy which is to be
made at the end of Prayer.*

THE Holy Ghoſt ſaith in the
Booke of Eccleſiaſtes, that the
end of Prayer is better then
the beginning. And the reaſon is, for
that then the hart is ſuppoſed to be
inflamed with meditation, and the
ſoule moued, taught, and eleuated
with the light, & heauenly wiſedom
communicated vnto her by God in
Prayer; ſo as then is the proper time
of Colloquy to ſpeake and conuerſe
familiarly with God, the time alſo
of petition, and requeſt of what we
deſire. And the ſayd Colloquies are
to be made according to the matter
which then we haue meditated, ſpea-
king ſometimes mentally, ſometimes
vocally, with the eternall Father, or
with his moſt holy Sonne Ieſus.

For example, If the matter of
our meditation hath beene ioyfull,
let vs reioyce with the eternal Father,
giuing him thankes for that by the
meanes

meanes and merits of such a Sonne
he hath communicated vnto vs such
graces, fauours, & benefits. If it be
of the payns & troubles of the Sonne
of Almighty God, we ought to grieue
and haue compassion, becaule he
hath sustayned such and so great afflictions for so vile and base creatures
as we are. And after this manner cō-
formably vnto the matter, the sayd
speach or Colloquy is to be made, &
therewith conclude our Prayer for
that tyme.

This is also the time to aske not
only for our selues but for others also
to whom we haue obligation, whose
life, health, and saluation we desire:
beseeching our Lord, to graunt them
his grace and loue, that they may liue
and dye therein. This is the tyme to
alke for the peace, increase, and conseruation of the Church, and for
those which be in mortall sinne, that
God will pleafe to haue mercy on
them, & bring them to a better state.
Finally this is the tyme to commend
vnto Almighty God all those which
remember vs, and haue commended
them-

themselues vnto our Prayers .

THE XVI. ADVERTISEMENT.

Of the care in obseruing these Aduertisements, and of the purity of Conscience requisite for Prayer.

HE that beginneth to vse mentall Prayer, ought not to afflict and discomfort himselfe in respect that the Aduertisements and Rules we haue heere prescribed for the better practising of mental Prayer be so many and diuers: for it is cleare that as the soule entring into the body, of it selfe is sufficient to informe, animate, and quicken all the members, exercising therin all the offices & functions of life, notwithstanding they be many and sundry : euen so the grace of the Holy Ghost entring into a soule , is alone sufficient to make it performe all the offices of a spirituall life . For by Prayer , our Vnderstāding is illuminated; Prayer instructeth and teacheth vs whatsoeuer we haue to do; Prayer moueth the Will, with all the interiour facultyes

tyes which depend thereon : Prayer
finally doth facilitate and make easy
whatsoeuer difficultyes do, or may
occur in this holy exercise, making
the way so plaine and easy, that we
need not feare them.

But if perchance it should happen, that setling our selues to prayer
we forget to obserue this order, or
misse in some of these aduises, and
rules. As for example, if we forget to
make in the beginning those three
Humiliations aforesayd, or to make
the Preparatory Prayer, and to put
our selues in the presence of God &c.
let vs not therfore trouble and disquiet our selues: for our intention &
endeauour only was, and is, to teach
euery one that which is best and most
profitable: which supposed, albeit
we sometimes misse in one thing or o-
ther, we do not therfore loose the
fruit of our Prayer: for the infinite
goodnes and liberality of God is not
tyed to these rules, neither will he
therefore omit to visit vs with his
diuine grace.

And wheras one of the thinges
which

which is chiefly required in Prayer,
is the purity of Conscience, wherof
Almighty God speaking by S. Mat-
thew sayd: Blessd are the cleane of
hart, for they shall see God. Therefore is it certaine, that how much
the more any shall purifye, and
cleanse themselus, so much the more
they shall see and enioy him. And
because this purity of Conscience is
by no other way better gotten, and
perseuered, then by the dayly examination of the same, togeather with the
act of Contrition: I haue thought
good to set downe in this place the
manner of performing it euery night
for the space of a quarter of an houre
before we go to rest and this done we
are to prepare our selues for the meditation of the day following, by reading the poynt, or poynts of the Exercise.

THE EXAMEN OF

our Conscience.

THE examen of our Conscience
that it may be done well, must
cosist in the fiue poynts following

ing heere briefly declared . The firſt
is, to giue thankes vnto Almighty
God for the benefits receaued at his
moſt liberall hand ; to wit , for that
he hath created, redeemed, and conſerued vs , and hath made vs Chri-
ſtians, and chiefly for thoſe which he
hath done vnto vs in particuler , for
which we owe vnto ſuch a moſt liberall Lord ſpeciall gratitude.

The ſecond is, to aſke of his diuine Maieſty light & grace, to know
and amend the faults committed a-
gainſt him that day .

The third is , to bethinke our
ſelues,& diligently to examine from
houre to houre , ſince the morning
we did riſe, vntill that preſent tyme,
all our thoughts, wordes, and deeds ,
what we haue done , ſpoken, or hath
paſſed in our mind .

The fourth is, to render harty
thankes vnto God our Lord for all
the good which we ſhall perceiue to
haue done, not attributing vnto our
ſelues (being ſo bad as we are) any
good thing of thoſe which we haue
done, but vnto God who moued vs to
C 5   do

do them .

The fifth and last is, to be sory with all our hart for the offences we shal discouer in our selues, committed against so good a Lord , crauing pardon for them. And so finally .(firmely proposing through the assistance of his diuinegrace to aměd) let vs repeate this Act of Contrition, to obtaine pardon for our sinnes.

O my Lord Iesus Christ, true God and Man , my Creatour and Redeemer, thou being whome thou art, & for that I loue thee aboue all things , I am sory withal my hart that I haue offended thee . And heere I firmely purpose neuer to sinne any more, & to auoyd all occasions of offending thee as also purpose to confesse and fulifill the pennance enioyned me for the same And in satisfaction thereof, I offer vp vnto thee thin owne sacred Passiō, the merits of thy B. Mother the Virgin Mary , and of al the Saints , and all my workes labours, and paynes, yea and my whole life . And I trust in thy infinite goodnes & mercy, that by the merits of thy most
precious

precious bloud and paſſion , thou
wilt forgiue me all my ſinnes , and
beſtow vpon me ſuch plenty of thy
grace, as therewith I may be able to
lead a holy life, and perfectly to ſerue
thee vnto the end .

Thus we are to make our Examen with all care and diligence euery
night ; the good and manifold fruits
wherof are ſuch and ſo admirable ,
that they cannot be worthily declared . For by this Examen we cut off
all culpable ignorance , and free our
ſelues from hidden ſins which thence
do ariſe , and do that which is in vs
to know the truth, the which Almighty God doth alſo the rather diſ-
cloſe vnto vs. By this Examen we
fullfill thoſe Commandements and
Counſels of Chriſt , ſo earneſtly and
often repeated by him in the Ghoſpel
ſaying : Watch and pray , becauſe
you know not the day and houre of
your death , nor of your iudgement.
Be you ready , for that what houre
you thinke not , the Sonne of man
will come to call you vnto his diuine
iudgment.

C 6   By

By this examen we keep watch
ouer our felues, efcaping the danger
and obligation of finnes paft, freeing
our felues from thofe to come. By
this we prepare our foule and confcience for death, though euen that
night it fhould ouertake vs, and
catch vs at vnawares (a thing very
poffible and perhaps to befall vs) as
it hath happened vnto many others.
And it may happen that one dying
on a fuddaine, if he had not examined himfelfe well, he had been loft
and condemned for euer, whereas
hauing examined himfelfe with contrition and forrow for his finnes, he
is faued eternally. That heerby we
may fee how much a diligent care
importeth in this bufines, and withall the great domage which may befal vs, if we negleɕto do it euery day.

THE

THE
FIRST BOOKE
OF MEDITATIONS,
which appertaine vnto the
Purgatiue Way.

THE PREAMBLE,
Concerning the three wayes, Purgatiue,
Illuminatiue, and Vnitiue.

EING now time to be-
gin to set downe in this
first Booke the Medi-
tations and Points,
which belong to the
Purgatiue Way, it will not be from
our purpose, before we declare in particuler what the way Purgatiue is,
to say somewhat in general (for more
perspicuity and clearnes sake) of the
three

three Wayes: which done I will treat
in the three bookes following of e-
uery one seuerally.

I say therfore, that as by sinne
(according as the Prophet Isay saith)
man is deuided & straieth from God,
who is his true way and last end; so
as the meanes which he is to vse to
reunite himselfe vnto him, is called
a Path, or Way: and the returning
againe, to Mooue, and to Walke.
And euen as in euery motion which
is made from one place to another,
there be three thinges : first, The
tovvne and place from whence the
traueller departeth. Secondly, the
Place whither he goeth. And thirdly
the Motion it selfe from one place to
another : Euen so, in the motion,
wherby a soule, separated from Almighty God, reuniteth it selfe with
him againe, we may consider three
other things alike. First the extreme
from whence it parteth, which is
sinne, and the euill state which therin it had. Secondly the place whither it tendeth, to wit God, to reunite it selfe vnto him. And thirdly
the

the paſſage from the one to the other,
to wit, the ſpace which is betweene
theſe two extremes, which is necceſ-
ſary for the attayning of the deſigned
end: and this is, that the Vnderſtanding be illuminated in the knowledg
of that good, which is to loue, and
wherwith it is to be vnited.

And as the way-faring man
firſt is to leaue the place where he
was, and then to continue going till
he come to the end of his iourney
which he pretended : ſo in this ſpirituall voyage, the firſt pace or ſtep, &
firſt part of the way, is to get out of
the ſinnes in which he was intangled,
thereby to come to Almighty God.
For if he would go forward in the
wayes, Illuminatiue and Vnitiue,
that is, to the height of Contemplation, and diuine Perfection, not paſ-
ſing firſt by the Purgatiue way, ex-
erciſing himſelfe in rooting out vices
and bad inclinations, it were to go &
proceed without any foundation or
ground at all; and ſo ſhould he alwayes remayne imperfect, as a ſchol-
ler that would paſſe to higher ſtudies,
not

not hauing groun ded himselfe suffi-
ciently in the lower schooles, and
mount vp vnto the last, not hauing
passed the first degree The way therfore to obtaine this good, must be by
going first the Purgatiue Way, which
may be declared as followeth.

THE PVRGATIVE WAY.

WE call that the Purgatiue
Way, which doth purge
and purify our soule and
conscience from vices & sinnes, and
doth replenish and fill the same with
that purity and cleanes, which is necessary to enter into the celestial Ierusalem, whither (as S. Iohn saith) no
polluted thing shall enter. But who
through his manifold sinnes and abhominations, shall find himselfe polluted and defiled, must know, that
the only meanes to wash and cleanse
himselfe from the same heere in this
life, is duely to consider them, and
with aboundance of teares to be sory
for them, togeather with the remem-
brāce of the good he hath lost, which
is God himselfe, and the present euill
which

which he suffereth. Also the confideration of Death, Iudgement, and Hell: for these and such like confiderations, are included in this first paffage or Purgatiue Way, which appertaine to beginners, & in which fo much time is tobe fpent by euery one in particuler as fhall feeme neceffary for him, to walke this way with purity and fruit: feeing that fome haue more finnes, and a more foft, and tender hart and confcience, then others.

Wherefore I remit the yong beginner (tothe end he go not aftray) to his prudent and difcreet fpirituall Father, to direct, guide, and inftruct him in euery thing, according as the courfe of his life hath beene more or leffe difordered. For it were no difcretion, to detaine one in the exercife of this Purgatiue Way, longer time thē is neceffary, which of it owne nature doth caufe in the foule feruile feare, that hindereth the perfection of Charity, and vnto which Charity we ought to endeauour to attaine, in the courfe of a fpirituall life: becaufe

as

(as S. Iohn faith) perfe&ct; charity ex-
pelleth feare . Wherefore it feemeth
conuenient and reafonable , that hauing fpent in thefe laudable and holy
exerciles fifteene or twenty dayes ,
we proceed to the Illuminatiue and
Vnitiue vvayes; out of which likewife, Motions of Sorrow , Feare, &c
Humilitv may be gathered, as out of
the Purgatiue For certaine it is, that
one wilbe grieued more that he hath
offended Chrift our Lord, confidering his excellent vertues of Humility , Patience , Charity,and the like ,
then if he fhould confiJer his ovvne
finnes, Death, Iudgment, and Hell .

And albei- thefe confiderations
be more proper to thofe who defire
of new to conuert themfelues to Almighty God, or be but beginners in
vertue; yet reafon it is,that the iuft
alfo, to purify themfelues the more
from the finnes prefent, & withal to
make furer the pardon of thofe which
bepaft, do now & then(as for exáple
once euery yeare) refrefh and renew
the memory of thefe Meditations :
following the counfaile which Ec-
clefia-

Ecclesiasticus doth giue vs, saying:
Be not hindred to pray alwayes, &
feare not to be iustifyed euen vnto
death. And our Sauiour sayth: He
that is iust, let him be iustifyed yet,
and let the holy be sanctifyed yet;
increasing dayly in purity of conscience, and in sanctity of life.

   The Meditations following of
the Purgatiue vvay will giue a good
beginning to this enterprise in which
I haue thought good and expedient
to follovv the counsaile & opinion of
S. Gregory and other Saints, who
say, that the firme and true foundation of a spirituall building, is the
knowledge of our selues; and they
proue it very well: for if one do not
first practise himselfe in the consideration and knowledge of his owne
misery and weaknesse, he shall remayne ignorant and blind, and not
know how to aske in Prayer that
which is conuenient for him. Wherfore I will beginne the Meditations
of this first Booke with this consideration, which shalbe the fundamentall stone of all this spirituall building
                                    wheron

whereon the reſt muſt ſtand . The
points and conſiderations wherof, I
haue gathered out of diuers places
of the holy Scripture and Saints, and
for ſuch they are to be eſteemed and
practiſed . And becauſe we all aſpire
vnto vertue and holynes of life, it is
expedient , that we alſo imitate and
follow them this way which they
haue ſhewed vs .

THE I. MEDITATION .
Of the Knowledge of our ſelues.

T HE Preparatory Prayer preſuppoſed (whereof we treated
in the eleuenth Aduertiſement)
two thinges are to be done in euery
Meditation contayned in this Manuall , to wit , Firſt the Compoſition of
place : Secondly the Petition, which
muſt be alwayes conformable to the
matter of the Meditation , as in this
and the reſt of this fi ſt Booke is ſaid.
The Compoſition of place.
T HE Compoſition of the place heer
ſhalbe, to behold & conſider with
the

the eyes of the foule, that the whole
compaffe of the earth, in comparifon
of the heauens & the greatnes therof,
is as it were a point or graine of fand:
which being fo, what fhalt thou then
be before thy God , Creatour of the
fame heauen and earth , in whofe
prefence thou art leffe then nothing?

The Petition.

THE Petition fhalbe to afke of our
Lord God , that he communicate
vnto thee his diuine light , therby to
know thy owne bafenes and mifery ,
and knowing it, to humble thy felfe ,
and in humility to ferue and adore
him as thy Lord and God : this done
begin thy Meditation as followeth.

THE 1. POINT.

TO confider the matter whereof
thy body was compofed & made,
and thou fhalt find that it was not framed either of the heauens, or of cry-
ftall, neither of the fupreme element
of fire , nor of water , nor of other
cleare, bright and tranfparent matter,
but of the moft vile and bafe element
of all , which is the earth , and hence
hath thy body his origen and beginning,

ning, which God himselfe remem-
bred our firft Father Adam of, when
laying this confideration before his
eyes, he fayd vnto him: Duft thou
art, and into duft thou fhalt returne.
Confider thou as much, and thou
fhalt receiue fight, and knowledge of
thy felfe, as he that was blind from
his natiuity receaued fight, whome
Chrift our Lord cured both corporally and fpiritually, laying vpon
his eyes the clay or earth wherof he
was firft framed and made -

Ponder, that it is the will of Almighty God, that men be alwayes
very carefull, & diligent in knowing
and vnderftanding his owne bafenes
and mifery: and that he haue continually the eyes of his foule fixed v-
pon the earth wherof he was framed,
to the end he alwayes keep himfelfe
in humility and fubiection: knowing
that he deferueth not to be efteem'd
and honoured, but rather to be trodden vnder foot and trampled vpon
as is the earth : this being the only remedy and meane to obtaine the vertue of Humility.

Hence

Hence shalt thou gather two
thinges. First, Confusion and shame,
seeing how contrary thou hast done
heereto, hauing euer desired and taken pleasure, not in submitting and
humbling, but in extolling and boa-
sting of thy selfe, as if thou wert
somthing : remembring those words
of the Apostle, If any man esteeme
himselfe to be something, whereas he
is nothing, he seduceth himselfe. Secondly, A firme purpose, continually
to exercise thy selfe in the base esteem
and acknowledgment of thy selfe, as
did S. Augustine, and S. Francis
&c. of whome the first was wont to
say vnto God, Lord, Let me know
my selfe, and know thee. The second, Lord, Who art thou, & who
am I?

THE 2 POINT.

TO cōsider what thy body is whilst
it liueth, and thou shalt find, that
it is a sack of earth, a continuall flowing water of all filth and stench, and
that there is not any part therof from
the sole of the foot, to the crowne
of the head, without impurity and
vnclean-

vncleaneſſe. For which cauſe Holy
Iob ſayd, as one who had throughly
entred into this conſideration, I haue
ſayd to rottenes, thou art my Father,
& to wormes, thou art my Mother
and ſiſter.

Weigh how much the trees &
plants of the field do ſurpaſſe thee in
this, for they produce flowers, leaues
and very good fruit: thou breedeſt
and engendreſt infinit vermine. The
trees & plants bring forth wine, oyle,
and balme, but thou auoydeſt out
a thouſand infirmityes, & al manner
of vncleanes. And what meruaile,
for according as the tree is, ſo is the
fruit: and an euil tree (like as man is)
cannot yield good fruit.

Of that which hath been ſayd,
thou mayſt gather a great deſire of
humbling thy ſelfe, ſeeing that the
miſeries of thy body be ſo great and
ſo manifold, beſeeching our Lord
to open the eyes of thy ſoule, that
from this day forward, thou ceaſe to
ſeeke delights and contentments for
thy body, which is ſo vnworthy of
them; chaſtiſing it with rigorous pennance

nance for what it hath already in-
ioyed.

THE 3. POINT.

TO confider, in what eftate this
thy body fhallbe, after the fe-
paration of thy foule : howfoeuer
beautiful & faire it was before, how
foule and filthy, how loathfome &
abhominable it fhall then remaine.

Ponder, that the caufe of all
thefe domages and euills, wiilbe the
abfence of thy foule, and into what
thy wretched body fhal prefently be
conuerted, to wit, into worms meate
into earth, and duft, to be trodden
vnder euery mans feet. Whereby
thou mayft fee wherein all flefh and
the glory therof doth end, and what
a foole thou art to pamper thy body,
permitting it to run after all defires,
purchafing with fhort and tranfitory
delights, euerlafting torments.

Hence thou mayft ftir vp in
thy felfe a great defire of knowing
thy owne mifery, and to fet before
the eyes of thy foule, the earth, of
which thy body was made, and into which it is againe to be refolued.

D   And

And if this be the port and hauen whereat shortly thou, and all men are to land after the tempestuous nauigation of this sea of miseries, it is a matter of no small importance for the knowledge of thy selfe, to be mindfull of what thou art, and what is to become of thee at last, that setting the eyes of due consideration, vpon the feet of this thy proud and haughty Statua made of clay (to wit thy body·) thou humble and submit thy selfe to the very ground : for by how much the higher the building is to be (as S. Auguſtine ſaith) ſo much the lower is the foundation to be layd.

THE 4. POINT.

TO conſider that to know thy ſelf perfectly and throughly, thou art not to reſt in the knowledge of thy body alone, but muſt paſſe further to the knowledge of thy ſoule, pondering firſt, that albeit in regard of thy ſoule thou mighteſt greatly eſteeme thy ſelfe, it being a creature wholy ſpirituall, and like in nature vnto the Angells, a liuely reſem-
blance

blance of Almighty God, an image
of the most Blessed Trinity, indued
with three most perfect powers and
one essence, able to vnderstand, loue
and enioy infinite goodes: notwithstanding thou wantest not wherin to
humble thy selfe, if thou call to mind
the foule and loathsome dungeon,
wherein thy soule is imprisoned, the
house of clay wherein it is detained
and liueth: remembring the saying
of the Apostle: What hast thou, that
thou hast not receaued? And if thou
hast receaued, what dost thou glory,
as though thou haddest not receaued?

Secondly ponder that before Almighty God created thy soule, to
put and infuse it into thy body, it
was nothing, nor was of any value,
and would instantly returne to the
same nothing againe, if Almighty
God should not continually keep &
conserue it, and so thou hast not
whereof to glory, but in thy miseries
and infirmities (as S. Paul sayd of
himselfe) seeing thou art compassed
about with innumerable temptatiōs

D 2   both

both within and without.

Reap and gather from hence
defires, to know and humble thy
felfe, and acknowledge thy felfe for
lefle then nothing, perceiuing now
what thy foule is, how little it is
worth, and how much reafon it hath
to feare.

The Speach, or Colloquy.

THE Speach, or Colloquy to end
the Prayer, is alwayes to be
drawne out of the matter of the Meditation : and fo we are to do in this
and all the reft, as aboue we haue noted in the fifteenth Aduertifement.

THE II. MEDITATION.

Of Sinnes.

THE preparatory Prayer fhalbe
like vnto the firft.

The Compofition of place
fhalbe, to fee with the eyes of thy
Vnderftanding, thy foule fhut vp &
imprifoned in the obfcure prifon and
dungeon of thy body, and thy felfe
banifhed into this vale of teares and
mifery,

misery, entangled with many snares
of sinnes and temptations.

The petition shallbe, to aske of
our Lord light, wherewith to know
the grieuousnes of sinne, to abhorre
and bewayle it, and the terriblenes of
Gods iustice in chastising it with e-
uerlasting paine and torment.

THE 1. POINT.

TO consider the chastisement,
which Almighty God shewed v-
pon the Angels for one only sinne,
and that only in thought, committed
against his diuine Maiesty, in matter
of Presumption and Pride : depriuing them in an instant of that supreme and high dignity wherein he
had created them, & throwing them
like thunderbolts from the highest
heauen into the lowest hell, without
respect either to the beauty of their
Nature, or to the greatnes of their
estate, or that they were his creaturs
made according to his image and
likenes.

Ponder, how great an euil Mortall sinne is, seeing that only one was
inough to obscure and defile so great

beauty of the Angels, Almighty God
permitting the same, to the end that
men should feare and tremble to liue
but one houre in mortall sin : knowing, that if God spared not the Angells, being notwithstanding so noble
and excellent creatures, how much
lesse will he pardon men, being so
vile and base as they are.

Hence raise in thy selfe feruent
desires of contrition togeather with
a great detestation of thy sinnes committed against Almighty God, firmely, purposing from this day forward
rather to dye a thousand deathes,
then euer to commit one mortall
sinne: for whatsoeuer can be suffered
in this life, is lesse without comparison, then the paine due to one only
sinne, which was sufficient to make
of a beautifull Angell, a most foule &
vgly Diuell.

THE 2. POINT.

TO consider who was the author
of this most grieuous euill of sin,
and thou shalt find it to be man, a
vile and abiect creature, who being
so much obliged to serue and loue

his

his Creatour and Lord, for so many
& so innumerable benefits receaued
from his diuine and most liberall
hand, to wit, his Creatiō, Conseruation, Vocation, and Redemption,
forgetting all this, hath only beene
mindfull to despise and offend, with
his manifold sinnes, his Lord and
God.

Ponder whence it proceedeth,
that so vile a worme, & so wretched
a creature as thou art, hath beene so
bold as to offend the infinite Maiesty
of thy Creatour, before whome the
most highest Saints do tremble ; and
thou shalt find that it is thy presūption and pride, and want of Humility, which maketh thee to stumble
& fall, not permitting to vnderstand
that to sinne, is worse then not to
be at all, and that, it had been better
not to haue beene borne, then to
haue sinned, as our Sauiour sayd
speaking of Iudas. For it is certaine
that there is no place so base & contēptible in the sight of God, among
either things created, or not created,
as is man who is in mortall sinne.

D 4   Gather

Gather hence a great defire to be defpifed and contemned of men, for that with thy finnes thou haft difhonoured & contemned Almighty God: and do fharp pennance for them, therby to incline thy Saviour to pardon thee, befeeching him, that feeing he hath not beene wearyed in fuffering for thee, he will vouchfafe to pardon thee, reftoring thee againe to his grace and friendfhip.

THE 3. POINT.

TO confider, how much the Sonne of Almighty God doth abhorre and deteft finne : for that loving & efteeming fo much his life (as it was reafon, that fo iuft and holy a life as his, fhould be loued and efteemed) did choofe neuerthcles to loofe and fpend it, to deftroy this bloudy and cruell beft Sinne, feeling more our faults, then his owne paynes.

Ponder, that if finne coft Almighty God fo much (in that for to deftray the fame, he imbraced the Croffe, offering on it his moft precious bloud and life, in fatisfaction cf finne) how art thou fo blind and foolifh,

lish, that thou wilt needs loue and
esteeme a thing so abhominable vnto God ? How art thou so besotted ,
as to choose death it selfe ? How so
bold and foole-hardy , as to aduenture the committing of a mortall
sinne, it hauing cost God himselfe so
high a price ? And if this be true (as
it is) is it not a madnes incredible, to
beleeue with faith what thou belee-
uest , and to liue in manner as thou
liuest ? that is to say , to beleeue that
sinne is so bad and detestable , and
neuertheles to commit the same so
desperatly? to beleeue that God is so
good, and notwithstanding to offend
him ?

Hence thou shalt gather a great
mislike and detestation of sinne, seeing that for the curing therof, human
meanes did not suffice, but diuine a-
lone . And know, that he who com-
mitteth it, as much as lyeth in him
(as S. Paul saith) doth crucify againe
the Sonne of God .

THE 4. POINT.

TO consider, the innumerable souls
that be now burning in hell for

one only sinne which they committed. Where ponder first, how all
those damned soules were men as
thou art, and many of them Christi-
ans, and were perhaps sometimes
highly in the fauour of Almighty
God, but by little & little they grew
carelesse, and came to fall into that
miserable estate, and by the iust iudgements of God, death ouertooke
them therin, and so were they most
iustly condemned for all eternity.

Secondly, with how much
more reason thou deseruest to be in
Hell, as those soules are, for hauing
offended God, in that very kind of
sinne, not once, but many times: &
how iust reason there was that death
should haue caught thee in committing the first sinne, and that God
should haue giuen thee no time of
repentance.

Hence thou shalt gather desires
and affections of loue and gratitude
towards Almighty God for the fauours and benefits done vnto thee,
in deliuering thee from the danger,
before thou didst fall into it. Also
                                    feruent

feruent defires of doing fatisfaction
for thy offences in this life, lamenting and bewayling them.

THE III. MEDITATION,
Of Death.

T H E Preparatory Prayer as before. The Compofitiõ of place
fhalbe ; to imagine the King of
heauen feated on his Royall throne,
difpatching thence his Iudges, Ser-
geants, Apparitors, and other his Officers to depriue of their liues all
thofe that are to dye. Suppofe that
the laft day of thy life is now come,
and that this is the laft houre therof,
and that thou prepareft thy felfe for
the finall account.

The petition fhallbe to befeech our Lord to open the eyes of
thy foule, giuing thee grace to liue fo
now, as thou wouldft then wifh thou
hadft liued: and fo compofing and
ordering now thy diforderd life,
that thou mayft dye a happy death.

T H E

The 1. Point.

TO confider, how doubtfull and vncertaine this day and houre of thy death is, ſo that thou neither knoweſt when, nor in what manner it will attach thee. For that ordinarily when a man is moſt careleſſe, and thinketh leaſt thereof, it then commeth: the diuine prouidence ſo ordaining to oblige thee to be alwayes watchfull, expecting this day, and fearing this houre. For as there is nothing more vncertaine then that houre, ſo thou muſt beleeue that nothing is more certaine, then that after health followeth ſickneſſe, and after life enſueth death.

Ponder, how this Verity is moſt ſure and vndoubted, yet thou liueſt neuertheles with ſo great careleſnes and negligence, not preparing for death; which dayly doth threaten thee. And mooue heere in thy ſelfe a great deſire to liue wel to day as one that is to dye to morrow: for the day will come, and that very quickly, wherein thou ſhalt liue to ſee the morning, but not the euening,

or

or the euening but not the morning,
and order thy life from this day forward, in manner as thou wouldeſt
wiſh to haue liued at the houre of
thy death. And if thou wouldſt not
that death ſhould ſeize vpon thee in
the ſtate in which now thou ſtandeſt,
procure forthwith to come out of it:
for it is not good to liue in that ſtate,
wherein thou wouldſt not dye.

The 2. Point.

TO conſider, of what importance
it is (as the Holy Ghoſt ſaith) to
haue alwayes in mind the preſence
of Death, thereby not to ſinne for
euer. For thou wert very vnwiſe, if
in a buſineſſe of ſo great conſequence
and importance (as is alwayes to
walke prepared, and armed with
this holy & wholſom remembrance)
thou wouldſt ſo much forget thy ſelf
as to deferre it to the very point and
inſtant of thy death : not knowing
how, or in what manner thou art to
dye, whether ſodainly, or by ſome
ſtone throwne at randon, or by a tile
of a houſe falling downe vpon thee,
by ſword, fire, or water : for doubtles

les thou art not certaine whether a fodaine and violent death will befall thee, as it hath befallen many others.

Ponder that euery finner who-foeuer, doth deferue to be chaftifed with this fodaine death, and to pe-rifh, and dye therein, as very many haue done. Seeing therfore thou art fo great a finner, how doft thou not tremble to be but one houre in mor-tall finne? Why art thou not careful how death may find thee well or ill prepared? that is, in mortall finne, or in the grace and fauour of Almighty God?

Hence raife in thy felfe, an ear-neft defire with a firme purpofe and refolution to do fo, and not to be fo carelefse, as hitherto thou haft been in this holy exercife of preparing thy felfe for death: it being a bridle for many euills, and a fpurre to all kind of vertue.

The 3. Point.

TO confider that it is a law ap-pointed by Almighty God (as S. Paul doth teftify) to all men once to dye, & not twice, or oftener. Wherupon

upon enfueth that the hurt and domage of an euill death, is irremedia-
ble for all eternity, as likewife the
profit of a good death is euerlafting.

Ponder, that if it be but only
once that thou art to dye, and thereon dependeth thy eternall faluation
or damnation, how liueft thou then
fo carelefly, not exertifing thy felfe
during life, in fuch manner that thou
mayft dye a happy death?

Gather hence a great defire to
mortify thy felfe, in whatfoeuer thou
difordinatly loueft: be they thy Parents, Brethren, Friends, honours,
riches or pleafures: feeing thou art
to leaue and depart from all at thy
death. And to the end thou mayft
feele it the leffe, procure often to dye
in thy life time, mortifying thy fenfes
and fhutting vp thy eyes, leaft they
may fee that which is not lawfull to
be defired for thy faluation, refray-
ning thy tongue, leaft it fpeake
things hurtful to thy Neighbour &c.
for fo dying and mortifying thy felf
in thy life tyme, thou fhalt find Almighty God fauourable vnto thee at
the

the houre of thy death.

THE 4. POINT.

TO confider, how perplexed and troubled thou wilt be in that trauce & agony of death, when thou shalt see a holy candle lighted at thy beds side, & thy winding sheetspread vpon thy bed, and the standers by calling vpon thee to prepare thy self for death, and to commend thy selfe with thy hart, if thou canst not with thy mouth, vnto the mercy of Almighty God.

Ponder, the terrour, anguish, and perplexity of mind thou art to feele in that passage, not so much for that thou art to leaue the beloued company and society of thy body, & other thinges which thou didst willingly enioy, as for to see and vnderstand that the dreadfull houre of account, and finall sentence doth approach, the which shalbe according to thy works, either of eternal saluation or damnation, to enioy for euer God Almighty, or to burne for all eternity in hell fire.

Gather hence a great feare and terrour

terrour, calling to mind the insupportable paines & trauailes that thy body and soule are to endure in the houre of death, and withall a liuely desire neuer more to forget the same whilest thou liuest. Reprehend and condemne thy carelessenes: demaund oftentimes of thy selfe, How, if I meane to dye wel, do I not liue wel? For it is a Law common and ordinary, that he that liueth well dyeth well, & he that liueth ill, dyeth also ill. Craue of thy Blessed Sauiour, that by his most holy death, he will vouchsafe to giue thee also a good & happy passage.

THE IIII. MEDITATION.

Of the particuler Iudgement.

THE Preparatory Prayer as before. The composition of place shalbe, to imagine Christ our Sauiour as the soueraigne Iudge, seated on a Throne of Maiesty ready to iudge thy soule, which is accompanied with thy good and bad deeds, **and**

and that on either side of thee stand
thy good and bad Angell, expecting
whose prey thou shalt be

The petition shalbe to beseech
our Lord God, that he wil vouchafe
to shew thee his goodnes and clemē-
cy, vsing toward thee not Iustice, but
Mercy, seeing he is (as S. Paul saith)
the Father of Mercyes.

THE 1. POINT.

TO consider the time and place,
wherin the particuler Iudgment
of euery one is to be, to wit, the very
instant of death, at the point when
the soule shall leaue the body des-
poiled of all the good it had, and in
that very time and moment the
whole iudgement shalbe concluded,
the sentence giuen and executed.

Ponder, how much it behooueth thee to haue alwayes before thy
eyes this houre and moment, as
which is to be a beginning of thy e-
ternall good, or euill. For in euery
moment of these thou maist merit or
demerit either life or death, which is
to endure for euer. The place of this
iudgment shallbe whersoeuer death
shall

shall first arrest thee, on the land, or
on the sea, in thy chamber, or in the
street, in thy bed, or on the way: for
as this soueraigne Iudge hath power
and iurisdiction in euery plece, so in
all places he hath his Tribunall, and
maketh his iudgement: that in euery
place thou mayst feare, because thou
knowest not whether that shalbe the
place of thy Iudgment. Out of which
thou art to draw a great feare of offending God in any place where he
may iudge thee.

THE 2. POINT.

TO consider, the most rigorous examen whereunto the Iudge shall
call thee, seeing it is to be vniuersall
of all thinges whatsoeuer, charging
thee withall thy sinnes, of deeds,
words, and thoughts : euen of those
which thou hast idly done or spoken,
though thou shouldst haue quite forgotten them; & this accusation shall
be so cleare & euident, as no manner
of doubt may be made therof. Seeing therfore thy selfe copassed about
with so many anguishes and strayts,
what canst thou do but say with the
Prophet

Prophet: The panges of death haue enuironed me, and the sorrowes of hel haue compassed me round about.

Ponder, the affliction, paine, & sorrow wherein thy poore soule shal find it selfe at so strait and rigorous an examination, in which it is to giue an account of whatsoeuer it hath fraudulently taken, euen of a pin, or tagge of a point. There thou shalt be asked account of thy life, thy goods, & family, of the inspirations of God; and aboue all, of the most precious bloud of Christ, and vse of the holy Sacraments.

Gather hence a great desire from this day forward to examine thy conscience with the greatest seuerity thou canst, chastising thy selfe rigorously for the faults thou shalt find, though they seeme but little, sith he that is afterwards to examine and iudge thee, is God, who seeth more then thou art able to see. Beseech him, that he will not enter into iudgment with thee, because no man liuing (as his holy Prophet testifyeth) shalbe iustifyed in his sight.

THE

THE 3. POINT.

TO consider, how sad and sorrowfull thy soule will be at the departing from thy body, into which God hath infused it, & wherwith it hath liued in so strait a band of loue and amity: for it shall be scarce out of the body, when as troopes of diuells will straight encounter it, cyting it forthwith to appeare in iudgment, before the Tribunall seate of God.

Ponder, the terrours and feares which then wil beset it on euery side, how then it shall feele true sorrow and paynes, which in comparison of those it hath sustained in this life, though otherwise great, shall seeme as it were painted. What griefe shal it haue, when it shall perceiue that there is no more appealing from the finall sentence which the supreme Iudge shall pronounce? How will it feare to know whether it be in Gods fauour or no? For of the sinnes it hath committed, it is certaine, but not of true repentance for them. And if then the mercy of God should leaue thee,

thee, what wouldst thou do (poore silly soule) enuironed with so many rauenous wolues, desirous to swallow thee vp at one morsell?

Hence raise in thy selfe a great desire, to gaine by some speciall seruice and endeauour the friendship of thy iudge, and to fullfill in all things his most holy will, obeying him, respecting him, fearing him, and most hartily louing him, and finally representing vnto him his manifold merits, that therby, & by thyne own good workes, the sentence may be giuen, not against thee, but in thy fauour : for thereon dependeth thy eternall weale or woe.

THE 4. POINT.

TO consider, how strait the Processe of this Iudgment shallbe, how vpright the Iudge, how busy and solicitous thy accusers, how few thy patrons and defenders. For then thos things which most thou louedst, and for which thou didst most, and which as it seemeth should most assist and ayde thee, will not only not help thee, but rather will entangle

and

and put thee in greater ſtraits.

Ponder how that thing which
faire Abſolom did moſt loue and e-
ſteeme, to wit, his haire (as the Holy
Scripture recounteth) Almighty God
by iuſt iudgment ordayned to be the
cauſe and inſtrument of his death :
Euen ſo it will befall thee if thou be
bad, that the thinges which in thy
life time thou moſt regardedſt, and
by inducement wherof thou offen-
dedſt God, the very ſame will then
plead moſt ſtifly againſt thee, and
make thy caſe more doubtfull, and
cauſe thee greater torment : ſo thy
goods, honours, delights and pleaſures which were thy Idols in thy
life tyme, ſhall there be executioners
and ſhall torment thee moſt cruelly,
being a meanes of thy perdition.

Gather hence a great deſire
that God will pleaſe to illuminate
thyne eyes, that thou ſleep not in
death at any time, and leaſt thyne
enemy ſay : I haue preuayled againſt
him. Beſeech Chriſt our Sauiour as
he is a moſt mercyfull Iudge, that
when he ſhall come to iudge, he condemne

demne thee not, nor deliuer thee into the bloudy clawes of those most
fierce lyons, which rage for hunger,
& are at all tymes ready to deuoure
thee.

THE V. MEDITATION,
Of the body after death.

THE Preparatory Prayer, as the
first . The Composition of
place shall be to behold thy self
with the eyes of thy soule, dead and
shrowded in a sheet, lying in some
hall, or chamber vpon a cloath or
couerlet, alone without company,
thy body couered with a blacke
hearse, and theron a Crucifixe lying, with two candles on either side.

The Petition shallbe, to aske
light of our Lord to make no reckoning at all of whatsoeuer is in this
life, but only of his grace.

THE I. POINT.

TO cosider, how thy body as soon
as thou hast giuen vp the Ghost,
will remaine without life, sense, or
motion, like vnto a block, al pale, disfigured,

figured, foule, cold, horrible, and
ſtinking, and finally in ſuch a ſhape
as euery one will fly from it.

Ponder, what is the end of all
beauty, eſtimation, honour, and delight of the fleſh, and how little whatſoeuer thou haſt enioyed hitherto,
will then pleaſure thee : for he who
a little before pleaſed the eye of the
beholder with his beauty and come-
lines, now cauſeth horrour & dread
vnto all that looke vpon him.

Procure hence a great deſire of
chaſtiſing thy ſaid body, and mortifying thy ſelfe : for pamper it neuer
ſo much, yet wil it ſtill remayne fleſh,
and what is fleſh, but (as ſayth the
holy Prophet Iſay) a little graſſe? &
what is the glory thereof but the
floure of the field, that fadeth and
withereth away with a blaſt? And
ſeeing that this thou art, and in this
thou art to end, it behoueth thee to
carry thy ſelfe as one dead to the
world, & to all that is fleſh & bloud.

THE 2. POINT.

TO conſider, how thy body ſhall
depart this world bound hand &

E   foot,

foot, not richely adorned with gor-
geous and precious garments, but
clad in a poore shroud, made of an
old sheet, or some rent and pacht habit : the house, chamber, and bed
they will allot it, shallbe the hard
earth, and a narrow pit of seauen foot
long and three foot broad, and with
this it shall, and must rest contented,
who through meer vanity and pride
(as another Alexander the Great) the
whole world could scarce containe
before.

Ponder, how the hard ground
shall succeed in place of a soft bed,
a poore shroud in lieu of precious &
richa pparell, stench and rottenes
for the fragrant smells and sweet o-
dours, wormes for delicacyes and
pleasures, which shall gnaw and consume that belly which before thou
heldest for thy God.

Reape hence great confusion &
shame for thy vanity and sensuality
in desiring costly apparell, soft bedding, and large habitation, encoura-
ging thy selfe to mortify thy ouer-
great lauishnes heerin, and beare patiently

tiently whatſoeuer want of theſe
things, or whatſoeuer is not ſuch, or
ſo good as thou couldeſt wiſh, ſith
what thou haſt at this preſent, how
little ſoeuer it be, is very much and
very large, cōpared with that which
expecteth thee, and thou art to haue
heerafter.

The 3. Point.

TO conſider, the iourney of thy
body towards the graue, and the
company that ſhall carry thee to be
buryed, how thou ſhalt be borne
vpō a beare, on other mens ſhoulders
vnto the Church, ſome weeping, o-
thers ſinging.

Ponder firſt, that he who but
a while before ſtroutted vp & down
the ſtreets, looking on euery ſide, &
entred into the Church, regiſtring e-
uery thing that paſſed therein, goeth
now vpon other mens feet, blind,
deafe, & dumbe. For then although
thou haſt eyes, eares, and tongue,
yet ſhalt thou neither ſee nor ſpeake,
becauſe thou art dead.

Ponder ſecondly, how after
the office of the dead being ended,
they

they will caſt thee into thy graue, &
couer thee with earth, leaſt the people
ſhould ſee thy filth & putrefaction,
where the greateſt benefit any friend
thou then haſt can do thee, ſhallbe to
honour thee with caſting vpon thee
a handfull thereof . Why therefore
art thou ſo deſirous of aboundance
in this life, ſith at that houre ſo little
will content thee?

Hence thou maiſt gather, that
thou art not to make any account of
the vaine honours of this life, but
deeply to humble thy ſelfe, and in
thyne owne eſtimation to put thy
ſelfe vnder the feet of all, ſith thou
art to be layd vnder the feet of the
poore man that ſhal bury thee, who
will not ſticke to trample and tread
vpon thee , and deale roughly with
thee, yea and to bruſe thy head with
his ſpade or mattock. Learne by this
not to contemne the poore, & little
ones, ſeeing in thy death thou ſhalt
ſoone be equall with them.

THE 4. POINT.

TO conſider thy body in the graue, couered with earth, and vpon
                                    it

it a heauy ftone, corrupted, confumed, and brought to naught, yea
made food for wormes, who before
didſt hunt after all kind of dainty &
fauory morſels, ſweet muſick, pleafant odours, and beautifull aſpects:
low all this ſhalbe vnto thee, as if it
were not, hauing loſt the inſtruméts
and organs whereby thou mighteſt
enioy them.

Ponder, what profit thy rotten
hands do now reap of thy riches ſo
greedily ſought and harded vp togeather. What fruit do thyne eyes
now enioy of all the vanityes which
they haue beheld? what will all thy
delicacies prouided for thy taſt then
auayle thee? of what continuance
haue thoſe caſtles of aire been framed
in that thy head? what end haue all
thoſe guſts and pleaſures had, procured by ſo heynous ſinnes vnto thy
wretched body? And turning thy
ſpeach vnto thy ſoule, ſay: Looke
and conſider well, what will be the
end of this fleſh thou now haſt,
Conſider whome thou cheriſheſt,
whome thou now adoreſt. O miſe-
E 3   rable

rable wretch that I am , wherfore are all these riches, if I am to be come so naked heere ? For what purpose are these deckings and braueries , I being to remayne at last so vgly and foule ? To what end are these delicacies and banquettings, if so soone after I am to be food for wormes ?

Gather hence desires that God our Lord would illuminate & cleare the eyes of thy poore soule with his soueraigne light, that it may behold the wretched end of thy miserable body , and contemne that which is present, at the inward sight of that which is to come.

THE VI. MEDITATION ,

Of the generall Iudgement .

THE Preparatory Prayer as the first. The Composition of place shalbe , to imagine a great and spacious field , and therein all the people that haue beene from the beginning of the world . In the midst whereof is erected a Tribunall, or
Throne

Throne made of a most excellent &
bright shining cloud, and thereon a
seate or chaire of Estate and Maiesty,
where Christ our Sauiour is to sit,
and to iudge all mankind.

The petition shallbe to craue
of Almighty God, grace to apprehēd
and feele now, that which thou art
then to see, endeauouring that, since
thou art one of those which are to be
there callled, thou maist also be of
the elect.

THE I. POINT.

TO consider, the great and fearful
signes, which shallbe in all creatures at the day of Iudgement. For
as Christ our Lord sayth, the Sunne
shallbe darkened, the Moone shallbe
turned into bloud, the stars shall fal
from heauen, and the sea shalbe troubled. Finally the dread and horrour
which then shall possesse the harts of
men, shallbe so great, that they shall
not find any place or corner secure
wherein to hide themselues, whereupon they will all waxe pale, dry, &
wither away for feare, and become
as it were a liuely picture of death it
E 4   selfe.

Ponder, that if when any great
tempest doth arise on the sea, or any
boysterous whirle-wind or earth-
quake on the land , men fall into a
maze, and are astonished , voyd and
destitute of all strength and counsail,
what will they do when the sea and
the aire, when heauen & earth shallbe turned vpside downe ? who will
haue list to eate ? who will sleep?
who wil be able to take one sole moment of rest amiddest so great per-
turbation of all thinges?

Gather hence a great feare of
Almighty God , and detestation of
thy sinnes, that obtayning pardon of
them, thou maist be freed from all
these euills, which are to come as tokens and fore-runners of God his
wrath and indignation : and that he
graunt thee, through his mercy , a
good and secure conscience , since
the day of thy Redemptiō doth approach, the end of thy labours , and
beginning of thy euerlasting repose.

T H E

THE 2. POINT.

TO conſider, how the laſt day being now come, an Archangel with a fearfull voice, in manner of a trumpet, ſhall ſummon all the dead to Iudgement. And in a moment all, both good and bad, ſhall riſe againe with their proper bodies which they liued in heere on earth, and come togeather in the valley of Ioſaphat, there to attend the Iudge that is to iudge them.

Ponder, the ſorrowes & paines which the damned will feele when their ſoules brought out of hell, ſhalbe againe conioyned with their bodyes : what will they ſay vnto one another, hauing been authours and cauſes of ech others torments and miſeries? O with what curſes will they vpbraid one another, being thē to be linked togeather, to be ech others executioner? Contrarywiſe, how great content ſhall the ſoule of the iuſt receaue at the good company of the body, which whileſt they liued togeather on earth, was a mean and help whereby ſhe might ſuffer

E 5 ſomewhat

somewhat for the loue of God . O
what wellcome and bleffings will
they with one to another, feeing that
the Iudge who is to iudge their caufe
is their friend, and will now beftow
vpon them the crowne and reward
of their feruice.

Out of which thou maift gather feruent defires & purpofes not
to liue any more negligently & care-
les of thy faluation , but comparing
that which fhall happen to the good,
with what fhall befall the euill , to
choofe in this life , that which moft
will help thee, to rife againe with
Chrift, to thy euerlafting blifle and
happines.

The 3. Point.

TO confider , how all being now
fullfilled, Chrift our Sauiour fhal
truely and really defcend from heauen, with moft foueraigne Maiefty ,
enuironed with an whole army of
Saints and heauenly fpirits , and approaching to the afore mentioned
Throne, fhall command the Angells
to feparate & deuide the good from
the bad .

Ponder

Ponder, how great the griefe and rage of the bad wil be, who were so much honoured in this life, when they shall see themselues on the left hand of God in such extremity of basenes, cast off, and set at naught by his diuine Maiesty. What inward feeling and sorrow will they haue, seeing the iust, whose life they esteemed madnes, and their end without honour, accounted now among the children of God, for to be eternally honoured and rewarded. And on the other side what ioy and content will there be among the good, when they shall see themselues by meanes of their humility placed on the right hand of Almighty God, singularly honoured and exalted.

Gather heerhence, not to make any account of the right or left hand in this world, that choosing in this life the lowest place amongst men, thou maist merit in the day of Iudgment to sit on high with God and his Angels.

E 6   T H E

THE 4. POINT.

TO consider, how all the sinnes of the wicked, euen of their most hidden and secret thoughts, and the vertues and good workes of the iust, being layd open to the view of the whole world, the Iudge will pronounce the sentence. And beginning with the good, will say with a gentle and amiable countenance: Come yee blessed of my Father, possesse yee the kingdome which I haue prepared for you. And to the wicked with an angry and seuere looke: Depart from me, you cursed, into fire euerlasting.

Ponder, these two contrary ends: he calleth the iust vnto him as if he should say: Seeing ye haue imbraced the Crosse, and Mortification to follow me, come and receaue the reward which is due vnto you, and take possession thereof with eternall rest. And to the wicked he will say: Seeing for your sake I receaued these wounds, and haue inuited you with pardon, and you haue not accepted therof, refusing to receaue me, therfore

fore depart from out of my fight.
But whither,ô Sauiour,doft thou caft
them? To the euerlafting torments
of Hell .

Hence thou mayft perceiue
how much it behooueth thee , to regard how thou liueft,and with what
care and vigilancy thou art to watch
ouer thy felfe at all times, feeing all
thy workes, be they good or bad ,
are to be ftrictly examined and iudged .

THE VII. MEDITATION ,

Of Hell .

T H E Preparatory Prayer fhallbe as before. The Compofition
of place fhallbe, to imagine in
the hart or center of the earth,a huge
pit , and moft darke caue, full of terrible fire , where neere at hand thou
mayft behold what paffeth amongft
thofe innumerable foules , which are
tormented by the Diuell .

The Petition fhallbe to befeech
our Sauiour, that he will enkindle in
                                    thy

thy foule a great feare, and horrour of euerlasting paines, that thou maist escape so hideous and so terrible a place.

THE 1. POINT.

TO consider, the dreadfullnes of this pit and dungeon of Hell, which is all obscure & full of darknes, whither neuer entreth any light of the Sunne, and the fire which is there, giueth no light at all, but only such as serueth for the greater paine and torment of those who there do suffer, being swallowed vp and plunged in most grieuous paines & torments.

Ponder how, if thou canst not for the space of one only houre, endure the darknes of a dungeon: if thou darest not touch for a litle while the light fire of a burning candle, how shalt thou be able to lye in a bed of perpetuall flames, shut vp and compassed round about with those Fire-brands of hell, both in soule and body, and that for all eternity?

Gather hence, how great the malice and heynousnes of one only

mortall

mortall finne is : for which Almighty God (being fo mercyfull as he is)
doth punifh fo many foules with fo
grieuons torments, becaufe they re-
fufed to fuffer fomething in this life
for their finnes, hazarding thereby
themfelues to fuftaine fo long and
grieuous paines in fo vnfortunate &
accurfed place.

THE 2. POINT.

TO confider the company which
thefe damned foules fhall haue in
that hideous dungeon. For though
they haue beene Emperours, Kings,
and Lords of the world, yet fhal not
any one frend of theirs now bewayle
or lament this their miferable eftate,
not any one be found to comfort
them, not any vaffall or faythfull feruant to attend vpon them but their
mortall enemyes, abhorring, dete-
fting and raging againft them, full
of wrath, impatience, and enuy. All
thefe things fhal caufe new torments
and paines vnto them, the which fhal
be alfo much augmented and increa-
fed with the horrible fight of the Di-
uels themfelues.

Ponder,

Ponder, what a torment it wil be vnto them to liue, or rather more truely to dy, amongst such cruel enemies, which long to drinke their very bloud . How much more excessiue will their paynes and griefes be , when they shall perceaue with how small, and short labour they might haue escaped so long, and so intollerable torments , which now they must abide without all hope of the least refreshing, or ceasing, and in comparison whereof the torments and paynes of this life, seeme rather painted , then true torments indeed ?

Gather hence a great feare of prouoking and enkindling Gods wrath against thee, and desire to establish friendship in his loue and charity, louing him aboue all-things , & mayntaynig true peace withall men, that thou mayst be deliuered from the wicked company of so many reprobate and damned persons .

THE 3. POINT.

TO consider the grieuousnes of payns of the senses, wherwith the damned

damned fhallbe tormented : for as
the finner hath offended God by all
his fenfes, fo fhall he be punifhed in
them all .

Ponder, how the carnall and
difhoneft eyes fhalbe tormented with
horrible and dreadfull fhapes and vi-
fions: The eares with wofull lamen-
tings, howlings, and blafphemies a-
gainft God, and his Saints : The
fmelling, with the intolierable ftench
that fhall proceed from the place it
felfe, & from the bodyes of the damned, a torment not poffible to be endured : The taft, with gall and fuch
like bitter drinkes which fhallbe giuen them . Finally, they fhall haue
heaped vpon them all manner of
paynes and torments, as of the head,
the ftomacke, the fides, the hart, and
all other griefes whatfoeuer are wont
to torment vs heere in this life .

And befides this, vpon euery
one of the damned, fhallbe inflicted
other particuler punifhments, contrary to the vices whereunto they
gaue themfelues in their life time .
The gluttons fhallbe tormented with
hungar

hunger more then dogs. The drunkard with vnsatiable thirst. Those that were ouercurious in trimming and setting themselues forth in silkes fine linen & gallantry, shall there be cloathed from top to toe in frying pitch and brimstone, which shall intollerably torment, but not consume them.

Hence it is good, thou raise in thy selfe a great courage and vigour of mind to contemne al the pleasures & delights of this life: seeing they are the cause of these torments, standing in feare of that sentence which sayth: As much as he hath gloryed himselfe, and hath beene in delicacies, so much giue him torment and mourning.

The 4. Point.

TO consider that the paine whereof we haue hitherto spoken, is not the most terrible of those which the damned are to sustaine : for there is another without comparison greater, which Diuines call, Of losse, and consisteth in being banished for euer from the sight of Almighty God.

Ponder

Ponder, how that this payne
alone fhall torment the foule, more
then all the reft togeather do torment the bodyes of the damned: for
fince God is an infinit good, and the
greateft of all goods, it is manifeft
that to be depriued for euer therof, is
an infinite euill, and greateft of all
euills. And fo euery one fhall curfe
his vnhappy ftate, and misfortunate
birth, gnawing and pulling in peeces
his owne flefh, and renting his very
bowells, and raging with fury and
rancour fhall turne himfelfe againft
Almighty God, not ceafing to curfe
and blafpheme his holy Name, becaufe he tormenteth him, and by his
fupreme power and authority, de-
tayneth him plunged and ouerwhelmed in that bottomles pit of fire, enclofed and fhut vp on euery fide, and
this not for one day, moneth, or
yeare only, but for all eternity.

Heere mayft thou moue in thy
felf a great affection & defire to feare
God and abhorre thy finnes: for by
them thou haft deferued already to
be caft into thefe moft grieuous pains

of

of hell: where many others be for
fewer and lighter sinnes then those
which thou haft committed againft
God . Shew thy selfe therefore gratefull , and serue him hartily , seeing
without any merit of thyne, he hath
set thee in the way of saluatiõ, if thou
wilt thy selfe .

THE VIII. MEDITATION.

Of the glory of Heauen .

THE preparatory Prayer as the
former . The Compofition of
place shallbe , to behold with
the eye of thy soule , that Celeftiall
Court, replenifhed with whole Ar-
mies & Quiers of Soueraigne fpirits
and Saints,adorning and beautifying
it , and the Holy of Holyes seated in
the midft of them with infinite glory and Maiefty .

The Petition shallbe , to beseech our Lord God , that seeing he
hath vouchsafed to create thee to enioy him, and so holy a society in that
heauenly

heauenly Court, he will giue thee
grace to liue in such sort, that departing out of this vale of teares and misery, thou mayst truely see and enioy
the same euerlastingly.

THE 1. POINT.

TO consider, the excellency and
the beauty of that glory, and of
that spacious, rich, and most fruitfull
and pleasant Land of Promise. The
length of the Eternity thereof, the
greatnes of Riches, the seruice of
their tables, the disposition and order
of those which serue, the diuersity of
their liueries, and finally the policy,
gouernement, & glory of that noble
Citty.

Ponder, how our Lord God,
though he be so bountifull and liberall as he is, notwithstanding to make
thee a way into this his glory & paradise of delights, he was not content
with any lesser price, after sinne committed, then of the most precious
bloud and death of his only Sonne
Iesus. So that, it was necessary that
God should dye to make thee partaker of that heauenly life, and that
he

he should endure griefes, paynes & sorrowes, that thou mightst liue in perpetuall ioy, and contentment. And finally, that God should be nayled on a Crosse betwixt two theeues, that man might be placed among the blessed Quiers of Angells.

Ponder furthermore, what, and how great that good is, which that it might be bestowed vpon thee, it was necessary that God should sweat so many stremes of bloud, be take prisoner by his enemyes, whipped, spit vpon, buffeted, and hanged vpon a Crosse.

Gather hence a great estimation of this glory, and an earnest desire to enioy the habitation of so soueraigne a Citty, and to walke the pathes and streets therof, that animated with this consideration, thou mayst endure with pleasure and delight whatsoeuer paynes and difficultyes may occur, for the attayning of so great a good, remembring what Christ our Sauiour performed and suffered in the whole course of his life, least thou shouldst loose the same.

THE

THE 2. POINT.

TO confider, that Almighty God did not prepare this houfe and pallace for his honour alone, but for the honour and glory alfo of all his elect, fullfilling that which himfelfe fayd : I honour and glorify thofe, who honour and glorify me. And not content with this, he doth, and will glorify, not only the foules, but alfo the bodyes of his elect, allotting them a place in that his Royall Pallace.

Ponder, that it is the will of the Father of Mercyes, that the flefh which deferued rather to lye like a brute beaft in a ftable, be placed & glorifyed amongft the Angells in Heauen : that as it hath holpen to carry the burden, it be alfo partaker of the glory, enioying the fame in all the fenfes of the body, which then fhallbe more pure and perfect then euer before : for euery one of them fhall haue their fpeciall dilight and glory, as the fenfes of the reprobate in hell, fhall haue particuler payne & griefe.

Gather

Gather hence feruent defires
to mortify thy fenfes, taking henceforward particuler care in the guard
therof, feeing that for the paines
which laft but a fmall while in this
life, thou fhalt be rewarded & crowned with that immenfity of eternall
glory, without meafure or end of fo
great ioyes.

THE 1. POINT.

TO confider the content which
thou fhalt receaue at that heauenly fociety and company of Saints, &
efpecially of the Saint of Saints Chrift
Iefus our Lord, and at the glory and
beauty of his facred body which was
before fo much diffigured vpon the
Croffe for thee.

Ponder, that notwithftanding
the multitude of the bleffed be innumerable, yet there is not any difor-
der or confufion among them, but
moft perfect peace and vnion, becaufe the vertue of loue and charity
is there obferued in the higheft degree, they being more perfectly vnited among themfelus, then the parts
of one and the felfe fame body, are
one

one with another, according to that
which our Sauiour demaunded of his
Father, faying: I pray thee (Father)
that they may be one (by loue) as
we alfo are one (by Nature.)

Ponder further more, that
although fo infinit number of heads
be adorned with moft precious
cownes, and euery one with a fcep-
ter in his hand, all notwithftanding
are content with that they haue, and
no one enuyeth at another, becaufe
that kingdome is fo great and fo ca-
pable, and their iurifdiction fo ample and large, as there is moft abundantly and completly inough for all.

Hence raife in thy felfe great
ioy with a burning defire to appeare
in the prefence of thy Sauiour, to behold his moft fingular beauty, and to
enioy that glorious cotenance, vpon
whome the Angells defire to looke:
for if thou on thy part benot backward in his feruice, he doubtles will
be large and bountifull in graunting
thee thefe fauours and benefits,
manifefting vnto thee his infinite
glory and beauty, togeather with the
F glory

glory of all thofe bleſſed Saints and
heauenly Courtiers . Let therefore
thy workes be ſuch as thou mayſt
deſerueto be one of the number of ſo
holy a company , and to liue euerla-
ſtingly with thofe beloued children
of Almighty God.

The 4. Point.

TO conſider the wonderfull and
excefſiue ioy which the ſoules of
the bleſſed vill receaue at the cleare
ſight of Almighty God, wherinconfi-
ſteth the eſſential glory of the Saints.

Ponder, how the only ſight of
that diuine countenance ſhall ſuffice
to giue perfect contentement to all
thofe bleſſed ſoules : for if the things
of this world delight vs ſo much, how
much will that infinite goodnes delight vs, which containeth in it ſelfe
the perfection and ſumme of all that
is good ? And if the ſight of the creatures alone be there ſo glorious, what
ſhall it be to ſee that face, and that
beauty, in whome all graces and be-
autyes do ſhine ? beholding once the
myſtery of the moſt bleſſed Trinity,
the glory of the Father, the wiſedom
of

of the Sonne, and the goodnes and
loue of the Holy Ghoſt.

Deſire from hence forward,
not to ſee, haue, or enioy in this
world any quiet, eaſe, riches, or content, in which thy affection may reſt,
but only in Almighty God, & being
moſt willing to depart from al earthly comfort, that thou mayſt not be
depriued of ſo diuine a ſight, and ſo
ſoueraigne a good, as is our God,
ſaying with the holy Prophet: One
thing I haue aſked our Lord, this will
I ſeeke : That I may dwell in the
houſe of our Lord all the dayes of
my life, that is, for all eternity.

F 2   THE

THE
SECOND BOOKE
OF MEDITATIONS,

appertayning to the Illuminatiue Way.

VVhat is the Illuminatiue VVay.

THOSE who be alrea-
dy iuſtifyed, & be de-
ſirous to go forward in
that which they haue
begun, & ſo gaine true
and ſolid vertues, increaſing dayly
therin, muſt walke this ſecond way,
commonly called the Illuminatiue
Way. The end of which way is to
illuminate the ſoule with the light of
ſundry truthes and vertues, & with
liuely and effectuall deſires of knowing

ing God, and to vnite himselfe with
him , exercising himselfe in the considerations of the diuine Mysteryes
of the life and death of our B. Sauiour: for by meditating of these, and
by carrving them alwayes in his hart
he shall stir vp and enkindle in himselfe , motions of deuotion , proper
and peculiar to this way, to wit, loue,
and desires of the vertues of Humility, Patience, Chastity, Obedience,
Pouerty of spirit, Charity & the like.
For to what vertue can any one be
inclined , wherof he may not find in
the life and death of our Sauiour
meruailous examples, it being as it
were a royall table, or banquet fur-
nished with all forts of meats, a paradise full of all delights, a garden
set forth with all manner of flowers,
a market abounding with all things,
and as it were a spirituall faire replenished with all good things that we
can with for, as in this second booke
shallbe seene.

An Aduertisement.

I T seemeth vnto me conuenient
for the better obseruing of our in-

tended breuity) not to treate from
hence forward in the ensuing Meditations, of the Preparatory Prayer,
of the Composition of Place, or of
the Petition,since it wil suffice to haue
done it in all the Meditations of the
first Booke, of which euery one may
make his benefit, and haue a general
knowledge & light, inough to make
alwayes the sayd three thinges, according as the subiects of the Meditation shall require : for more perspicuity whereof let vs put an example or two.

    Will you meditate vpon the
Birth of our Sauiour Christ, or on
the pennance which he did in the
desert &c. In the former the composition of place may be as followeth.

    Imagine that you see with the
eyes of consideration, as it were a
house or cottage vnhabitable, forsaken of all, open on euery side, full
of cobwebs and filth, exposed vnto
the wind and snowy weather, and in
a corner therof on the ground, vpon
a little straw the only begotten Sonne
of Almighty God, Iesus Christ our
                Lord,

Lord, crying like a little infant, tre-
bling and quaking for cold, the moft
Bleffed Virgin our Lady , and her
Spoufe S. Iofeph full of deuotion ,
admiration, and aftonifhment, adoring him on their knees.

Let thy Petition be to obtaine
grace of his Maiefty, to performe the
like with them, and to know, ferue,
and be gratefull for the fauours and
benefits he commeth to beftow v-
pon thee, thou being fo vnworthy of
them .

In the Meditation of the defert,
The compofition of the place may
be made thus : Behold with the interiour fight of thy foule, Iefus Chrift
our Lord, all alone in a defert, com-
paffed with high mountaines , and
craggy rockes, doing for the fpace of
forty dayes hard and rigorous pennance, not eating any thing at all,
enuironed with the fierce and wild
beafts of the woods , caft vpon the
ground vnder a hedge, or at the foot
of fome tree (for fuch was his fhelter
and place of repofe) treating day &
night with his Eternall Father about

F 4   thy

thy saluation and remedy .

The Petition shalbe , that his
Maiesty will vouchsafe to do thee so
great a fauour as thou mayst serue &
accompany him in that desert and
wildernes : for such holy company
willbe to thee a paradise and glory .

And after this manner thou
mayst alwayes make in the beginning and entrance of thy Prayer, the
Composition of place , and Petition,
according as the passage or Mystery
which thou dost meditate shall require, humbly crauing ayd , and fauour of the Holy Ghost, who (as a
most excellent maister of spirit) will
teach thee far better, then I can .

But one thing is specially to be
noted , that when thou art to make
the Composition of place in some
passage or Mystery of Christ, either
newly borne, or bound to the pillar,
ornayled to the crosse, thou must not
imagine as though it happened a far
of, in Bethelem, or in Ierusalem , a
thousand, and so many yeares since ,
for this doth weary the imagination ,
and is not of so much force to moue .
But

But rather imagine thofe thinges, as if they were prefent, and euen now did paffe before thyne eyes : feeing and beholding with the eyes of thy foule the infant Iefus weeping and crying in the cradle or manger . And as it were heare the ftroks of whips, and knocking of the nailes, whereby thou fhalt both pray with more facility, fweetnes, attention, and deuotion, and be moued more, & reap more aboundant fruite and profit thereof .

THE I. MEDITATION.
Of the Conception of our B. Lady .

THE I. POINT.

TO confider, and with the eyes of thy vnderftanding to behold the three diuine Perfons, Father, Sonne, and Holy Ghoft, in the Throne of their glory and Maiefty, (in whofe prefence do affift an innumerable number of Angells) ordayning and decreeing in that fupreme Counfell, that feeing the ruine and

perdition

perdition of mankind, and the for-
getfullnes of their eternall weale and
faluation, was fo great, to redreffe
the domage and vniuerfall hurt, the
fecond perfon of the moft B. Trinity
the only begotten Sonne of the Eternall Father, fhould become Man to
redeeme vs.

    Ponder, the exceffiue loue
which did borne and inflame his diuine breaft, for hauing many other
meanes to redeeme thee, which
would haue coft him farre leffe, he
would notwithftanding make choice
of no other, but of that which fhould
coft him moft of all, the more to declare his vnfpeakable loue towards
thee, making himfelfe Man, that he
might be more humbled therby, and
inuefting himfelfe with the bafenes
of thy flefh to communicate vnto
thee his greatneffe: he that was before impaffible, became mortall, he
that was Eternall, temporall, and of
a Lord, aflaue, of the King of heauen,
a worme and reproach of the earth.

    Hence thou mayft gather the
great longing defire our good Lord
                 had

had of thy saluation, seeing he would
vndertake so much for thee, for thy
soules health . Stir thou vp likewise
in thy selfe feruent desires of humiliation, the better to serue him , for
that he so humbled himselfe to redeem
thee .

THE 2. POINT.

TO consider , how Almighty God
hauing determined to make himselfe Man, and to be borne of a Mother , as other men are , ordayned
that his holy spirit should begin to
build the house , wherein he was to
dwell, creating the sacred Virgin our
B. Lady, pure, and without spot or
blemish, free from all staine of sinne,
originall or actuall . And certainely
it was meete that such a priuiledge
should be graunted her , in whome
God was to lodge and dwell, as in his
holy Temple .

Ponder , that as all our hurt
and perdition entred into the world
by a man and woman , God in like
manner would that our Redemption
should haue beginning by another
man , and another woman . And as

F 6   death

death entred into the world by Adam
and Eue when they sinned : so the
life of grace should enter by Iesus &
Mary which neuer sinned, vnto
whome men should repaire for remedy of their wants, with like confidence as they would haue recourse
to their owne Father and Mother.

Gather hence, an earnest desire
of the loue of God, who by such
meanes and remedyes, vouchsafed
to restore thee vnto his grace, and
friendship, making thee (as S. Paul
sayth) his child & member of Christ,
and heire of heauen. Acknowledge
the good thou hast receiued of him,
and be thankefull for so great a benefit: behaue thy selfe withall humility and subiection towards thy Parents and Superiours, sith he, who
was supreme and absolute Lord of al
thinges, did subiect himselfe & obey
his creatures, with so great an example of humility.

THE 3. POINT.

TO consider, how in the very instant that God created the soule
of the Blessed Virgin Mary, forming
there-

therewith that little and tender body
of hers, in the wombe of her Mother
S. Anne, in that very moment he
did alfo enrich and beautify it with
his foueraigne grace, fanctifying her
from the very inftant of her Conception, & preferuing her from original
finne, which as being the daughter
of the terreftrial and finneful Adam,
fhe was naturally to haue incurred.

Ponder, how great a glory and
how fingular an ornament it is to al
mankind, that a pure creature, being
naturally conceiued of man & woman, fhould be fo highly aduanced,
and adorned with fuch plenty of
grace, and chofen of God, as a moft
precious veffell, wherin to place and
beftow all thofe his diuine and foueraigne treafures, which was fit fhe
fhould haue, who was predeftinated
to be the Mother of God, & to crufh
the Head of the infernall Serpent.

Inuite the Bleffed Angells, the
Heauens, the Earth, and al Creaturs
to the prayfe of our Lord God, for
fo fingular a fauour beftowed on the
Bleffed Virgin, and in her vpon al the
world

world. For that he chose her to be
his Mother, wherby she is also made
thy Mother, and Aduocate for all
sinners, by whome thou, and we all
find accesse to the Throne of hi * infinite mercy : for none hath beene
truely and sincerely deuout vnto her
who hath not at last arriued at the
port of euerlasting Blisse.

The 4. Point.

TO consider, how Almighty God
hauing created this glorious Virgin, besides that first grace (aboue
mentioned) of preseruing her from
sinne, and sanctifying her soule, he
did both then, and afterward from
time to time endue her with new
prerogatiues of singular priuiledges,
giuing her from thence forward the
title and claime to the dignity of Mother of God, to which dignity in due
time he intended to aduance her.

Secondly, graunting her that
she should feele no kind of bad incli-
natió, or disordered appetite. Thirdly confirming her in grace in such a
singuler manner, as in seauenty and
so many yeares which she liued, she
                                neuer

neuer committed any mortall sinne,
not so much as in thought. Fourthly
preseruing her also from all veniall
sinne, a thing wonderfull aboue all
wonders. Fifthly causing her to conceiue the Sonne of God by vertue of
the holy Ghost, and bring him forth
without any payne at all, or detri-
ment of her Viirginall purity &c.

Ponder, how conuenient it was
that Almighty God should exalt and
honour withall these graces and priuiledges and many more, this most
pure Virgin. For it is his generall custome and manner of proceeding to
make thinges proportionable to the
end for which he createth them.
Wherefore our Blessed Lady being
chosen to the highest dignity that can
be imagined, next to the humanity
of the Sonne of God, to wit, to be
his Mother, there were also graunted
her the greatest graces and priuiledges, the greatest sanctity and perfection, next after him.

Reioyce and be hartily glad of
the infinit and soueraigne fauours,
which God hath bestowed vpon this
Blessed

Blessed Virgin . Inuite the Angells, that afterwards adored the Sonne of God, when he entred into the world to come now withal ioy and gladnes to reuerence her that is to be the Mother of God , and their heauenly Queene . And ioyning thy selfe with them, salute her in the wombe of her Mother with the words which after were spoken vnto her by the Angel Gabriel : Haile, full of grace, our Lord is with thee. Beseech him also o Blessed Lady, that he will likewise be with me, to purify my soule, bridle my flesh, and replenish me with his grace and vertues.

THE II. MEDITATION.

Of the Natiuity of our Blessed Lady, and her Presentation in the Temple.

THE I. POINT.

TO consider, how the whole world being before ouerwhelmed with darknesse and ignorance, couered with an obscure and fearfull night, at the birth of this most

moſt Bleſſed Virgin it began to ſhine
with a new & vnwonted brightneſ,
the day as it were breaking vp, and
this ſoueraigne morning-ſtar ſprea-
ding her beames ouer the whole face
of the earth, the Angels of heauen &
the iuſt that liued heere on earth reioycing and exulting, when they vn-
derſtood that the day did now approach, and the Sonne of iuſtice to
be at hand, who with his heauenly
light would illuminate the world, &
deliuer it from all the euils and miſeryes which it did then ſuſtaine.

Ponder, that with great reaſon
our Holy Mother the Church, guided by the Holy Ghoſt, doth ſay in
the office of this day: That the Natiuity of the B. Virgin hath brought
ſingular ioy & gladnes to the world.
For if the Angell Gabriel truly ſayd
to Zachary, that many ſhould reioyce and take pleaſure at the Natiuity of his Sonne S. Iohn Baptiſt,
becauſe he was to be the fore-runner
of the Meſſias, and to point him out
with his finger, and ſay, Behold the
lambe of God: how much more may
the

the whole world now reioyce, celebrate, and keep Holy day on which
this moſt glorious Virgin was borne,
ſhe being to ſhew vnto vs our Lord
and Sauiour in a far nobler ſort then
S . Iohn, not only poynting him out
with her finger, but bearing him in
her armes, and feeding him at her
breaſts, ſaying: Behold this is my
wellbeloued Sonne in whome I am
well pleaſed .

  Stir thy ſelfe vp to affection of
ioy, and to the prayſe of God, congratulating him forthe glorious birth
of this bleſſed Virgin which he hath
choſen to be his Mother, and haitily
thanking him for that he hath exalted her to ſo great a dignity and honour, as neuer before or after was
graunted to any pure creature. Thou
ſhalt likewiſe congratulate all mankind, for that now the happy houre
of their Redemption is at hand. Ieſus
Chriſt our Lord being ſhortly to be
borne of this immaculate Virgin, &
made man, to exalt man to the dignity of the Sonne of Almighty God.
        THE

THE 2. POINT.

TO confider how the parents of this Bleffed Virgin gaue her the Name of Mary, that is to fay, A fea of Graces, and fuch and fo great were thofe fhe found in the fight of God, that the celeftiall fpirits aftonifhed therat, demaunded one of another: What is fhe that commeth forth like the morning rifing, faire as the Moon elect as the Sunne, to whome none in the earth can be compared, none found her equall?

Ponder, how pleafing it was to the moft Bleffed Trinity to behold a Creature fo beautifull, fo faire, and gracious in the fight of the diuine Maiefty, and a Creature who with the fplendour, and fhining light of her vertues, was to giue a happy beginning to the bleffed day of the Eternall weale and Redemption of mankind, the true Sonne of Iuftice Chrift Iefus being foone after to be borne of her, and to rife out of her facred wombe.

Defire moft ardently and affectuoufly, to honour and ferue this
heauenly

heauenly Lady, and to haue continually in thy mouth and hart her
moſt Holy Name. For as the Name
of Ieſus is as an oyle powred out, for
the curing and healing of all thoſe
that are ſtroken and bitten by the infernall ſerpent, the Diuell: ſo the
Name Mary hath ſuch a vertue and
force, that being called vpon with
deuotion, like a moſt ſoueraigne oyle
it illuminateth, comforteth, healeth
and reioyceth the hart of man, and
ouercommeth and vanquiſheth the
Diuells themſelues, who as her ſworn
enemies do vtterly abhorre, and de-
teſt the ſweet ſound of this her moſt
ſacred Name, and all thoſe that are
deuoted vnto her.

THE 3. POINT.

TO conſider, how this moſt Bleſſed
Child being borne, and now three
yeares of age, her parents S. Ioachim
and S. Anne, for the fullfilling of
the vow which they had made to Almighty God, to offer vp vnto him
the fruit of the benediction which he
ſhould beſtow vpon them, brought
her to the Temple, ioyfull and much
comforted

comforted that fhe was to go to fuch a place, and to remaine, and ferue her Creatour, and Lord all her life time in that holy place. Yea not content with this, out of her exceeding loue to Almighty God, fhe would alfo be the firft that euer made vow of perpetuall Virginity, and hauing made it, fhe kept it fo exactly and fo perfectly, that fhe might iuftly feem rather an Angell without a body, thē a tender Lady in mortall flefh.

Ponder the great deuotion, wherewith this Bleffed Child prefented and gaue vp her felfe to Almighty God, offering her felfe wholy to his feruice For being come to the Temple fhe was firft receaued by the high Prieft, & by him placed on the loweft ftep of the fifteene which mounted to the Altar, from which, with wonderfull ioy, alacrity, and grace (not ayded or led in hand by any) fhe mounted vp the reft of the fifteene with great feruour of fpirit, with an vndaunted courage, and refolute mind to afcend by al degrees of vertue to the higheft top of perfection.

Stir

Stir vp in thy selfe a feruent desire to present thy self to Almighty God, and to offer thy selfe in like manner wholy to his seruice, with a constant resolution to mount vp and increase euery day more and more in purity of soule and body, and neuer to separate thy selfe from him. And if his diuine Maiesty shall do thee so much fauour as to heare thy prayer, and to withdraw thee from the occasions and perils of this world to serue him in his holy Temple and house, acknowledge it with much gratitude and thankes, as a most euident signe of his special loue towards thee, and a most certaine token that he hath a particuler care and prouidence ouer thee, as a most louing Father of his dearest child.

THE 4. POINT.

TO consider how this most holy Virgin spent the yeares of her childood in the Temple. Doubtles she was a most absolute patterne of holynes, and of all kind of vertue to the rest of the Virgins liuing in place with her, so carefull, so solicitous, & feruent

feruent fhe was in the feruice of God
and in obferuing all points of his
holy Law: the firft no doubt in the
vigill of the night, in Humility and
all humble, offices the moft humble,
in purity the moft pure, in euery
vertue the moft perfect.

Ponder, the great admiration
and aftonifhment which the dayly
conuerfation and vertuous exercifes
of this moft Bleffed Child did caufe
in her companions, and in thofe who
did treat and conuerfe with her, beholding fuch eminent vertue & fanctity in fo tender yeares: Ponder alfo with what feruour and diligence
fhe fpent a great part of the day in
afcending the myfticall ladder of the
Holy Patriarch Iacob, which reached
from the earth vnto the heauens, the
degrees wherof are, Reading, Meditation, Prayer, and Contemplation,
in which holy exercifes fhe there
wholy imployed her felfe, being often vifited by the Bleffed Angels,
defcending and afcending by this
heauenly ladder, yea and by the
Lord of Angells ftanding and view-
ing

ing her from the top thereof : in which , as in many other notable thinges she seemed rather an Angell sent from heauen, then a Virgin heer borne on earth .

Stir vp in thy selfe a great desire to imitate this tender and B . Virgin in those excellent vertues which she did exercise in the Temple : which among others were Silence , Solitarines, Quiet of body & mind, Prayer and Contemplation . Be ashamed to see thy selfe so far from imitating her in any sort whatsoeuer, so remisse & slothfull in the seruice of God , and in all vertuous exercises .

THE III. MEDITATION.

Of the betrothing of the Blessed Virgin to Saint Ioseph .

THE I. POINT.

TO consider the desires which the Blessed Virgin had , being in the Temple , to liue all the dayes of her life in subiection and o-bedience, vnderstanding by instinct

of

of the Holy Ghost, how dangerous
a thing liberty is for all, & espe ially
for women, wherefore she besought
him very earneftly, that if through
any occasion she were to depart out
his House and Holy Temple, she
might notwithstanding haue whom
to obey and ferue.

Ponder, how few there be,
who defire that which this Bleffed
Virgin defired, or that demaund of
Almighty God that which she demaunded, to wit, the vertue of Obedience and Humility, choofing rather to ferue and obey, then to be a
Miftreffe & comander ouer others.
Wherefore when the diuine prouidence ordayned, that she should
come from vnder the Obedience of
her Superiour in the Temple, he
placed her vnder S. Iofeph, whome
she was alwayes after to obey, reuerence, and refpect. And this she vnderftood to be the will of God, when
he was made her husband, to wit,
that it was to the end she should performe thofe offices of Obedience towards him.

G   Defire

Defire therefore and purpofe
to be duely fubiect and obedient to
thy Superiour, whomfoeuer he be
that God fhall giue thee, learning of
this moft Holy Virgin true Humility
and Obedience, who being Queene
of heauen & Mother of God, obeyed
and ferued, not only her Superiour
in the Temple from three yeares of
age till fhe was thirteene, but many
yeares after S. Iofeph her Spoufe,
that walking the path which fhe did
and following her footfteps, thou
mayft ariue whither fhe did, that is
to fee and enioy God for euer in heauen and endles bliffe.

The 2. Point.

TO confider, how little more then
ten yeares being paft that the B.
Virgin liued enclofed & recollected
in the Temple (her parents being
now dead) the high Prieft thought
good for the fullfilling of the receaued Law, and Cuftome, to fettle
her in fome determinate ftate of life,
and fo they betrothed her to a certain man called Iofeph, who though
he were poore, yet was he nobly def-
cended,

cended, and of the bloud Royall, &
withall a vertuous and holy man.

Ponder the great Obedience,
which this Holy Virgin shewed in
accepting that state of life, which o-
therwise was much against her best
desires : but vnderstanding that it
was the will of Almighty God, she
espoused her selfe to this Holy man,
being certifyed by diuine reuelation,
that it should be without preiudice
of her integrity & Angelicall purity.
The day therefore being come in
which this most chast mariage should
be contracted, behold with what
excellent composition of body and
mind, with what virginall bashfull-
nes and modesty she gaue her hand
to her earthly Spouse, hauing been
long before espoused, and wholy
dedicated to an Heauenly King.

Desire most earnestly to imitate
the most Blessed Virgin according
to thy estate, perswading thy selfe
that obaying Almighty God, and
trusting in him, thou shalt not want
vertue, nor comfort, nor any thing
whatsoeuer with reason thou mayst
desire

desire for thy saluation, because God
as his knowledge and power is infinite, so he can ioyne Virginity with
Wedlock, Contemplation with
Occupation, and the beauty of Ra-
chel with the fecundity of Lia, so that
the one shall nothing preiudice or
endomage the other.

The 2. Point.

TO consider how conuenient it
was that this sacred Virgin should
be espoused to S. Ioseph, both in regard of her selfe and of her most B.
Sonne: for hauing from all eternity
determined to be borne of her, he
would not that her honour & fame
should be subiect to calumniation, as
doubtles it would haue beene, if she
had had a Sonne without a husband.

Ponder the great Humility of
the Sonne of Almighty God, who
chose rather to be accounted the Son
of a poore artificer (being the Sonne
of his eternall Father) then that the
same of his most chast mother should
receaue the least blemish or staine, she
being the example and patterne of al
vertue and purity.

Seeke

Seeke hence forward to maintaine the good name and fame of others, euer speaking wel and honorably of thy Neighbours, though they deserue it not, and especially of those who in any sort be thy Superiours: for as thou hast need of a good conscience in the sight of God, so thy Neighbour hath need of a good name in the sight of man, so conserue and maintaine his honour and reputation. For as the Holy Ghost sayth: A good name shalbe more permanent to thee, then a thousand treasurs precious and great. And if thou faile in this, thou deseruest most iustly to be punished of God, as a transgressour of his holy Law, which consisteth (as our Sauiour Christ sayth) in two Commandements, to wit, in louing of God, and our Neighbour.

The 4. Point.

TO consider, that Almighty God would, that S. Ioseph should not only be the defender and guard of the person, chastity and fame of the most Blessed Virgin, but also which is more to be admired, that he should

G 3   be

be withall her Spouse , and Husband .

Ponder the depth of the diuine
Counsel and Ordination in recom-
mending so great a treasure and so
precious a relique , as the sacred Virgin was, to the charge and custody of
so poore a man, the being so highly
fauoured and esteemed of God ,
as that he particulerly chose her to be
his Mother. For if our Lord keepeth
the soules of his Saints , as Dauid
sayth : and he himselfe sayd to Abraham , I am thy Protectour wheresoeuer thou art; the defence and custody of man might seeme wholy need-
les in her , of whome God and his
Angeils had so speciall protection .
Neither is it lesse wonderfull, that his
diuine Maiesty should appoint and
ordayne, that the lesser and inferiour
should help and keep the greater &
more eminent, and that he who was
lesse perfect and able , should haue
care of her that was more able and
perfect: giuing vs to vnderstand, that
there be subiects in this life higher in
grace , then be their Superiours , and
sheep

sheep more exalted then their Pa-
stours and Sheepheards.

Gather hence desires to hum-
ble thy self in imitation of the excellent humility of our Blessed Lady,
who hauing so many pledges and
tokens of the infallible protection of
God and his Angells, did notwithstanding with all Humility liue in
subiection, and vnder the gouernement not of some rich man, or some
Earle, Duke, or King, but of a poore
Carpenter, who was faine to get his
liuing by his dayly labour, & maintaine himselfe as he could by his
trade, and sweate of his browes.
And in this mans company she was
to liue at home and abroad, & whither soeuer he went, that so her fame
& chastity might be secure. Whence
thou mayst vnderstand, that seeing
Almighty God would not leaue his
owne Mother without a guard, he
will not also keep or protect any one
that shall presume of himselfe, as sufficient of himselfe: and much lesse
will assist him, who shallbe ingrateful
for the guard and superiour appoin-
G 4   ted

ted him already by God himselfe,
whether he be lesse or more eminent
in vertue, learning, or whatsoeuer
naturall or supernaturall parts.

THE IIII. MEDITATION,

*Of the Annunciation of the B. Virgin,
and of the Incarnation of the
Sonne of God.*

THE 1. POINT.

TO behold the most Holy Virgin in her secret closet wholy attending to Contemplation, and (as some Holy men do obserue) meditating the sacred Mystery of the Incarnation of the Sonne of God, which had beene reuealed vnto her, though it had not beene told her in what manner, or tyme it should be executed, nor who should be the Virgin that was to conceaue, and to bring forth so noble a Sonne.

Ponder, how gratefull this her prayer was in the sight of Almighty God, when risirg in the night tyme (her Blessed Spouse S. Ioseph perceauing

ceauing no such matter, though he
tooke his rest in the selfsame chamber) she kneeled downe in the darke
in some corner of the same chamber, and beginning to speake with
God from the very bottome of her
hart, she brake forth into these like
words with farre greater feruour thē
euer Moyses did; saying : If I haue
found grace in thy sight, O Lord, I
beseech thee haue mercy on mankind, redeeme the many soules that
do dayly perish, send downe from
aboue the Blessed Lambe of God to
take away the sinnes of the world,
let the desired of all Nations come
now at last. Vouchsafe to create her
that is to carry in her armes and bosome thy most Blessed Sonne our
Redeemer. O how happy should I
be (O my Lord) if thou wouldest
vouchsafe to make me the hand-
mayd and poorest seruant of thy B.
Mother. More would I esteem such
a fauour then to become Queene of
the whole world. Thus did the B.
Virgin speake vnto God, and obtayned doubtles more of him by such

G 5   prayers

prayers then euer Iacob or Moyses did by theirs. And answere was returned her as to that other woman of the Ghospell : O woman, great is thy fayth, be it vnto thee as thou wilt. And Almighty God dealt so bountifully with her, that insteed of making her his hand-mayd as she desired, he chose her for his Mother.

Meditate therefore often those thinges which this most pure Virgin did meditate vpon, and wish for that which she most humbly craued, to wit, to serue her, yea to be as her hand-mayd that was to be the Mother of the liuing God. Sir vp in thy selfe speciall deuotion to this Blessed Virgin, that though thou hast beene a most wretched sinner, yet she may notwithstanding for thy diligent seruice heerafter account thee as one of her adopted sonnes.

THE 2. POINT.

TO consider how that God hauing determined to make himselfe Man, and to be borne of a woman, he beheld from aboue all the women that were to liue from time to tyme
in

in this world : among all which, this
most chaft and pure Virgin Mary
was moft pleafing & gracious in his
diuine fight. And to her alone he
decreed to fend that fo glorious Em-
baffy which afterwards he did by the
Angel Gabriel.

Ponder firft, how many Queens
and principall Ladyes were then in
the world, on whome men had caft
their eyes, and were by them highly
efteemed, of whom there was much
fpeach and talke, who were much
regarded and greatly refpe&ed of al,
yea and accompted alfo happy a-
mongft women : yet vpon none of
thefe did Almighty God vouchfafe
to looke, but on her alone that was
forgotten of all, poore, retired, and
wholy vnknowne to the world : fhe
I fay alone was chofen, and called by
God himfelfe : Bleffed among al women : Full of grace, and the like.

Ponder fecondly, how the Angell, entring into the chamber of
the Bleffed Virgin, kneeling on the
ground, faluted with great reuerence
this Princeffe of Heauen, the ele&ed
Mother

Mother of Almighty God, the
Queene of Angells, & the firft word
he fayd vnto her, was: Hayle full of
grace, our Lord is with thee.

Gather hence an earneft defire
that our Lord would vouchfafe to
caft his diuine and gracious eyes v-
pon thee, to the end that as thou art
of thofe who are called, thou mayft
be alfo of the elect, although thou
deferueft it not, defiring and reque-
fting him to do thee the fauour and
grace, that (feeing thou art not an
Angell but a poore and filly worme)
thou mayft fpeake with his diuine
Maiefty, and his moft holy Mother
in thy Prayer, with great reuerence,
feare, and loue.

THE 3. POINT.

TO confider, how the Bleffed Virgin was troubled, not at the fight
of the Angell, though he appeared
in a moft refplendent and glorious
fhape (for it is credible that the B.
Angell vifited her many tymes, and
treated familiarly with her (but fhe
was troubled at fo wonderfull and
fo vnwonted a falutation, and to
heare

heare the prayſes which were ſpoken of her.

Ponder, what a meane conceit this moſt holy Virgin had of her ſelf, for being in her owne ſight ſo meane as out of her great Humility ſhe held her ſelfe to be, ſhe could not be per-ſwaded that ſuch greatnes could be contayned in her littleneſſe, and ſo ſhe deſired to be the hand-mayd vnto her that ſhould be the Mother of Almighty God. And thereupon was confounded and troubled, becauſe whoſoeuer is truely humble, is trou-bled at nothing ſo much, as hearing his owne prayſes; but the Angell ſayd vnto her: Feare not Mary, for thou haſt found grace with God, which ought to take all dread and feare from thee.

Gather hence, how meane and how baſe a conceit it is reaſon thou ſhouldſt haue of thy ſelfe, being as thou art, ſo vile and ſo miſerable a creature: ſhut out from thy hart whatſoeuer vaine prayſe men ſhall giue vnto thee, attributing the glory therof wholy to God, and the con-

fuſion

fusion to thy selfe: desire and be glad
that they intreate and handle thee as
thou deseruest, that exercising thy
selfe by this meanes in Humility,
thou mayst prosper & increase both
in the sight of God and man, as did
this most Holy and pure Virgin Mary.

THE 4. POINT.

TO consider the most prudent answere which the Blessed Virgin
made to the Angell, full of so great
Humility and Obedience, yeilding
that ioyfull consent vnto his speaches
which reioyced both heauen and
earth, saying vnto him: Behold the
hand-mayd of our Lord, be it done
to me, according to thy word. And in
that very instant the Sonne of the E-
ternall Father Iesus Christ our Lord
was incarnate in her sacred wombe
by vertue of the Holy Ghost, to whō
this worke is especially attributed.

Ponder first, that although the
dignity and office of being the Mother of God was so high and so excellent, yet because it had annexed vnto
it imminent labours, trauells and afflictions,

flictions, it was the will of A'mighty
God, that it should not be imposed
vpon her without her consent and
good will, but rather that she should
of her owne freewill accept the same
dignity, togeather with the charge)
that so she might merit a great deale
the more.

Ponder secondly, how this B.
Virgin being chosen to be the Mother of the Sonne of God, she termed
her selfe a hand-mayd, and not a
Mother, as who did accept this office
to serue as a hand-mayd, not to be
serued and attended vpon as a Lady
and Mistresse. Agreeing in this with
that which afterwards her B. Sonne
sayd of himselfe: That he came not
to be serued, but to serue his creaturs
and to put himselfe euen vnder their
feet.

Enkindle in thy selfe inflamed
desires of the loue of this vertue of
Humility, and of subiecting thy selfe
wholy to the will of Almighty God,
and neuer to resist any thing which
he shall commaund or enioyne thee,
how hard and paynefull soeuer it
                              shallbe,

fhallbe , but alwayes and in euery
thing; faying : Gods will be done.
Pouerty , aduerfity, troubles, payns
neceffity , and whatfoeuer want of
thinges in this life , receaue them as
fent by the hand and prouidence of
Almighty God himfelfe, & imbrace
them with alacrity and loue , faying
with the Bleffed Virgin : Gods will
be done .

THE V. MEDITATION.

Of our Bleffed Ladyes Vifitation of Saint Elizabeth .

THE 1. POINT.

TO confider how the Angell hauing taken leaue of our Bleffed
Lady , fhe remembring what
had beene told her of her Cofin S.
Elizabeth being great with child, did
greatly reioyce, and comming out of
her clofet , arofe and went vnto the
Citty of Iuda, and entring into the
houfe of Zachary , faluted there S.
Elizabeth her Cofin German .

Ponder , how the loue and
earneft

earneſt deſire which this Holy Virgin had to pleaſe Almighty God, brake through whatſoeuer difficultyes, & though ſhe ſaw that the way was long and payneful, the time cold and her ſelfe tender of complexion, all this notwithſtanding ſeemed eaſy vnto her. And preſently without any ſtay, ſhe departed towards that high and hilly Countrey, to accompliſh the diuine will, and not regarding the dignity to which ſhe was newly exalted, being choſen the Mother of God, ſhe deſired and reioyced to viſit, and ſerue her that was far inferiour vnto her.

Gather out of this example of ſo rare Humility, firſt a great deſire to ſubmit thy ſelfe, & to put thy ſelf vnder the feet of all, chooſing rather to ſerue, then to be ſerued, in imitatiõ of this Bleſſed Virgin, who being Lady and Miſtreſſe of all the world, went to viſit her ſeruant.

Secondly, deſire to imitate the great Charity of the Bleſſed Virgin, reioycing at that great good, and contentement which S. Elizabeth had receaued,

receaued, & for the fauour which Almighty God had bestowed vpō her: for this is an admirable and most noble vertue, to reioyce and be glad at our Neighbours good, & the contrary is the sinne of enuy, a vice proper to the Diuel, who is alwayes sory and repining at the good of others. Be thou glad therefore and reioyce, becausethis Blessed Virgin our Lady is made the Mother of Almighty God, & congratulating her, beseech that the will vouchsafe also to be thy mother: and seeing she is so humble, that she will visit and comfort thee with her most sweet and gracious presence.

THE 2. POINT.

TO consider the entrance of the B. Virgin our Lady, and of her most Holy Sonne into the house of S. Elizabeth: whome the Blessed Virgin as being most humble, saluted first, replenishing both her and the little infant in her wombe S. Iohn Baptist, and all the whole house, with many heauenly gifts : for therby the infant was cleansed from originall sinne,

finne, & filled with the Holy Ghoſt,
S. Elizabeth his mother receaued
the gift of propheſy, and S . Zachary
his Father the vſe of his tongue to
prayſe Almighty God withall: for
where his diuine Maieſty , and his
Bleſſed Mother do enter, there cannot be wanting true ioy, and perfect
comfort .

Ponder, what a holy ſalutation
this was , and how different from
thoſe which now adayes are vſed in
the world, full of vanity and flattery,
where ſo much time is loſt , and ſo
many ſinnes and offences are committed againſt Almighty God .

Gather hence a great deſire to
be viſited of this thy ſoueraigne King
and Lord , that with his diuine preſence, the greatnes of his mercyes
may be made manifeſt in thee, who
art ſo vnworthy of them, beſeeching
him to giue thee, as he did to his
Precurſor S . Iohn, light and knowledge of the high Myſtery of his Incarnation, and reioyce at his ſacred
preſence. Intreate alſo the Bleſſed
Virgin to obtayne for thee of her
moſt

moſt Holy Sonne, ſome of thoſe
heauenly fauours, which by her only ſight he beſtowed in ſuch plenty
& aboundance on this thrice happy
babe, and on his parents, that now
and for euer thou mayſt imploy
thy ſelfe in her prayſes, as they did

THE 3. POINT.

TO conſider, how S. Elizabeth
vnderſtanding by diuine reuelation, the Myſteryes of the Incarnation of the Sonne of God in the ſacred wombe of the moſt B. Virgin
Mary, ſhe began to praiſe and magnify her, ſaying: Whence is this to
me, that the Mother of my Lord
doth come vnto me? But the Bleſſed
Virgin, the more ſhe was prayſed,
the more ſhe did humble her ſelfe
attributing the glory of all to Almighty God, breaking forth into this
Canticle: My ſoule doth magnify
our Lord &c.

Ponder, that as all holy and iuſt
men do neuer attribute any good
thing whatſoeuer to their owne de-
ſerts, ſo out of the like affection of
Humility, S. Elizabeth wondering
at

at the graces & fauours which Chrift
and his Mother had done vnto her,
cryed out : Whence is it, that fo
great a fauour hath beene fhewed
me, I being fo vnworthy therof?

Defire thou likewife to do the
fame, when thou fhalt be honoured
and praifed by men, humbling thy
felfe the more, and acknowledging
that all the good thou haft wholy
commeth from Almighty God, and
is not of thy felfe. And fay with S.
Elizabeth : Whence is it, that God
vouchfafeth to remember me, I hauing beene fo vnmindfull of him?
How happen thefe things, O Lord,
to me, I hauing fo often offended
thee, and been fo vngratefull to thy
diuine Maiefty? which thou muft
practife, not only in wordes, but alfo
in workes and deeds, as the Bleffed
Virgin did, when fhe ferued her Cofin Elizabeth almoft three monthes
with great care and diligence, euen
in humble and bafe offices, exerci-
fing thy felfe willingly, yea & delligh-
ting therein, as Chrift our Sauiour
& his B. Mother did al their life time.

THE

THE 4. POINT.

TO côsider the great good which
the B. Virgin did in the house of
her Cosin , how much she did profit
all those that liued therein with her
heauenly discourses and rare examples of Modesty , Humility , and Charity . For if her only sight and presence was cause of so many & so ex-
traordinary graces both in the Mother and the child , what would (as
S . Ambrose well noteth) the company & communication of so many
dayes and months as she stayed with
S . Elizabeth , worke and effect in
them ? How pious may we imagine
their conuersation to haue beene?
how singular the exampls of vertue?
how would they exhort one another to prayer, & to inward communication with Almighty God ?

Ponder, that if by reason that
the Arke of the Testament was three
moneths in the house of Obededom,
God heaped vpon him and vpon all
his family so great benefits : with
how much more reason may we iustly beleeue that this diuine Arke of
the

the new Teftament (within which
Iefus Chrift himfelfe repofed) remayning as many moneths in the
houfe of Zachary and Eliz-beth,
would fill it with a thoufand benedictions and heauenly fauours.

Gather hence a conftant and an
vndoubted hope, that whenfoeuer
thou fhalt come to receaue Almighty
God in the moft Bleffed Sacrament,
with a liuely faith, though thou be
fo poore & miferable as thou art, he
will replenifh thy foule, in which his
diuine Maiefty defireth to make his
habitation and aboad, with many
celeftiall benedictions and fpirituall
fauours.

THE VI. MEDITATION.

*Of the reuelation made by the Angell
vnto S. Iofeph concerning
this Myftery.*

THE 1. POINT.

TO confider how noble & worthy a man this Patriarch S. Iofeph was, being of a Princely
race

race, and lineally difcended of King
Dauids houfe. But that which did
moft commend and honour him,
was not his pedegree & defcent, but
that he was true heire of the vertues
of that Holy King, as of his Meeknes,
Iuftice, and Holynes of life &c. and
finally becaufe he was a man truely
according to the hart of God. And
fuch a one doubtles it was conuenient he fhould be, who was to be exalted to fo great a dignity, as to be the
Spoufe of the Mother of Almighty
God, and to whofe cuftody was to be
commended fo great a treafure as
was his moft Holy Sonne.

Ponder, how the Bleffed Saint
knew to negotiate and to help himfelfe with the gifts which he had receaued, dayly augmenting and in-
creafing them more and more : only
one thing did caufe in him great fad-
nes and forrow of mind, to wit, to
fee his facred Spoufe after her returne from Zacharies houfe, to be great
with child, he hauing no part therin.
But as he was a iuft man, and liued
in feare of Almighty God, he would
                              not

not speake of it to any body, but
thought secretly to abandone and
leaue her. But far greater was the
affliction of the B. Virgin his Espouse, who could not but perceiue
his intention of forsaking her, and
casting her off, and be much grieued
to see him so sad & troubled in mind
whome she so deerly loued & much
respected for his holy nes of life: and
knowing on the other side her selfe
to be free from any fault, wherof she
was suspected by him, she liued in
continuall payne and griefe.

Out of which thou mayst gather, that albeit one be very holy, &
conuerse alwayes with holy persons,
yet in this life he shal not want cause
of humiliation & afflictiõ, by which
Almighty God will try his vertue,
and loue towards him as they were
not wanting to our Blessed Lady and
S. Ioseph.

The 2. Point.

TO consider the secret iudgments
of Almighty God, in not reuealing this Mystery of the Incarnation
of his only begotten Sonne to S. Io-
H   seph

feph as he had reuealed it to Zachary and to S. Elizabeth. And the cause was, thereby to take occasion to exercise the vertues of the Blessed Virgin, and her Holy Spouse.

Ponder, the great good which is contayned in Humility and affliction: for they are as it were the precursors of great consolation & comfort, as we may see in this present passage: Almighty God ordayning, that the Blessed Virgin should suffer this humiliation and infamy, to dispose her therby, and to make her more fit for those fauours which soone after she was to receaue in Bethleem.

Hence thou mayst gather, that though thou couldest cleare thy selfe when thou art accused, and shew thy innocency, yet oftentimes thou must haue patience, and relying vpon God his diuine prouidence suffer for his loue some infamy and shame. And if this be to be done when thou art innocent, with how much more patience oughtest thou to endure the same when thou art in
fault

fault, and blame-worthy : following
the example of the Blessed Virgin,
who though she were innocent, did
not seeke to excuse her selfe, but imbracing humility and silence, chose
rather to be esteemed naught, then
to discouer those hidden Mysteries,
& that most excellent treasure which
Almighty God had committed vnto
her, putting her honour into his
hands, & teaching thee therby how
thou oughtest to exercise thy selfe in
all humility and silence.

The 3. Point.

TO consider, that though Almighty God concealed that Mystery
vnto S. Ioseph for a time, & knowing that he could not find out the
cause of her being with child,
vnles he should reueale it vnto him,
he determined so to do, thereby to
defend the honour of the most B.
Virgin, sending an Angell vnto S.
Ioseph to free him from all scruple,
and suspition, and to reueale vnto
him the most hidden and ineffable
Mystery of our redemption.

Ponder, how with this reuela-

tion Almighty God conuerted the
griefe and sorrow of this Holy Patriarch, into exceeding great ioy and
comfort. And it is credible, that he
did go and prostrate himselte at the
feet of the Blessed Virgin, crauing
humbly pardon for the suspition, &
for the errour which he had comit-
ted, acquainting her with the Mystery which the Angell had reuealed
vnto him.

Hence thou mayst gather two
thinges. First, that although truth
sometimes lye hidden for a while,
yet it shallbe at length discouered &
knowne. Secondly that when at any
tyme thou shalt be suspected or accused of some fault vndeseruedly, thou
oughtst to humble, and not alwayes
to defend or excuse thy selfe, vnles
thou shouldst sometymes be bound
in conscience, for the honour of God
or good of thy Neighbour. And perswade thy selfe certainely that neuer
any thing was lost by putting thy
trust and confidence in Almighty
God, as we see the Blessed Virgin
receaued greater honour by concea-
                                    ling

ling the Myftery, thē ſhe ſhould haue
done if otherwiſe ſhe had diſcloſed
it.

THE 4. POINT.

TO conſider the faithfullnes of the
diuine prouidence, in comming
then to remedy the affliction of his
friends, when they are brought into
greateſt extremity, applying diuine,
when human meanes do faile, as
heere he did, reuealing this ſecret
Myftery to S. Ioſeph, and giuing
him to vnderſtand, that the Bleſſed
Virgin had conceiued by vertue of
the Holy Ghoſt, and that ſhe ſhould
bring forth a Sonne, of whcme he
was to haue a tender care, whoſe
name he was to call IESVS, which is
as much to ſay, as Sauiour.

Ponder the ſingular ioy and
content which this Holy Patriarch
receaued at the hearing of theſe ſo
happy tidings, how thankefull he
was to Almighty God, for hauing
giuen him an Eſpouſeſo Holy, and of
ſo great worth and dignity: & committed to his charge the care of his
only begotten Sonne. But aboue
H 3   all

all this, what and how great was the
spiritual comfort of the moft Bleffed
Virgin, feeing her Spoufe whom fhe
loued fo tenderly , and whofe affliction and trouble fhe had felt fo
much and taken fo heauily , now to
be fo full of ioy and comfort. What
thankes and prayfes did fhe giue vnto Almighty God for fo great a benefit, as was the declaring of her innocency, and affifting her in fo great
a tribulation .

Gather hence how much it
importeth thee to rely vpon the prouidence of Almighty God , and to
haue great fecurity and confidence
in the middeft of thy afflictions : feeing it is moft certaine, that his diuine
Maiefty at fit and due time wil come
and remedy all things , and fet thee
free from all trouble and moleftati-
on, to thy great comfort, and con-
folation .

THE

THE VII. MEDITATION.
Of the expectation of our Blessed Lady her deliuery.

THE 1. POINT.

TO confider that as our Bleffed Lady was a Virgin, in conceiuing the Sonne of Almighty God, fo likewife did fhe know fhe fhould fo remayne in bringing forth the fame Sonne : for the experience of what was paffed , affured her of what was to come .

Ponder the fpirituall ioy which fhe conceaued in her foule, breaking forth into thefe or fuch like words of admiration and thankefgiuing : Is it poffible that I haue conceaued in my wombe that very Sonne of Almighty God, whome the Eternall Father contayneth in himfelf! I giue thee moft hûble thanks, moftmighty Lord, for that thou haft chofen me, thy hand-mayd for thy Mother. O that the houre of thy birth were now come, that I might fee thee be-

H 4   fore

fore me, that I might haue thee in
my armes, that I might nourish thee
at my breasts, and with my milke.

Gather hence, & stir vp in thy
selfe the like desires, and in imitation of this Blessed Virgin, say: Is it
possible, o Lord, that I being who I
am, so vile and so wretched a creature, thou hast neuerthelese chose me
to be thy sonne! to receaue and enclose thee in my breast, to hold thee
in my handes, to kisse and imbrace
thee a thousand tymes! and leauing
many others, who would haue byn
more thankefull vnto thee, & serued thee much better then my selfe,
hast abandoned them and receaued
me! I render thee o my Lord God
infinite thanks for so great a benefit
and mercy. Graunt I beseech thee,
that I may duely prepare my selfe
these dayes to receaue thee, and wellcome thee into the world, as this
most Blessed Virgin thy Mother and
our Lady, did diuinely dispose and
prepare her selfe for thy comming.

THE

THE 2. POINT.

TO consider the liuely and inflamed desire which our Blessed Sauiour had in the wombe of his most Holy Mother, to manifest himselfe to the world, for the redeeming of mankind, and to giue vs the repast and food of life euerlasting.

Ponder, that his small and tender body was not so pressed and straigtned in that narrow prison of the wombe of his Mother, as was his louing hart kept in, and straitned with the force of his vehement desire: and though euery day seemed vnto him a yeare, yet he would neuertheles remayne therein the full tyme of nine monethes, and admit no priuiledge which might exempt him from suffering, or shorten the tyme of his durance therein.

Gather hence, how much it importeth thee, to dispose thy selfe these dayes to celebrate with deuotion the feast of his Holy Natiuity, imitating the inflamed desires wherwith those ancient Fathers disposed themselues for it. For so thou shalt

reap in thy hart the blessed fruit of
thy hopes.

THE 3. POINT.

TO confider how greatly the moft
facred Virgin defired at length to
behold with her eyes the only Son
of Almighty God, & the fruit of her
wombe, to adore and ferue him in
way of gratitude and thankfullnes
for the great fauour he had done her
in electing & choofing her to be his
Mother.

Ponder, with how loud and
often cryes of her hart fhe repeated
with ardent affection of defire and
loue, that which the Holy Church
doth often fing : O would to God
thou wouldeft breake open the heauens, and defcend : and the clouds
raine downe the Sauiour! And with
the Efpoufe : O my Sonne, that I
might fee thee out of this thy enclo-
fure, fucking the breafts of thy Mother, that I may kiffe, cherifh, and
imbrace thee ;

Hence thou maift gather like
affections, and defiring that thy Sauiour would come vnto thee, endeauour

uour to imitate this Bleffed Virgin
our Lady,to the end thou mayft fee,
and enioy the diuine treafure which
fhe did. And with thefe or the like
words moue and quicken thy defirs
to adore and ferue the Sonne of
God, borne newly in thy foule, as
the moft Bleffed Virgin his Mother
did ferue and adore him.

THE 4. POINT.

TO confider, what S . Iofeph did,
what his thoughts and meditations were thefe dayes : doubtleffe
through the great defire which he
alfo had to fee his Lord God , he often fpake thefe or the like words :
Come at laft O hope of all Natiös,let
my eyes behold thee before they be
clofed vp! when fhall this be ? O that
it were now: that I might once come
to kiffe and imbrace thee moft tenderly !

Ponder, how this Holy man ,
perceiuing the Bleffed Virgin to be
neere her deliuery, ferued, and che-
rifhed her, in whatfoeuer his fmall
forces , power, and ability was able ,
refpecting and honouring her as the
Mother

Mother of Almighty God, and his most chaſt Eſpouſe, of whoſe vertue, holvnes, and purity he had now ſo high a conceit and eſteeme.

Gather hence deſires to do the like, eſteeming and reuerencing this moſt pure Virgin, ſeruing her with purity of body and ſoule, and performing theſe dayes ſome particuler ſeruice towards her, that ſhe may obtaine for thee of her Sonne, a good preparation to receaue him, as this Holy Patriarch by her meanes obtayned.

THE VIII. MEDITATION.

Of our Bleſſed Ladyes iourney from Nazareth to Bethleem.

THE 1. POINT.

TO conſider how the Sonne of the euer-liuing God, being to be borne into this world, he ordayned to leaue and depriue himſelfe of thoſe commodityes which he might haue had in Nazareth, being to haue beene borne in his Mothers

thers house, & amongst his kindred
and friends, where he could not haue
wanted the shelter of a warme lodging or chamber, yea and further
commodity and attendance, such as
was not wanting vnto S. Iohn,
borne at home in his Fathers house.

Ponder, how Christ Iesus our
Lord abandoned, and contemned
whatsoeuer the world loueth, to
wit, contentments, pleasures, and
pamperings of the flesh, and sought
for all that which the world abhorreth and flyeth, as he demonstrated
in the pouerty and want of al things,
in which he alwayes did exercise
himselfe, and choosing to be borne
in Bethleem, at the time when all
things should be wanting vnto him,
in an houre and season so incommo-
dious, sharp, and rigorous·

Heere confound thy selfe, beholding so rare an example, and be
ashamed to see thy selfe so great a
louer of thy owne commodityes &
delicacyes. Humbly beseech him to
giue thee grace, that thou mayst renounce whatsoeuer pleasures and delights

lights of the flesh, and loue and imbrace pouerty and want of al things,
as he alwayes did.

THE 2. POINT.

TO consider the occasions which
Christ our Sauiour tooke to mak
this his iorney, that therby all might
know he came to obey, and serue,
and not to do his owne will, but
the will of his Father who had sent
him.

. Ponder, that as Christ our Sauiour was borne in obedience, so he
also dyed in obedience, that thou
mightst learne to obey. In regard of
which obedience his holy will was,
that his Mother and himselfe in her
should professe seruice and alleagiance, and submit themselues to the
commaundement of Augustus Cæsar, who as Emperour and Lord of
the world had commaunded that all
his subiects should be enrolled for
the paying him tribute.

Gather hence that if the King
of heauen entred into the world
humbling himselfe, and professing
alleagiance to a temporall King, it
                              cannot

cannot be much for thee to humble
and subiect thy selfe to a heauenly
King, and to thy Superiours, his sub-
stitutes on earth, to whose will thou
must endeauour to conforme al thy
actions : for this is the will of Almighty God .

THE 3. POINT.

TO consider the discommodityes
which our B. Lady suffered, who
being poore, the way long, the season sharp and cold, and in the hart of
winter , comming to Bethleem all
wett, and destitute of humane comfort , yet she carryed all with admirable patience and conformity to the
will of Almighty God ,

Ponder, how the Blessed Virgin
and S. Ioseph went that iourney all
alone, vnknowne and forgotten of
the world, notwithstãding they were
the most precious iewels the world
had euer yeilded, & inhighest esteem
in the sight of God · O how little did
the Blessed Virgin and S. Ioseph
regard the world, with al the pompe,
and honour thereof.

Gather hence desires to be forsaken

saken of men, and be ashamed of the little loue which thou hast to suffer, and that thou so easily dost complaine of the least discommodity, which is offered. Learne from this day forwards to set all thinges at naught, but only vertue & holynes of life.

The 4. Point.

TO consider, how that after two or three days iourney these holy pilgrims ariued at Bethleem late in the euening, and going from house to house, and from Inne to Inne, did enquire after lodging, either for money or for Gods sake, but found none that would receiue or lodge them, all being taken vp by persons of better esteeme and fashion then they were thought to be.

Ponder, how often this soueraigne Lord hath called at the gates of thy hart, and sayd vnto thee that which he sayd to his chast and Holy Espouse in the Canticles: Open to me, my beloued, my sister, my doue. But such was thy obstinacy, and rebellion that thou wouldst neuer intertaine tertayne nor lodge him, yea rather hast shut the dore most vngratefully against him.

Gather hence a great desire now at last to harbour and receiue this thy Lord, and Maister, and giue him some place in thy hart that he may be spiritually borne in thy soule: for doubtles he will most aboundantly requite thy good hospitality and entertainement, as he requited Martha and Zacchæus. Beseech him to come once more and knock at thy dore, for that thou wilt now open it vnto him, and giue him the best part of thy house, to wit, thy hart, that he may repose and remaine therein as long as it shallbe pleasing vnto him.

THE

THE IX. MEDITATION.
Of the Natiuity of our Sauiour Chriſt in Bethleem.

THE I. POINT.

TO conſider how the moſt B. Virgin not finding any other, was faine to take vp her lodging in a poore & forlorne cottage, yea which is more, in a vile & loathſome ſtable, the which S. Ioſeph hauing accommodated after the beſt manner he could, they there reſted very well contented, rendring to Almighty God many thanks for that ſory ſhelter and aboad.

Ponder firſt, that a poore and baſe habitation is nothing diſpleaſing vnto Almighty God, ſo it be quiet and free from all worldly vanityes. For God had rather come and remayne with a poore and humbly man (if he giue him his hart, quiet, and free) then with any Prince or King, that hath his mind buſied and diſquieted with worldly affaires.

Ponder

Ponder secondly, how the B.
Virgin miraculously perceiuing the
time of her deliuery to be at hand,
in place of sorrow and payns which
other women do feele, she was filled
with ioy and gladnes of soule and
body, contemplating the present benefit, which Almighty God bestowed
vpon the world, for the redemption
thereof: and so she brought forth her
only Sonne, and the only begotten
of God the Father, without any pain
or griefe, or losse of her Virginity :
wherat being wrapt with profound
admiration, she cryed out : Is it possible, that with these eyes of myne
I do see God who created me, now
become a child for my sake, in this
most vile & abiect place of the earth,
a stable / Is it possible that I behold
the Sonne of the Eternall God, become a tender babe ! And the splendour and brightnes of the glory of
his Father, layd vpon a little straw,
and hay ! That I heare, and see him
weep, who is the only comfort of
the miserable, and the ioy of the Angells !

Gather

Gather hence a great defire to
feele, and experience that which the
Sonne of Almighty God fuffered &
felt at this his entrãce into the world
endeauoring to get at the leaft fome
one of the vertues which then he
difcouered of Humility, Pouerty,
Patience, and contempt of all things
which this moft miferable world
doth yield.

The 2. Point.

TO confider, how the facred Virgin, beholding that Bleffed babe,
whom the Seraphims & all the bleffed Spirits do ferue and adore, lying
vpon a litl- ftraw, fhiuering for cold,
and in all chinges behauing himfelfe
as an infant, the teares trickled down
her cheeks, and bowing with great
deuotion her knees to the very
ground, with moft profound reuerence fhe adored him as her God, &
kiffed his facred feet as of her king,
his hands as of her Lord, and his
face as of her deereft Sonne, and
imbracing him and laying him at her
virginall breafts, did reioyce with
him, and fay : O child of gold, O riches

ches of heauen , O ioy of Angels, O
mirrour of beauty , thou art moſt
welcome into the world vtterly loſt
without thee : In good time art thou
come into this land of perdition, to
be a meanes for vs all to aſcend into
heauen .

Ponder , with how ſweet and
cheerfull a countenance this Bleſſed
Infant would behold his beloued
Mother, & ſmiling vpon her, would
diſcouer vntò her how the immen-
ſity of God did there lye hidden in
ſo ſmall a corps, his infinite wiſedom
in a téder babe that could not ſpeak,
his whole omnipotency in thoſe
weake and feeble members .

Gather hence feruent deſires
to adore and ſerue, as the Bleſſed Virgin did, this thy Lord and Creatour
ſeeing he debaſed & humbled himſelfe ſo much for thee ſo vile a ſeruant of his, becauſe by thus offering
thy ſelfe to ſerue him, body & ſoule,
and with all thy ability and power,
he will moſt willingly accept of this
thy good will, and giue thee grace to
ec effect it .

THE

The 3. Point.

TO confider the ioy, deuotion &
teares of the Bleffed Virgin, and
the care, and diligence wherwith fhe
did performe whatfoeuer appertay-
ned to the feruice of her Sonne, and
Lord. She fwathed him in poore,
yet cleane and handfome fwathing-
bands and cloathes, fuch as fhe had.
She with moft tender loue, and incomparable ioy imbraced him, fhe
gaue him a thoufand kiffes of ioy,
faying : My King, my Prince, my
Loue, my Lord, and my God, and
forthwith layd him downe in the
manger

Ponder how this Bleffed Infant, though he fpeaketh not a word,
doth notwithftanding from the mä-
ger, as from out of a chaire or pul-
pit, teach and read vnto thee a leffon
of Pouerty, and negleĉt of whatfoeuer is in this world : for he being a
moft mighty and potent King, hath
neuertheles no other throne or place
but only a ftable, and in lieu of rich
and coftly hangings, and cloath of
gold, the fpiders webbes, and his
bedding

bedding ftraw and hay, infteed of
the fofteft and warmeft fethers.

Gather hence confufion and
fhame, for that thou doft alwayes
defire, procure, and feeke for thy
felfe whatfoeuer is beft, whereat
Chrift our Sauiour did alwayes for
himfelfe choofe whatfoeuer was
worft: as to be borne, he chofe a
ftable, a moft loathfome place, an a-
boad of brute beafts:to dye he made
choice of an infamous place, ap-
pointed for the execution of theeues
and malefactours: for to be borne he
felected a fmall and filly Village, &
the depth of midnight, when no body might fee him: to dye he appoin-
ted the midday, and the greateft and
faireft Citty of the world. When
he was to be borne in Bethleem, he
ordayned that there fhould be great
concourfe of people which might be
an occafion that his Mother and S.
Iofeph fhould not find any lodging
or commodity for his birth, and
when he was to dye, that the Citty
of Ierufalem fhould be ful of people
that it might be vnto him an occafion
that

that his Mother and S. Ioseph should
not find any lodging or commodity
for his birth, and when he was to dy
that the Citty of Ierusalem should
be full of people, that it might be vnto him an occasion of more infamy.
To conclude, if this our Lord his election, choice & iudgement of things
be alwayes best, as doubtles it is, it
behooueth thee in imitation of him
euer to make choice of the worst for
thy selfe, flying whatsoeuer tendeth
to thy honour and estimation, and
imbracing whatsoeuer may be for
thy dishonour and contempt.

THE 4. POINT.

TO consider, what this B. Child
hath in heauen, as he is Almighty
God, and what in the stable, as he
is man, & who he is in both places.

Ponder, how this poore little
Infant who is heere lodged in so vile
a cottage, and reposeth in a manger,
is a God of infinite Maiesty, whose
seate is heauen, whose throne are the
Cherubims, whose seruants are al the
Angells, and whom all do adore and
serue. This babe is the vniuersall
Lord

Lord and eternall word in all things
equal with the other two diuine per-
√ons, who afterwards was √o glori-
ou√ly tran√figured in the mount Tabor betweene Moy√es and Elias, and
who in the day of iudgment √hall √it
in a throne of Maie√ty, amidde√t
the good & bad. He, the very √ame,
now in this his entrance into the
world, lyeth in the cribbe in a hard
and abiect manger, betweene two
brute bea√ts, preaching and √aying
vnto thee, not by word of mouth,
but of √pirit, not with many √peeches,
but with deeds: Learne of me, be-
cau√e I am meeke & humble of hart.
Behold, how euen from my cradle
votill my dying day, I haue cho√en
for my in√eparable companions, pouerty, contempt, √orrowes and afflictions.

Hence may√t thou gather, that
√eeing God him√elfe, √o great a Lord
became for thy √ake √o little, thou
mu√t al√o endeauour to humble thy
√elfe and to become little: for vnles
thou become as this little one, thou
√halt not enter into the kingdome of
heauen

THE X. MEDITATION.

Of the ioy which the Angells and men
had at the Natiuity of the Sonne of
Almighty God .

THE 1. POINT.

TO consider what passed in heauen at such tyme as Christ Iesus our Lord was borne on
earth . Then the eternal Father gaue
commandment that all the Angells
should adore him (as the Apostle S.
Paul sayth) and all of them singing
in the aire hymnes and prayses to
this new borne king, adored him
with most humble and profound
reuerence : acknowledging that litle
babe to be the only begotten Sonne
of the eternall Father, the king and
Lord of heauen and earth .

Ponder how much this worke
of the Incarnation of the diuine
word, was for the glory of Almighty God : for in regard therof, he was
glorifyed by all the celestiall spirits,
both

both in heauen and earth, who like
vnto so many flakes of most white
snow did descend from aboue, as it
were a ladder from heauen to the
little porch of Bethleem, and in token that they did acknowledge him
for their king and Lord, they kissed
his sacred feet.

Gather hence a great ioy to see
this soueraigne king adored by his
holy Angels · and be hartily greeued
to see him so much forgotten & neglected amongst men, yea so hei-
nously offended by them. Beseech
him, that thou mayst not be of the
number of those vngrateful persons,
but mayst glorify & adore his most
holy Sonne on earth as the Angells
did, and do alwayes in heauen.

THE 2. POINT.

TO consider how the Eternall Father did manifest the birth of his
most holy Sonne to the shepheards,
who were watching over their flocke
in the night time, sending his Angels
to bring them the happy tidings of
it, and to declare so high a mystery
vnto them, of which company one

l 2   approa-

approaching neere vnto them, fayd:
Reioyce, for behold I fhew vnto
you great ioy, that fhallbe to all the
people : becaufe this day is borne
to you a Sauiour which is Chrift our
Lord, in the Citty of Dauid. And
this fhallbe a figne to you, you fhall
find the infant (wathed in cloths: and
layd in a māger. And prefently thofe
heauenly fpirits brake forth into a
moft diuine melody , manifefting
therby the fingular content which
they receiued, and fayd: Glory in the
higheft to God, and in earth peace to
men of good will. The fhepheards
hearing this fo happy newes , with
great defire and loue inuited one another to feeke out him whome they
heard fo much prayfed , faying : Let
vs go to Bethleem, and let vs fee this
word that is done, which our Lord
hath fhewed to vs.

Ponder the admiration of thefe
holy fhepheards, when fo lowing the
direction of the Angell , they found
all to be fo as they had told them, yet
were they greatly aftonifhed to fee
that things fo meane & bafe, as were
a

a poore stable, an oxe, an asse , and a
manger, should be the signes to find
out the Lord of Maiesty . But far
greater was the admiration which
this very same caused in the holy
Prophet Isay , foreseeing in spirit
long before these shepheards, and
this great God and Lord so litle, and
so much humbled; wherfore he said:
Who euer heard such a thing ? and
who hath seene the like to this? God
an infant , God in swathing bands ,
God to weep ? a thing so vnbesee-
ming his Maiesty and greatnes , a
thing so strang , a worke that doth
amaze and astonish the iudgements
of men and Angells.

Gather hence desires to be
humble and lowly, as God Almighty
vouchsafed to humble himselfe: for
he manifesteth himselfe freely and
of his own accord to the humble she
pheards, but not to the proud Scribs
and Pharisies . He is willing to be
found of those who carefully watch
ouer their owne soules, but not of
those who are ouerwhelmed & buryed in the dead sleep of sinne . Haue

I ﬁ a

a care therfore to watch and pray, &
thou shalt find our Lord as these
shepheards did.

THE 3. POINT.

TO consider, the great desire which
these holy sheepheards had to
bring home with them to their cottage and cabines (if they could haue
obtained so much) those lights of
the world, the Sonne and the Mother, seeing them so solitary, poore
& vnprouided of all human meanes,
to serue and cherish them as far as
their small forces and ability would
reach, in token of gratitude for the
high fauour which they had receaued of them when they disclosed &
manifested themselues vnto them.

Ponder that for the finding out
of Almighty God, is not required,
either a sharp wit or a good vnderstanding, much learning or great
parts; neither will he be found by
such, if togeather therewith they
seeke honour and vaine glory, and
not God alone, but he is sooner foūd
out by an humble Cooke or seruant
in Religion, or by a poore & simple
swine-

swineheard, and doth most bountifully communicate vnto them his
celestiall gifts and fauours, as the
Holy Ghost himself testifyeth in the
Prouerbs.

Hence thou mayst gather desires to seeke Almighty God with
true loue and diligence, that thou
mayst also find him as these silly
sheepheards did. Beseech him that
seeing he is the soueraigne shepheard
and thou his sheep, marked with his
owne most precious bloud, he will
vouchsafe to take from thee all presumption and pride: which is the di-
sease and infection that doth wast
thee away, and make thee so leane:
and that he will shew thee, as he did
his holy and chast Espouse, where he
feedeth, where he lyeth in the midday, to wit, in the manger: that seeing thou hast made thy selfe a beast
through sinne, thou mayst find him
in the stable, a place proper for
beasts.

THE 4. POINT.

TO consider that the Eternall Father sent this multitude of Angels

I 4   to

to honour his only Son, who had so
much humbled himselt for his loue:
& to teach & instruct vs by their example, what infinite thanks we owe
vnto God for so soueraigne a benefit
as he now had bestowed vpon vs, in
giuing vs his best beloued Sonne not
only as a Sauiour, King, or Lord,
but (which is more wonderfull) as
our Brother, our flesh, and bloud.

Ponder what care the Eternall
Father euer had to exalt his most Holy Sonne, when he did most humble
and debase himselfe, as is to be well
seen both heere, and in al other passages and mysteries of his most holy
life. He was circumcised, and a Name most honorable and most glo rious was giuen to him, to wit the name of Iesus. He was baptized, and
the heauens were opened for him,
the Holy Ghost descended vpon him,
and the Eternall Father honoured
him, saying: This is my beloued
Sonne. He was crucifyed betweene
two theeues, and presently the heauens grew darke, the earth quaked,
the rockes rent, the dead rose, all the
                                elements

elements altered: finally he was acknowledged of his enemies for the Sonne of God .

Gather hence a great and earnest defire to imploy thy felfe wholy all thy life tyme in honouring and prayfing fo good a God, and he will haue care to exalt and honour thee, as he had of his moft holy Sonne, who humbled himfelfe fo much for his honour and glory . And fo doing thou mavft alfo fing the hymne of the Angells with the like fpirit and deuotion as they did.

THE X. MEDITATION.

Of the Circumcifion, and of the Name of IESVS.

THE 1. POINT.

TO confider, how God Almighty hauing fent his only Sonne into the world in habit & likeneffe of a finner, he was not content to take only vpon him humane nature, and to feeme leffe then the Angells in our mortall fleíh, but would

I 5   alfo

also on the eight day after his most
holy Nativity, subiect himselfe to the
Law of Circumcision, which was
the badge of a sinnefull child, & shed
not only teares from his eyes, but also sacred bloud from out his veines.

Ponder how great loue to-
wards vs he doth dayly discouer, for
he cannot endure that his suffering
for our weale and remedy should be
any whit delayed, though those who
were to see him circumcised, might
iudge and account him a sinner, as
taking vpon him the marke & badge
of a sinner.

Whence thou mayst gather very
great confusion, that being so great a
sinner as thou art, thou wilt not seem
to be accounted so, but rather iust
and a very Saint, and to that end
of en excusest thy sinnes. Wherfore
thou must humble thy selfe, and giue
thanks vnto this thy Lord, who hath
so wonderfully humbled and sought
to hide himselfe. Beseech his diuine
Maiesty, that as he subiected himself
to carry vpon his tender shoulders
the old Law of Circumcision, so hea-

uy

uy and painefull, thou mayſt likewiſe carry, and haue before thyne
eyes, and in thy hart, the ſweet **Law**
of his diuine Commandments: and
that he will vouchſafe to ſeaſon it
with one drop of his moſt precious
bloud, which he ſo liberally ſhed v-
pon the ground, to the end it may
looſe all the hardneſſe, and diſtaſt
which it hath.

The 2. Point.

TO conſider, that it is Gods will &
pleaſure, that thou circumciſe
thy ſelfe ſpiritually (that is) that thou
cut off all ſuperfluityes in pampering
thy fleſh, in honour and commodityes of this world, circumciſing and
mortifying thyne eyes, not ſuffering
them to behold that which is not
lawfull to deſire; circumciſing thy
tongue, making it to keep ſilence,
from vaine and idle wordes; circumciſing thy taſt, that it feed not it ſelfe
with gluttonies and delicacies.

Ponder in how much need thou
ſtandeſt of this Circumciſion, how
much thou art giuen vnto thyn own
will, and how much it behooueth
thee,

thee, alwaves to carry in thy hands, that is in all thy actions, the knife of Circumcision.

Gather hence also a great and earnest desire, to suffer willingly, & that others both Superiors & Inferiors may circumcise thee (if thy selfe shouldst be remisse and slacke therin) and help thee to cut away whatsoeuer may hinder thee from comming vnto this thy Lord whether they do it with a good or bad intention, bearing it patiently, when they shall depriue thee of thy delight, honour, pleasure and content, euen to the sheading of thy bloud for him who first hath shed it for thee.

THE 3. POINT.

TO consider how they imposed vpon this child the Name of Iesus which is to say, Saviour of sinners: as one who was to deliuer them not only from all euill, but also to bestow vpon them most excellent fauours and riches, that their remedy and saluation might be most abundant.

Ponder that this glorious Name was imposed vpon him for his greater

ter honour. For his Eternall Father
feeing him fo humbled and marked
with the badge of a finner, would
that he fhould euen then be exalted,
& haue giuen him (as S. Paul faith)
a Name which is aboue all Names,
that is I E S V S. And whereas our
faluation was to coft him the fheding
of his moft precious blcud, he gaue
leaue to whatfoeuer inftrumets were
fit for the drawing of bloud to work
their effect vpon him. to the knife at
his entrance into this world, and at
the end therof to the whips, fcourges,
thornes, nayles, and fpeare.

Hence thou mayft gather affec-
ctions and defires to adore and reuerence this moft holy and moft fweet
Name of I E S V S, hauing it alwayes in thy mouth and hart, thereby to obtaine victory ouer thyn enemies. For the Diuells do fly from
this holy Name, and the infernall
powers do tremble at it, and by it &
in it finners haue their hope & confidence, becaufe IESVS is as much
to fay, as Sauiour. And if to faue thee
and truely to beare that Name, coft
him

him so deare, as the sheding of his most precious bloud, and the spending of his life for thy sake; what is it meet thou shouldst do for thyne owne saluation? And seeing all is but little, though it should cost thee thy very hart bloud and life, say vt to him with the Prophet: My hart is ready, o God, my hart is ready so to do, so that thou vouchsafe to make me partaker of that sacred pledge.

THE 4. POINT.

TO consider, how the Circumcision being performed, & the knife of grief hauing pierced the tender flesh of thy Sauiour, they restored him vnto our Blessed Lady all bloudy, and the teares trickling down his cheeks.

Ponder with what griefe of hart, with how many teares gushing out of her eyes this most B. Virgin receiued her beloued Sonne, endeauouring to comfort him, taking him in her armes, laying him at her virginall breasts, giuing him to sucke of her mof pure milke, and saying: O spouse and king of glory, how deare

doth

doth the finne of Adam coſt thee,
how ſoone doſt thou performe the
office of a Redeemer, ſuffering pains
& ſheding thy bloud for mankind.

Stir vp in thy ſelfe a deſire to
accompany this Bleſſed Virgin in her
tears and good offices towards her
Sonne. And ſhedding aboundant
teares of compaſſion, bewayle thy
ſinnes and offences, that thou mayſt
obtaine pardon of them. And render
vnto Chriſt our Sauiour moſt humble thanks for the bloud and teares
which he ſhed for thee; auoyding
heereafter to increaſe his payne with
other new offences. Beſeech the B.
Virgin to obtaine for thee grace of
her moſt holy Sonne, that at the entrance and beginning of this new
yeare, thou mayſt renew thy life,
forſaking and caſting off thy old garments, wherein thou haſt been hitherto wrapped, to wit, thy luke-
warmneſſe, ſloth, and negligence in
thy ſpirituall exerciſes: putting on
from hence forwards feruour, loue,
and charity towards God and thy
neighbour.

THE

THE XII. MEDITATION.
Of the comming of the three Kings,
and of their gifts.

THE I. POINT.

TO confider, how the fame day
on which Iefus Chrift our Sauiour was borne in Bethleem,
he fent to thefe Kings or Sages a new
and moft bright fhining ftar, giuing
them therby to vnderftand, that the
true King & Redeemer of the world
was borne in Iury; and they illuminated with that heauenly light, and
inflamed with diuine loue, much re-
iovced at the fight therof, congratulating and inuiting one another to
go & adore that true King of Kings:
and forthwith leauing their Countrey they went with much content
and ioy to feek Chrift Iefus in a for-
raine Land, & to behold with their
corporall eyes, whome they had already feene with the eyes of fayth:
knowing very wel how bleffed thofe
eyes fhould be, that fhould behold
him.

him .

Ponder how great the deuotiō was of these Kinges, which moued them to leaue their owne Countrey, to vndertake so long and so dangerous a iourney, & to breake through so many difficultyes, which they might well imagine would befall them therein : wheras many though they be no Kings, because they will not depriue themselues of their cōmodityes, and vndergoe some small difficultyes for the loue of God, will not so much as set one foot before another for his seruice, and so do not find him . And it falleth out oftentymes, that those who are very far from Christ do by litle and litle draw ne er vnto him and find him, as may be seene by these holy Kings : and that those who be neere at hand, are cast backe and left of Almighty God for their ingratitude, as it happened vnto Herod, and to those of his Court.

Gather hence a liuely desire to seeke, find, and adore this great King & soueraigne Lord of al things
as

as often as thou shalt see the star of his diuine inspiration, to wit, the voice of thy Superiour, & the rule of thy profession, following it with great alacrity, though it bring thee to the stable, becaufe there thou shalt certainely find Almighty God.

THE 2. POINT.

TO confider how the Kings being come to Bethleem, the star stood ouer the place where our Sauiour was borne, and sparckling cast forth bright beames of light, as it were saying vnto them: Loe heere he is, whome you do seeke. And entring the place they found the true Lambe of God, who taketh away the sinnes of the world, reposed in the armes, and sucking at the breasts of his B. Mother. Who illuminating their vnderstanding with a celestiall beame of diuine light, discouered vnto thē, how that little babe, though in exteriour shew the most poore and contemptible in the world, was trueGod. and Lord of all.

Ponder the goodnes & mercy of this our Lord, who vouchsafed to
impart

impart the fayth of this facred Myftery of the Incarnation, in fuch plenty, vnto the Gentils; and communicated himfelfe vnto them fo grati-
oufly, as to call them vnto him,
though they had no knowledge at al
of him before; to feeke them out in
fo far countreyes, though they liued
without thought of him, and to call
as it were at their dores, and enter
into their harts, as if he had need of
them, and not they of him .

Hence thou mayft gather that
he hath often done the fame to thee:
for thou being neither able to defire
him, nor to taft of any fuch matter,
he hath fought, called & chofen thee
euen when thou wert moft carelefe
of him and didft fly away from him.
Be therefore thankfull and feruice-
able towards him for it, as thefe holy
Kings were. And if thou haft nothing
els to offer, take all thy finnes toge-
ther, and with harty forrow and repentance for thyn offences committed againft this thy Lord God, offer
them vp vnto him that they may be
confumed with the fire of his diuine
charity

charity, and thy soule remaine perfectly cleane and pure from them
all.

THE 3. POINT.

TO consider, that albeit these holy
Kings saw this poore infant lodged in a vile stable, wrapped in poor
ragges, layd in a hard manger, so de-
stituce and forsaken of all humane
help and comfort; yet they stedfastly
beleeued that he was the true King
and Lord of heauen and earth, and
forthwith cast their Scepters and
Crownes at his feet and prostrate on
the ground with great humility and
reuerence, adored him, and off-red
him gold as to their King, incense as
to their God, and myrrh as to a mortall man.

Ponder that as these holy Kings
offered vnto this heauenly King and
blessed infant these three mysticall
gifts: so it were meet thou didst offer
him whatsoeuer thou hast receiued
from his most bountifull hands. And
prostrating thy selfe before him, and
adoring him as thy King and Lord
with feruent loue, in lieu of gold
wouldst

wouldst offer vnto him all the riches
& goods of the world : so that if they
were thyne, thou wouldst most willingly lay them at his feet . In lieu of
incense, all the smoke and vanity of
the honours and glory which the
world can affoard thee . And insteed
of myrrh the delights & pleasures of
the flesh, wholy and most willingly
renouncing them , & desiring not to
haue or enioy them , although they
were offered thee .

Hence thou mayst gather great
confidence in the liberality of this
Soueraigne Lord, that he wil receaue
this thy present, and returne thee a-
bundance of spirituall riches for the
pouerty which thou hast promised
him, victory ouer thy passions and
thy flesh , for the vow of Chastity
which thou hast made vnto him .
And for the vow of Obedience , his
diuine loue & grace, that thou mayst
alwayes keep his holy Law , and
Commandements . And thou mayst
offer thy selfe vp wholy and entierly
in euery thing to thy Lord God , as
these holy Kings his disciples did offer

fer themselues, and all that they had.

THE 4. POINT.

TO consider, that after the offering was made, before these holy
Kings tooke their iourney homward
they receiued answere in sleep, that
they should not returne to Herod,
nor the same way they came.

Ponder that after thou hast once
found God, and dedicated thy selfe
to his seruice, thou oughtest not to
do as thou wert wont to do before,
nor walke in those rough and crooked pathes which before thou didst
tread : but must change thy course,
imbracing humility and detesting
pride, casting away anger, and reioycing in patience &c.

Gather also hence how necessary it is for thee to withdraw thy
selfe from all vice and sinne which
lead thee headlong into hell, and to
follow and imbrace all manner of
vertue which will bring thee to heauen, as the holy Kings did. For so,
doing Almighty God, who is the true
light and way which leadeth to life,
will illuminate and guid thee, as he
did

did illuminate & guide these his seruants, and fill thee with the like gifts
of his grace, with which he did replenish them, if thou dispose & prepare thy selfe to receiue it as they
did.

THE XIII. MEDITATION.

Of the presentation of the Child IESVS
and of the Purification of our
Blessed Lady.

THE 1. POINT.

T O consider how the most B.
Virgin, though after the birth
of her dearest Son, she remayned more pure and immaculate then
the stars of heauen, did not withstanding subiect her selfe to the Law of
the Purification, not being obliged
therunto; yea though in some sort it
were preiudiciall to her honour.
Wherefore as if she had beene like
to other women vncleane, comming
out of the stall of Bethleem, where
she was deliuered, in company of
her Spouse, shed carryed her only
begotten

begotten Sonne to the Temple of Ie-
ruſalem, there to preſent him to the
Eternall Father, and to offer ſacrifice
for him .

Ponder how different this entrance and obligation is, which the
Sonne of God this day maketh inthe
beginning of his life,from that which
he made in the end of the ſame : for
now he entreth intoIeruſalem borne
in the armes of the moſt B . Virgin,
but afterwards he ſhall enter a foot
carrying the Croſſe vpon his ſhoulders whereon he is to be crucifyed.
To day he entreth to be offered in
the armes of Holy Simeon : then to
be offered in the armes of the Croſſe.
To day he ſhallbe offered and redeemed with fiue ſicles (a certaine
coyne of that time) then as Redeemer he will offer himſelf for the loue
of men , to be whipped , crowned
with thornes , nayled and crucifyed
vpon the Croſſe, & to a moſt painefull and ſhamefull death .

Gather hence great and earneſt
deſires to offer thy ſelfe , togeather
with this thy Lord vnto the Eternal
Father

Father: alwayes to execute his most
holy will, and to carry thy Croffe
and the aduerfities which befal thee,
after his most Holy Sonne : feeing
that he and his Bleffed Mother being most innocent and most pure,
fubmitted themfelues to the law of
finners, as if they had beene themfelues alfo finners, with such and fo
heroicall acts of humility. And be a-
fhamed, feeing thy felfe fo foule and
fo abominable a finner as thou art, to
be fo proud and haughty ; defiring
to be reputed and regarded of all as
pure, holy, and iuft.

The 2. Point.

To confider the fpirit & deuotion
wherwith the Bleffed Virgin performed this obligation or offering
for all mankind to the Eternall Fa-
thar. And in imitation of her, offer
thou alfo vnto our Lord the facrifice
of his Sonne in remiffion of thy fins.
For it is better, and more gratefull in
his fight, then were all the facrifices
exhibited in old tyme by the Patri-
arches and Prophets. And if Almighty God had refpect to Abel and to

K   his

his gifts , how much more will he
respect the Blessed Virgin,& that B.
lambe her Sonne which this day she
offered vnto him .

Ponder the little spirit and deuotion wherwith thou makest thyn
offerings in Masse and Communion:
not offering to the heauenly Father,
his Eternall Sonne with such deuotion and thankesgiuing as it behooueth thee to do , in regard that he
hath giuen thee him for thy Redeemer and Maister, yea which is more
to be admired , hath deliuered him
into the hands of death it selffor thee
and for thy sinnes .

Stir vp in thy selfe affections of
deuotion with a great desire of amē-
dement of thy life : beseeching our
Lord to accept this thy offering. For
though on the one side in regard of
thy selfe who doest make this offer ,
thou mayst iustly feare to be reiected
as thou deseruest:yet because he doth
also make offer of himselfe for thee ,
trust and haue great confidence that
thou shalt be admitted,and haue thy
sinnes forgiuen thee .

THE

THE 3. POINT.

TO consider that although at the same tyme at which the Blessed Virgin our Lady entred into the Temple with her most Holy Sonne in her armes, there were many more of all sorts and conditions, Priests & learned men, noble and of the vulgar sort, yet to Simeon and Anna the Prophetesse only, God imparted his heauenly light to know the Sauiour of the world, in reward of their good life, and holy desires.

Ponder first with what seruour and alacrity that Holy old man Simeon came with stretched-out arms to receiue his Sauiour, and sayd as we may piously beleeue vnto the B. Virgin: Giue me, ô Virgin, your only Sonne, for he is my God, and Lord: he is the desired of all Nations: who is to pay for my trespasses and sinnes: who must open me the gates of heauen, and who must saue me.

Ponder secondly, when this holy old man sayd these or the like words, what floods of tears trickled

K 3   downe

downe his venerable cheeks? What
thanks and prayses did he yield vnto
him who had reserued him for so
great a fauour? How tenderly did he
imbrace the Infant in his armes,
saying with the Espouse in the Canticles: I haue found him whome my
soule loueth : I hold him, neither wil
I let him goe .

Gather hence the like longing
desires to receiue thy God, and to
place him within thy very bowells,
& to put him with the Holy Espouse
as a seale vpon thy hart: for so doing
thou mayst iustly hope that because
he is faythful in his promises, though
he stay awhile, he will come at last &
comfort thee, as he comforted S.
Simeon in reward of the feruour and
deuotion wherwith he serued him in
his holy Temple .

THE 4. POINT

TO consider, that this Holy old
man Simeon receiuing the child
in his armes, made oblation of him,
to the Eternall Father : for that he
had a very great desire to see Christ
our Lord in mortall flesh , and Almighty

mighty God had made him promise
thereof. And not only this his desire
of seeing him was fullfilled, but also
it was granted him to take him in his
armes, to kisse and imbrace him, &
to vnderstand by reuelation of the
Holy Ghost, that within that little
body was included all the greatnes,
Maiesty, & immensity of Almighty
God himselfe.

Ponder, that God Almighty is
not wanting in performing his promises : but rather doth performe
more then he promiseth, wheras the
world, the flesh, and the Diuell contrarywise, do promise that which
they cannot giue vs, they proffer
that which is good but perform that
which is euill, they promise pleasurs
and contentments, and giue disgusts
and sorrowes, finally in lieu of life,
they bring eternall death.

Gather hence an inflamed desire, with this Holy old man S. Simeō
to haue in thy armes this most sweet
babe, the heire & king of the world,
the only begotten Sonne of God, the
eternall weale and saluation of mankind,

kind, the summe of all happynesse, the author of thy euerlasting blisse; seeke, craue, and sigh after this : for if it be graunted thee , this alone wil aboundantly supply all other wants, and fulfill thy desires .

THE XIIII. MEDITATION.

Of the flying into Ægipt.

THE 1. POINT.

TO consider how King Herod , hauing vnderstood by the Sages of the birth of Christ our Sauiour, King & Lord of the whole world, fearing least he should take from him the kingdom which he had vsurped , determined to seeke him out, and to make him away : though he knew by the Holy Scriptures , that he was to be at least a great Prophet sent by God for the saluation of the world .

Ponder , how soone our Sauiour Christ beginneth to be persecuted : for he was scarcely borne, when presently Herod sought his life, the
Eternall

Eternall Father so ordayning, that
his most Holy Sonne and his Blessed
Mother should from their infancy
walke the way of persecution and
affliction: which ought to be a great
comfort vnto thee, if peraduenture
thou see thy selfe persecuted in regard of thy vertue; remembring that
which our Sauiour Christ sayd to his
Disciples: The seruant is not greater then his Maister: if they haue persecuted me, you also will they persecute. For they hate not those who
are of their owne crew and faction,
but those who are contrary vnto the
and resist them.

Heere, out of compassion lament, and be sorry, that there should
be found any so wicked, and vngra-
cious, as to seeke Iesus Christ with
intention to kill him: whereas he
commeth to giue life vnto the dead,
and an eternall kingdome of heauen
for a temporall. Take heed lest thou
doe not the same (that wicked King
did) through thy sinnes: for they do
seeke to persecute and kill him.

THE 2. POINT.

TO consider how S. Ioseph being
a sleep, an Angell appeared vnto
him and sayd : Arise, and take the
child , and his Mother, and fly into
Ægipt.

Ponder, the punctuall obedience of this Holy man in putting in
execution the diuine will : for being
a sleep, and reposing (at which tyme
trauaile is most yrksome vnto vs) he
forth with arose and obeyed in that
which he was commanded, not being scandalized nor troubled with
such a nouelty and sodaine flight. To
teach thee, that in the middest of thy
ease and prosperity , thou art to be
prepared for afflictions, & at al times
to leaue thy bed and rest, whenso-
euer Almighty God shall command
thee : esteeming it a thing of highest
price, to know and fullfill the diuine
wil, whether it be manifest vnto thee
by reuelation of God or his Angells,
or by ordination of men. For albeit
the first be more glorious , yet in the
second is exercised more humility.

Conceiue a great desire to obay
Almighty

Almighty God, as S. Ioseph did, because heerein consisteth true iustice
and sanctity, that thou do not reply,
nor contradict the Commandement
of God in any thing, but speedily
fullfill the diuine will : reioycing to
subiect thy iudgement, not only vnto God, but also vnto men for the
loue of God.

THE 3. POINT.

TO consider the small security
wherwith Iesus Christ our Sauiour liueth amongst those of his own
Countrey. For comming to remayne
with them, they receiued him not,
wherefore it was necessary an Angell should aduise S. Ioseph to take
the child, and his Mother, and to fly
into Ægypt, amongst a strang and
barbarous Nation.

Ponder how Christ our Lord
being to fly into the desert, he might
haue gone to the contry of the three
Sages, where he should haue beene
knowne, respected, and serued : he
would not do so, but went into Æ-
gypt amongst his enemies & stran-
gers, where he had neither house,

K 5　　　　　　　nor

nor harbour, nor any maintenance at all, that by wanting all commodities, he might haue occasion of more to suffer.

Gather hence how pleasing it is to God, that his elect (especially such as be Religious persons) remaine where his will is they should, and not where they, guided by their owne fansy, desire to dwell: because the true security of the soule, doth not cosist or proceed from the place, but from the assistance and protection of Almighty God.

Consider also, that the Angell sayd vnto S. Ioseph: Be there, to wit in Ægypt, vntill I shall tell thee: that is, that he should remayne in Ægypt vntill he should heare further from him: giuing therby to vnderstand that in matter of afflictions and desolations, and also in whatsoeuer offices and imployments he imposeth vpon thee, thou ought est not to assigne, nor seeke to know the time, how long they are to continue, but must leaue this care vnto Almighty God, be it litle or much, who

knoweth

knoweth much better what is befitting vs then we our selues.

THE 4. POINT.

TO consider how the most Blessed
Virgin, as soone as she vnderstood by S. Ioseph the diuine will,
being most humble and obedient,
she forthwith obeyed, and fearing to
fall into the hands of Herod, and so
endanger that precious Iewel, which
was all her riches, not standing vpon
labours or paynes, nor vpon the in-
commodityes of the way, she pre-
senly arose, and withall speed tooke
the Blessed babe in her armes & fled:
not regarding that she leaueth her
countrey, parents, and friends, her
house, and whatsoeuer she had there
so that she might keep and assure that
which of her was far more esteemed
then all the rest.

Ponder how the most Blessed
Virgin and S. Ioseph trauailed all
along that wearisome way vnprouided of all commodityes, in great
pouerty, vpon some little beast, or
asse, carrying a few cloaths of the B.
child, and some tooles of S. Ioseph,

K 6   the

the rest he carryed on his backe. Also what extreme cold the B. Virgin endured, being tender and of a delicate complexion, it being then the depth of winter. Behold the foule wayes & durty passages which they met withall: and finally how after long trauaile and paynes taken they came into Ægypt, & betooke themselues to some poore cottage, vnknowne & neglected of the world: but very much comforted, for that the Blessed Infant had escaped the hands of his enemies.

Gather hence a great loue to pouerty, and to be contemned and forgotten of the world; and seeing in this world thou art as a way-faring man, desire to ioyne thy selfe with this holy company in their iourney, and see if thou canst serue them in any thing. Peraduenture the Blessed Virgin wil giue thee her sonne sometymes to carry in thy armes. O happy art thou, if it be graunted vnto thee.

THE

THE XV. MEDITATION.

Of the murder of the holy Innocents. Of the aboad of the child Iesus in Ægypt: and of his returne into Israël.

THE 1. POINT.

TO confider how King Herod perceiuing that he was deluded by the Sages, to fecure his kingdome, determined to kill him whom he feared might depriue him thereof. And becaufe he knew not where he was, and leaft the child he fought for with rage & diuellifh fury fhould efcape him, he commanded all the young children borne at that tyme, to be murdered, and executed it with barbarous cruelty & impiety, to the end Chrift Iefus our Sauiour fhould not efcape, but dye among them. But it fucceded not as he defired, neither was the Tyrant able to compaffe his intent, albeit he omitted no diligence for the accomplifhing therof: for although all the world perfecute vs, if God protect

and

and defend vs, we cannot suffer losse
of the least haire of our head.

Ponder the griefe that our Sauiour had in Ægypt, seeing from
thence the murder of so many Infants for his sake. but on the other
side, how he was glad and reioyced
that by the meanes of temporall
death which passeth in a moment,
they obtayne life euerlasting, which
now they enioy. many of them by
this meanes being deliuered from
the danger of eternall damnation,
because if they had not dyed by this
occasion, peraduenture they might
haue beene of those that consented to
the death of our Sauiour, and so
should haue beene damned.

Hence thou mayst gather a
great desire to put thy life and death
in the hands of God, endeauouring
to confesse and manifest him with
thy workes, though it should cost
thee thy temporall life to gaine eternall, as these holy and thrice happy
Infants did.

THE

THE 2. POINT.

TO confider how S. Ioſeph , and the moſt Holy Virgin with her Sonne being now in Ægypt , began to treat with that barbarous people, and to gayne their good wills . And it is credible, that the Bleſſed Virgin went to aſiſt & help other women when they needed , and as rich women do call for the poore to haue their aſſiſtance, and do giue them ſome thing for their paynes , ſo it is likely they vſed her help.

Ponder how through her good behauiour, ſpeaches, & celeſtial conuerſation, the richer ſort tooke affection to this poore Virgin, and alſo to the child Ieſus , who in like manner was much beloued for his beauty & ſweet countenance .

Gather hence how thou oughteſt to behaue thy ſelfe with ſtrangers, ſuperiours, and inferiours .

Ponder likewiſe how S. Ioſeph did worke, & earne his dayly wages, therewith to maintayne the Bleſſed Virgin, and her Sonne . Make account that the office, paynes or function

ction wherein thou imployest thy
selfe, thou performest it to maintaine
these poore exiled and banished persons : for that which thou doest for
thy brethren and neighbours, our
Sauiour esteemeth it as done to his
owne person ; as himselfe sayth in
the Ghospell ·

The 3. Point.

TO consider how after fiue or seauen yeares were past of this exile
in Ægypt(as some Authors say) an
Angell of our Lord appeared againe
in sleep to S . Ioseph, saying : Arise,
and take the child and his Mother, &
go into the land of Israel for they
are dead that sought the life of the
child .

Ponder that at length the per-
secutor dyed, and the banishment of
the Innocent Child Iesus ceased ,
wherby thou mayst perceiue that the
paynes, perils, and persecutions of
this life, shall haue an end, and the
banishment therof : and they which
persecuted vs shalbe iudged & their
intentions examined .

Whence thou mayst gather
also

also that if thou remayne faythfull
towards God, and beare with patience the afflictions which he sendeth
thee for proofe and crowne of thy
vertue, after the exile of this world,
thou shalt enioy and possesse the
eternall rest of heauen, which God
hath prepared for thee.

THE 4. POINT.

TO consider the prouidence of Almighty God in sending presently
his Angell, to bring these so happy
tidings to S. Ioseph, and to free him
from the banishment of so many
yeares.

Ponder what confidence he had
in Almighty God, and how contented he was, seeing the care God had
of them, and how ready God was to
heare his prayer, and to release him
from his doubts, difficultyes, and
cares.

Purpose to haue recourse to
Almighty God in thy difficultyes,
with prayer and confidence in Him:
for thou mayst securely put of all anxious solicitude of the successe of thy
affaires, casting thy selfe into the
hands

hands of God : for in them (as Dauid
sayth) are thy strong & prosperous
successes .

Likewise thou mayst consider
the griefe of those of Ægypt among
whome these holy Saints had liued,
when they were to take their leaue
of them , by reason of the singular
content they receaued in their vertuous conuersation , and for that it is
credible that they left many (who
were blind and ignorāt euer before)
enlightned with the light and knowledge of the true fayth .

Gather hence desires , that Christ
our Lord neuer depart from thy
soule, but euerlastingly remaine with
thee . Beseech him, as those two disciples did , saying vnto him : Tarry
with vs because it is towards night,
and the day is now far spent .

THE

THE XVI. MEDITATION.

How the child Iesus remayned alone in the Temple of Ierusalem.

THE I. POINT.

TO consider how that after the most Blessed Virgin with her Sonne and S. Ioseph had been in the Temple of Ierusalem, and therein adored Almighty God their Creatour, the Blessed Virgin departed towards Nazareth, and S. Ioseph followed some houres after (because the men went not togeather with the women) wherein children might go indifferently with the one or the other: and so the Blessed child remayned behind them in the Temple, they not perceiuing it.

Ponder how the Blessed Virgin being now come a good way on her iourney, stood expecting her most beloued sonne, & Spouse with great desire of their comming: but when she saw that her Spouse S. Ioseph brought not with him the B. Child, being

being much perplexed and troubled, she asked him where he was? And he likewise much afflicted, answeared that he thought he had returned with her: but finding it otherwise, they began to lament and weep incessantly: and not without great reason for the losse was not small of so great a treasure.

Gather hence two things: The first what griefe thou oughtst to haue when thou shalt chance to loose Almighty God through thy owne default, seeing the most B. Virgin and S. Ioseph greiued so much, when he absented himselfe from thé without any fault of theirs.

Secondly, with what care thou oughtest to seek Almighty God not ceasing nor omitting any occasion, but seeking him in all places whersoeuer thou mayst haue any tidings of him, as the Espouse did in the Canticles when she sayd · I will rise, and will go about the Citty, by the streets and high wayes. I will seeke him, whom my soule loueth. For that which costeth vs nothing is

not

not esteemed, and that which is
worth much (as God is)must cost vs
much.

THE 2. POINT.

TO consider wherein this moſt
blessed child did ſpend thoſe dayes
which he was in the temple from his
parents,how he watched and prayed
there all the night, offering himſelfe
vp to his Eternall Father for the ſaluation of the world.

Ponder that his bed whereon
he repoſed al that while was the hard
ground, or ſome ſtoole or bench in
the Temple,and yet thou muſt haue
thy bed ſo ſoft. His dyet was a little
bread gotten of almes, and thou ſee-
keſt delicacies and ſuperfluityes. yea
it is more probable he paſſed all the
time without eating: for of all theſe
temporall matters he made but ſmal
reckoning: where contrary wiſe thou
wilt that nothing be wanting vnto
thee, but wilt abound in all.

Hence thou mayſt gather affections and purpoſes of imitating
our Sauiour, by inbracing the pouerty and want of all things : ſeeing
the

the Lord of them all endured and
suffered in himselfe so great penury
of them Haue also compassion of his
pouerty and solitarines, because for
thy sake he put himselfe in these
straits of extreme necessity.

THE 3. POINT.

TO consider, how the day following the most Blessed Virgin returned with S. Ioseph to seeke her
beloued Sonne our Lord in Hierusalem.

Ponder with how great solicitude, with what sighes, groanings,
and tears, and with how much care
she sought him, demanding of al she
met, whether they had seene whom
her soule loued: and giuing them
signes whereby they might know
him, she sayd with the Espouse in
the Canticles: My beloued is white
and ruddy, chosen from amongst
thousands. But when no body could
answere her demand, she turned her
selfe to the Fternal Father, with most
feruent and deuout prayer, beseeching h m not to chastice her so rigorously, if she had committed any
negli-

negligence in the seruice of his Son
and her God : acknowledging her
selfe not worthy to be his hand-
mayd.

From hence thou mayst gather
two things: First, that a most certain
& assured meanes to find Almighty
God is to acknowledge that thou deseruest not to find him, and peraduenture he hath left thee through
thyne owne default, albeit thou
knowest it not.

The second is, that Christ our
Lord is not to be found among the
delightes and pamperings of the flesh
but in afflictions, paynes and desolations : not among kinsfolkes and acquaintance, but in his holy Temple,
and there thou art to seeke him, if
thou desire to find him.

The 4. Point.

TO consider, how that after our B.
Lady, togeather with her Spouse
S . Ioseph had sought her beloued
Sonne both within and without the
Citty of Ierusalem, at last after three
dayes, they found him in the Tem-
ple it selfe, sitting in the middest of
the

the Doctors, hearing them, and asking them, with so great modesty, with such grauity & prudence, with so singular wisedome and eloquence that all were astonished that heard him, demanding of one another: Who is this ? What child is this? What wisedome is this in so tender yeares? Whose sonne is this child ?

Ponder how great ioy and content our Blessed Lady receaued when she found her most holy Sonne, and saw him so much honoured & esteemed, and her hart being not able to endure any delay, she entred among the middest of the Maisters and Doctors, and approaching vnto him, she spake these moanefull and tender words : Sonne, why hast thou so done to vs ? Behold thy Father and I sorrowing did seeke thee. He answered her, that he had done so, that he might attend, and imploy himselfe in the affayres of his Father.

Gather hence a desire, that all thy whole life and endeauours may be imployed, not in the affaires of this world, or of selfe-loue, but in
those

those which are of God, and for God.
Be ashamed to see how far thou hast
hitherto beene from obseruing this
aduise, and procure from this day
forward, euer to imploy thy powers
and senses in the seruice of Almighty
God : seeing his diuine Maiesty alwayes imployed himselfe in that,
which was for thy good and benefit.
For by so seeking our Lord God,
thou shalt find him, and neuer loose
him.

THE XVII. MEDITATION.

Of the life of Christ our Lord till he was thirty yeares of age.

THE I. POINT.

TO consider, that as Christ our
Lord grew euery day in years,
so likewise he increased in wisdome and grace with God and men.
Not that he properly receaued any
more wisedome, grace, or sanctity,
as he did incease in age (for nothing
could be added to that which he had
in these things, because from the very

L   instant

instant of his conception, he was endued with all plenitude of grace)but
he increased in the exercise thereof,
giuing dayly greater demonstration
of knowledge and vertue, of wisedome and sanctity to all the world.

Ponder, how gracious our Sauiour was in the sight of his Eternall
Father: and how pleasing a thing it
was vnto him to see his only Sonne,
not only in that height of al wisdom
and grace, wherewith he was replenished: but also to see him to proceed therein in the sight of men to so
high a perfection.

Learne to desire to proceed &
dayly increase in vertue: endeauouring to be perfect in that state wher-
unto thou art called, whether it be
religious or secular, and be ashamed
considering how often thou hast
gone backe in the way of vertue: remembring that (as S. Bernard sayth)
in the way of God, not to go forward
is to go backward.

THE 2. POINT.

TO consider how our Sauiour for
the space of thirty years was sub-
ject

iect to His Holy Mother, and to S. Ioseph vntill he dyed, obeying them
in all they commanded him.

Ponder who he is that obeyeth
and subiecteth himselfe, & to whom
and in what things. He that obeyeth
is God, Lord and Creatour of all
things, whome all are obliged to o-
bey, and be subiect vnto. Whome
doth he obey? Not only the Blessed
Virgin who was his true Mother,
but also for her sake he obeyeth S.
Ioseph, who though he were not
indeed his Father, yet was he so accounted, being a poore Carpenter.
In what thinges doth he obey? To
witt, in meane and base things, such
as are wont to be done in the house
of a poore Artificer, as to saw & hew
timber, and other things of the like
nature. Be confounded and greatly
ashamed, considering thy Sauiour
Christ Iesus hewing timber, driuing
nayles &c. and beholding thy selfe
how thou refusest to do such things.

And gather hence that the excellency of a spirituall life consisteth
not so much in doing workes which

L 2   of

of themselus be glorious (as to preach
to gouerne, to teach &c.) as in doing
those workes which God commandeth vs to do, by meanes of our Superiours, though of themselues they
be but base and very meane. And be
ashamed of thy pride, and little obedience, in not subiecting thy self, nor
obeying thy parents and Superiours
for the loue of God, euen in little
matters, seeing the King of Heauen
(as S. Bernard sayth) subiecting
himselfe to the very dust of the earth
the Creatour of al things to his creatures: and be ashamed to desire and
seeke after honourable offices and
imployments, seeing Almighty God
to exercise himselfe in things so base
and humble.

The 3. Point.

TO consider how Christ our Lord,
vntill he was thirty yeares of age,
exercised himselfe in the trade of a
Carpenter: for he was not only called the Sonne of a Carpenter, but also a Carpenter, as S. Marke sayth.
And whereas he might haue chosen
to himselfe some more honorable
imploy-

imployment, he vndertooke this
meane office, therein to exercise humility, and to be dealt with, as noble
and principal men do deale with me-
canicall artificers : that so, the treasures of wisedome and knowledge
of God, which are al in this our Lord
(as his holy Apostle sayth) might be
hidden from the eyes of the world.

Ponder the rare silence of
Christ our Lord, who during al this
tyme, would not make himselfe
knowne, but did so long hold his
peace: and being the Wisedome and
Eternall Word of his Father, would
not speake, nor make knowne who
he was by publike preaching, vntill
he was thirty yeares of age, leading
in the meane while, a life full of pouerty, humility and silence, couering his graces and other prerogatiues with rare humility.

Learne by this patterne & example how to keep silence in thy ex-
ternall businesses and corporall exercises, if thou art imploye d in any,
imitating Iesus Christ our Lord, who
labouring in body, prayed in mind.

3   Endea-

Endeauour likewise to conceale the
gifts and talents which God hath giuen thee, when there is no need to
publish them: laying firft deep root
in humility, feeing thy Redeemer
vouchfafed to walke this way for fo
long tyme togeather.

THE 4. POINT.

TO confider, how the B. Virgin
did profit and benefit her felfe in-
creafing in all fort of Vertues, but
efpecially in Humility, feeing her
moft Bleffed Sonne and her God, being wifdome it felfe, and yet concealed vnder fuch fignes and exercifes
of Humility.

Ponder how our Bleffed Lady
was euer contemplating and obferuing him and his examples, keeping
and ruminating all thefe thinges in
her hart: and calling them often to
mind, fhe endeauoured to imitate
her Sonne, and after his example to
increafe in humility, wifedome, and
grace. O how contented did fhe liue
hauing in her company fuch an
incomparable mirrour and patterne
of vertues! How ioyfull was fhe to
haue

haue him alwayes at her side, to see him dayly at her table: to heare his words: to enioy his presence!

Gather hence a great desire to haue Christ our Lord present, and before thyne eyes in all thy workes. Beseech him that he vouchsafe neuer to depart from thee, nor thou from him, that thou mayst performe thy actions with spirit and life, as his diuine Maiesty desireth thou shouldest.

THE *XVIII.* MEDITATION.
Of the Baptisme of our Sauiour.

THE I. POINT.

TO consider, how Christ our Lord hauing liued in company of his most Holy Mother (who was, now a widdow) thirty yeares, such a life, as we may well imagine doubtles to haue been more diuine then human, the time being now come wherein he was to manifest himselfe to the world, performing the office of a Redeemer and

L 4   Maister,

Maifter, he came one day to our B. Lady, & with moft tender affection difclofed vnto her the whole matter, & as an obedient fonne craued leaue of her and her benediction, that h might go and attend to the worke o our Redemption. The Bleffed Vigii through the great defire fhe had o the faluation of mankind, not reque-fting him to deferre it any longer time, with perfect refignation to the diuine will, denying her owne will to conforme it to the will of Almigh-ty God, fayd vnto him that which her moft Holy Sonne fayd to his eter-nall Father in the Garden : Let not o Lord, my will, but thyne be done : and imbracing her fonne & her God moft tenderly, fhe gaue him her blef-fing and licence, wherewith he de-parted, and remayned with teares trickling faft down her cheeks alon, a poore widdow, and without her Sonne.

Ponder the punctuall obedi-ence of the fonne, in thus abando-ning that chaft doue his mother, and the pleafant and contented life he led
with

with her, to lead his life among wild
beasts: and the sacrifice of the mother,
depriuing her selfe of such a Sonne.

Take example from hence and
learne of Christ our Redeemer so to
loue thy parents and kinsfolkes, that
whersoeuer the glory or seruice of
God shall require, they may not stay
nor hinder thy good purposes and
desires, neither Father nor Mother,
kinsfolks nor friends, no nor all the
world : procuring , if they attempt
any such thing , to fly from them as
from domesticall enemies : for so
Christ our Sauiour calleth them.

THE 2. POINT.

TO consider, how our Sauiour, as
soone as he was departed out of
the presence of his beloued Mother ,
tooke his way towards Iordan ,
where S. Iohn was baptising the Pu-
blicans and sinners.

Ponder first how poore , how
solitary, & how destitute of all company our Sauiour goeth on his way,
and about all, how he placeth himselfe in the number of sinners, thereby to giue vs another example of hu-
L 5   mility,

mility, and not desiring to be known
besought S. Iohn to baptize him.

Secondly how great the ioy &
content of this Saint was when he
knew by the spirit of prophesy Christ
our Lord, how he leaped againe for
ioy as he did when he acknowleged
him in his mothers wombe; beholding him there so humble.

Gather hence desires to humble
and submit thy selfe to the very dust
of the earth, not desiring from hence
forward, to iustify thy selfe, nor pre-
ferre thy selfe before others, seeing
thy Sauiour so humble, going to be
baptized, as if he had beene a great
sinner: and seeing thou art indeed a
sinner, desire to vse conuenient remedyes, though therby thou be noted and knowne to be a sinner.

The 3. Point.

TO consider, how S. Iohn refused
to baptize our Sauiour: saying
vnto him: I, ô Lord, ought to be
baptized of thee, and commest thou
to me?

Ponder the admiration and a-
stonishment of S. Iohn, seeing our
Sauiour

Sauiour fo humble, and thofe fhort, but myfticall wordes : Thou commeft to me to be baptized ? Thou God infinite , Thou Sauiour of the world , Thou forgiuer of finnes, Thou who fanctifiedft me in my mothers wombe, commeft to me , thy creature, a vile and filly worme, and thy feruant ?

Hence thou mayft gather, that vertue and fanctiry confifteth in humlity and obedience (that is) in obeying God and his vice-gerents (I meane) thofe which be in higher degree of dignity , office , age , and fcience. Alfo our equals, giuing them greater honour and the better place . And our inferiours , delighting to fubiect thy felfe vnto them as if they were thy fuperiours : taking example by Chrift our Lord , who humbled himfelfe fo much this day , obeying and kneeling downe before his Precurfor S. Iohn Baptift to be baptized of him .

THE 4. POINT.

TO confider, how while S. Iohn baptized our Sauiour, the Eter-

L 6   **nall**

nall Father authorized & honoured him most wonderfully, fullfilling the truth of that saying : Whosoeuer humbleth himselfe, shalbe exalted. And to this end the heauens were opened, and there descended a doue, and rested vpon our Sauiours head, to declare his innocency and sanctity that he was the Lambe of God, that taketh away the sinnes of the world, & a maiesticall and graue voice was heard from the heauenly Father, saying: This is my beloued Sonne, in whome I am well pleased, by whome I am appeased, and reconciled vnto mankind .

Ponder, that although Christ our Lord desired to conceale himselfe, permitting himselfe to be accounted but an ordinary man and a sinner, yet the Eternall Father manifested his innocency, declaring who he was by a voyce from heauen : for it was not reason that so great humility should passe without testimony of great glory . And it is the condition of Almighty God to glorify the humble.

Gather

Gather hence desires to please this our Lord, humbling thy selfe, as Christ humbled himselfe, hiding & concealing thy selfe for his loue, as he did for thy example, which if thou dost he will haue care when occasion shall serue, to manifest, honour, and exalt thee before God and men.

THE XIX. MEDITATION.

Of the temptation of Christ in the desert, and of his victory.

THE I. POINT.

TO consider how that after our Sauiour was baptized by Saint Iohn, moued of his owne holy spirit, he betooke himselfe to the desert, as to a place ministring occasion of temptation, there to be tempted; where he performed most holy and retyred exercises, and remained there forty dayes, and forty nights, neither eating nor drinking. And this to satisfy for thy riotousnes and delicacies : exercising himselfe in

continuall

continuall prayer and fasting, and
other corporal austerities: liuing not
in company of his Blessed Mother,
or of S Iohn by the riuer Iordan,
but all alone among sauage and
wild beasts, being Lord of Angels, to
humble himselfe for man, who
through sinne was become a brute
beast.

Ponder how the Holy Ghost
led our Sauiour into the desert, to
challenge the Prince of darknesse
to enter into the field, and to fight &
vanquish him; that knowing by experience, what it is to be tempted of
the Diuel he might haue compassion
of those who are tempted, and that
with the victory of his temptations
he might instruct thee to withstand
and ouercome thyne with magnani-
mity and courage.

Gather hence a very feruent &
earnest desire to giue thy selfe to
prayer, fasting and mortification (especially when thou art tempted) according to the example of this thy
Lord, who armed himselfe for the
combat and temptation with these
                                    spirituall

spirituall weapons, and taught thee
how greatly he alwayes esteemed
these vertues, that exercising thy self
in them, thou mightst to obtaine victory ouer thyne enemies.

THE 2. POINT.

TO consider how those forty dayes
of fasting being ended, our Sauiour was hungry, to wit as he was
man, and forthwith the Diuel was at
hand, who watched and obserued
whatsoeuer he did, and vnder colour
of pittying him, sayd vnto him: If
thou be the sonne of God, command
that these stones be made bread, and
eate: which he sayd to try if by this
meanes he might deceaue him.

Ponder that the Diuell perswa-
deth that the stones should be conuerted into bread and not into some
other more dainty meat : for that
which he pretendeth in temptations,
is not thy gust and pleasure, for if he
could deceaue thee by giuing thee a
tedious life full of a thousand bitter-
nesses & disgusts, he would not giue
thee any contentment all.

From hence gather, that thou
must

must neuer be carelesse how thou liuest, because the solicitude and care wherewith the Diuell goeth about to entrap thee is great and continual. For our Blessed Sauiour was no sooner hungry, but he was ready to tempt him, thinking to ouerthrow him. Take heed, for so will he deale with thee: marke well how much it importeth thee, to watch, and pray, (as our Sauiour sayd vnto his Disciples in the night of his so great afflictions) that thou enter not into téptation.

The 3. Point.

TO consider how the second temptation was of vaine glory, when the Diuell in his owne likenesse carryed our Sauiour from the desert, to the pinnacle of the Temple, perswading him to cast himselfe downe headlong from aboue, because much people being below, and seeing so strang a thing, that falling so high he receaued no harme, many of them would beleeue in him.

Ponder the meeknes of our Lord God, in permitting himselfe to
be

be carryed by the Diuell, without
refiftance, and concealing for the
prefent his omnipotency, that the
Diuell might not know him for the
Sonne of God.

Refolue and purpofe firmely,
that whenfoeuer the Diuell fhall
tempt thee by himfelfe or others, to
vaunt thy felfe of thy vertues, thou
wilt rather hide them by common
and ordinary behauiour and conuerfation, and couer the interiour and
hidden iewels of thy foule with the
precious veile of Humility. For
where this vertue is, there is alfo (as
the Wifeman fayth) wifdome, and
fo by his diuine ayd thou mayft obtaine thy defired victory.

THE 4. POINT.

TO confider how the third temptation was of couetoufnes & am-
bition, procuring to ouerthrow our
Sauiour at laft by this way, and fo he
tooke him vp intoa very high moū-
taine, and from thence he fhewed
him all the kingdomes of the world
prefenting thē al vpon condition that
falling downe he would adore dim.

Ponder

Ponder the vnsatiable thirst the Diueli hath of thy perdition : for he would giue thee the whole world if it were his, so that thou wouldst cõmit one only mortall sinne against Almighty God .

Gather hence a great esteeme of thy saluation, with a firme purpose not to do any thing in preiudice therof for all the world : for against this temptation our Lord sayd : What doth it profit a man, if he gaine the whole world , and sustaine the domage of his soule ? Wherefore putting him away with vehemency, he sayd vnto him: Auant Satan : for it is written, the Lord thy God shalt thou adore, and him only shalt thou serue. Whereby our Lord giueth thee to vnderstand , that if thou shalt preseuere in the combat , with his grace thou shalt ouercome whatsouer tẽptation : and the Diuell being vanquished, shall depart confounded , and leaue thee with the crowne of victory in thy hands, as he did (in spite of his teeth) in this cõflict with our Sauiour, vnto whome the Eternal Father

sent

sent after his conquest, not one Angel alone to minister vnto him in that necessity, but many to congratulate him the victory, and spreading the table, they attended on him at dinner, as seruants on their Lord and Maister.

Learne hence to confide & trust in God, and he will nourish thee and remedy thy necessity, when, and in what manner, it shallbe most fitting for thee.

THE XX. MEDITATION.

Of the vocation and election of the Apostles.

THE I. POINT.

TO consider how Christ our Sauiour being to choose twelue men, that might be the twelue foundations, or vpholders of his Church, himselfe in person, not trusting therein to any other, made choice of them, and called them.

Ponder how absolute and perfect in all points this election of our Sauiour Christ was, who being the infinit

infinit wisedome that cannot erre, made choice, not of the noble, rich, and mighty of the world, neither of the learned and Doctors of the Law, not because he contemned or despised either of them in respect that himselfe was more mighty & more wise, but because he being God had made himselfe man, and of so mighty a Lord was become a seruant, and being himselfe so great, had vouchsafed to become so little in our Nature; he chose rather humble, fraile, poore and contemptible persons, and such as got their liuing by fishing & mending of nets, that they might not attribute vnto themselues, those great gifts & graces which he intended to impart vnto them, nor those glorious acts which he meant to bring to passe by their meanes. Finally he made this so miraculous an election, that the couersion of the world might not be ascribed to humane force, but to vertue diuine. And this was the cause of choosing those whome he did choose, and leauing those whom he did leaue.

Gather

Gather by this how much it importeth thee to ground thy selfe in profound Humility, if thou wilt that God make choice of thee to performe great matters in his seruice, and make thee partaker of his diuine & sacred mysteries.

THE 2. POINT.

TO consider how Christ our Lord called Peter, Iames, and Andrew, and by them others to make them Apostles and Disciples of his schoole and his greatest fauorits, and Princes and pillars of his holy Church.

Ponder how great grace and fauour God did them heerein, in choosing them and leauing many others their equalls and companions that fished in the same places, whereas if he had not chosen them, they had still remayned in their obscure condition, and their memory had beene now quite forgotten, and they peraduenture eaten vp and deuoured by fishes of the sea. But God Almighty reserued them & called the to be the Fathers of the beleeuers, & that their memory should endure and be cele-

brated

brated for all eternity.

Hence thou maiſt gather, how
great a fauour it was of Almighty
God to make thee a Chriſtian, and to
take thee for his ſeruant, vouchſa-
fing to be ſerued by thee, & to chooſe
thee before many others, to whom
if he had done this fauour and benefit, they would haue ſhewed themſelues more gratefull, and ſerued him
a great deale better then thou doeſt.

THE 3. POINT.

TO conſider, how S. Peter, & S. Andrew, while they were caſting
their nets into the ſea, and the Sonnes
of Zebedæus while they were in the
ſhip of their Father, and S. Mathew
ſitting in the Cuſtome-houſe, being
called by our Sauiour Chriſt, forthwith leauing all, followed him euen
to death, in hunger, thirſt, and po-
uertv, being much perſecuted and
calumniated, and neuer ſhrinking
backe, but bearing all with great patience.

Ponder the excellent obedience
of the Apoſtles at the voyce and calling of Ieſus Chriſt. for they negle-
                                        &ed

&ed and held all as nothing, in respect of his seruice, and to become his
Disciples, putting off all carnall affection towards their Parents, friends
and goods, which though they were
but slender and little, yet in will and
resolution they left much for it all
the whole world had beene theirs
they would haue left it all in like
manner.

See therfore that when Almighty God shall vouchsafe to call thee &
knock at the doore of thy hart, thou
become not deafe, but presently and
without delay, leauing all thou hast
(which in deed is but very little)
thou follow and serue thy God, as
the Apostles did, in afflictions and
persecutions vntill death: that after
this life thou mayst enioy with them
euerlasting prosperity and blisse,
which God hath prepared for thee in
heauen.

THE 4. POINT.

TO consider how great fauours
Christ did to his Apostles for this
their prompt obedience: he exalted
them to the greatest dignity, which
be

he had inſtituted in his Church, he choſe them for his perpetuall compinions: he made them his Legats and Embaſſadours : he entred into very ſtraight league with them and inward familiarity, he made them partakers of his ſecrets. And finally ordayned them for ludges of the twelue tribes: and gaue them the firſt fruits of the Holy Ghoſt.

Ponder how for hauing obeyed the voyce of Chriſt, and forſaken whatſoeuer they had, or could poſſibly haue, honours, riches, and pleaſures to follow him that was more worth then all, they were far more honoured and eſteemed of all.

Gather from hence a great deſire to do as the Apoſtles did: for ſo God wil reward thee as he rewarded them with an hundred fold in this life, ouer and aboue that which thou haſt left: and afterwards with life euerlaſting.

THI

THE XXI. MEDITATION.

Of the miracle which our Sauiour did at the marriage in Cana of Galilee.

THE 1. POINT.

TO confider, how Iefus Chrift our Lord being inuited to a certaine marriage, togeather with his Blſſed Mother and Difciples, excufed not himſelfe, but went to the banquet to honour them (who by all likelyhood were poore, and kinsfolke or acquaintance to the B. Virgin) and to take occafion to do fome good to others, reaping thereby fome fpirituall gaine, not only for them which were prefent, but alfo for vs all.

Ponder how holy a marriage that was, wherein Chrift & his moft Holy Mother and the Apoftles did affift, giuing authority and honou-ring with their prefence, that which was to be one of the Sacraments of Holy Church, for remedy of thofe that are fraile. But at the beſt tyme of

M   dinner,

dinner, wine was wanting, and they that were inuited being many, the bride and bride-grome poore, those that serued were troubled and very anxious not knowing how to remedy the want.

Gather hence how that all the pleasures, gusts, and contentments of this life (signified by this banquet) neuer endure for any long tyme, & that when they are at the best, and as it were at the daintiest bit, they vanilh, and finally become bitter and distastfull when death commeth: wherefore it were a great deceipt to place therein our affection or confidence.

The 2. Point.

TO consider how the most Blessed Virgin perceauing the want of wine, of her selfe, and not requested by any, bethought her of a remedy, and had recourse vnto her B. Sonne, and sayd vnto him: They haue no wine.

Ponder how the Blessed Virgin performeth the office of aduocatrice in behalfe of those that are deuoted

vnto

vnto her, and hath compaßion of
their neceßities, and bringeth to paße
that the waters of tribulation and affliction, be couerted into moſt ſweet
and pleaſant wine of ſpirituall conſolation. And if ſhe be ſo ready to ayd
vs in our neceßityes being not aſked
(as heere ſhe was) how much more
will ſhe be being requeſted and moued by our prayers.

Purpoſe to be thankefull towards the Bleſſed Virgin: for ſeeing
ſhe had ſuch compaßion at the want
of terreſtriall wine, ſhe doubtles will
haue far greater at our want of ſpirituall wine: and ſeeing ſhe ſought remedy for the firſt, ſhe will more willingly craue it for the laſt, ſaying:
Sonne, this my ſeruant hath not the
wine of thy loue, graunt it him. I
beſeech thee, that he being filled with
it, he may ſerue thee with more feruour. After this ſame manner thou
mayſt repreſent vnto Almighty God
thy neceßityes with great confidence
that thou ſhalt find help, and in place
of the word Wine, thou mayſt put
any other, ſaying : O my God, I want
humility

humility, I haue not patience, I need
obedience &c. behold my necessity
and misery, and haue compassion on
me.

THE 3. POINT.

TO consider, how that although
our Sauiour could haue remedied
this want, without the help of any
body; creating new wine or multi-
plying that little which was left; yet
notwithstāding it being the pleasure
of God that we cooperate in part to
the remedy of our owne necessities,
he commanded the ministers to fill
the stone-pots that were there at
hand, full of water, which when they
had done, their anxiety and sorrow
was turned into ioy, and the water
into delicate, and most excellent
wine.

Ponder the obedience of the
seruants, and submission of their vnderstanding, when being commanded by our Sauiour to draw water,
and to fill the pots that were there
with the same, they did not only
reply but performed punctually that
which Christ commanded them.

Hence

Hence thou mayſt conclude how pleaſing a thing it is to God, that thou ſubmit thy vnderſtanding, vnto him, and mortify thy iudgment, & become tractable as a ſilly beaſt before his diuine Maieſty, and in the preſence of thy Superiours, who are in his place.

Likewiſe thou mayſt conſider the omnipotency of God, who with his will only, without touching the water changed and conuerted it into moſt excellēt wine. But what wonder is it that he ſhould make one thing of another, who hath made al things of nothing. Beſeech him to change thy hart, and ſeeing he is omnipotent deſire him that he will vouchſafe to alter it from cold to become feruent, from imperfect to be perfect, from naught to good: for he hath power to conuert water into wine, and of ſtones to raiſe vp children to Abraham.

THE 4. POINT.

TO conſider how our Sauiour in that banquet would not mingle two kinds of wine togeather, but ex-

M 3   pected

pected till the earthly wine was spent
before he would haue them tast of
the miraculous wine .

Ponder that vntill we renounce
the comforts of this world, and the
pleasures of the flesh, Almighty God
will not giue vs to tast how great the
multitude of that sweetnes is , which
he hath prepared for them that feare
him .

Gather hence a linely and effectuall desire to mortify thy carnall
passions, subiecting them to reason,
& forthwith thou shalt tast the celestiall comforts , and be made partaker of the diuine sweetnes: for if one
only draught of this precious wine,
which is giuen in this life by God
Almighty to some of his speciall
friends and fauorits , doth so rauish
and bereaue them as it were of themselues, as it did S. Peter in the Transfiguration, and S. Paul in his extasies
in what abundance will Iesus Christ
our Lord bestow this so precious
wine vpon his elect, when they shall
eate and drinke with him at his table
in the Kingdome of Heauen .

                                    T HE

THE XXII. MEDITATION.
Of the eight Beatitudes.
THE I. BEATITVDE

TO consider how Christ Iesus our Lord, to teach and informe his Apostls concerning the loue & esteem he had of pouerty (wherin consisteth the summe of all perfection) did separate and withdraw them from amongst the rest of the people, and sayd vnto them in priuate: Blessed are the poore in spirit for theirs is the kingdome of Heauen.

Ponder that those are poore in spirit, who in will and affection, neither haue, nor desire to possesse any thing: imitating in this our Sauiour and heauenly Maister, who being riches it selfe, alwayes gaue vs most rare examples of pouerty in all his life. for in his infancy he made choice of a poore Mother, of a poore countrey, and to be borne in a poore stable, and layd in a poore manger. In

M 4 his

his youth he exercised a poore and contemptible trade : and when he preached, he liued of alms as a poore man. He chose poore diciples, he conuersed familiarly with the poore: finally at his death, his pouerty arriued to that extremity, that he dyed naked vpon the Crosse, & in so great want and necessity, that desiring but a draught of water he could not haue it.

Gather hence a great desire to be poore in spirit, in imitation of Christ our Lord, who taught thee how thou mayst with rich and voluntary pouerty, cut off at once the roots of all sinne, and also the cares, afflictions and troublesome busines of the world : for Couetousnes (as the Apostle sayth) is the root of all euills. And moreouer, for so doing our Lord doth promise thee the kingdome of heauen, and will infallibly giue it thee.

THE 2. BEATITVDE.

THis Beatitude appertaineth to the meeke, wherein is to be considered, that meeknes cosisteth principally

cipally in three things. First in repres-
sing the violent passions of anger,
which maketh both for the interiour
and exteriour quiet and repose of
soule and body. Secondly it consisteth in being affable and courteous
towards all, not iniurying nor vsing
distastful words towards any. Thirdly in not rendring euill for euill, but
contrarywise good for euill. And
such Almighty God calleth blessed.

Ponder how Christ our Lord
proposeth vnto vs his own meeknes
that we may imitate him therein,
saying: Learne of me, because I am
meeke, and humble of hart. And
as he sayd it, so he shewed it in the
middest of so many raging wolues,
especially at his blessed Passion, not
once opening his mouth, not defen-
ding himselfe, not repining or dis-
dayning therat.

Learne how greatly it behooueth thee to shew thy selfe meeke &
gentle towards all, towards thy Superiours, equalls, and inferiours, if
thou desire to be blessed and to possesse the land of thy hart, and thy
M 5   passions,

passions, and the harts of all men, and most of all the land of the liuing, thy celestiall countrey.

The 3 Beatitvde.

TO consider how Christ our Lord calleth Blessed those that mourne or weep, not with corporall teares (as many worldlings do) for temporall losses, of honour, life and goods: but such as lament for their sinnes, and for the losse of so many soules, which are separated from the knowledge of Almighty God: wheras contrarywise, the foolish world calleth blessed those that laugh & liue in mirth and pleasure: but Iesus who is truth it selfe, sayth that they be accursed, because after their laughing, endles sorrow shall succeed: but happy be those who weep, because their sorrow shallbe turned into euerlasting ioy

Ponder how much it importeth thee to bewayle thy sinnes and defects, and that thou hast so often lost God and our Sauiour, whome thou art to imitate and accompany in this holy exercise of teares, of whom

it

it is not read (as S. Basil noteth) that
he euer laughed, but we reade that
he wept many tymes, in the manger,
at the death of Lazarus, vpon Hierusalem, and on the Crosse.

Gather hence a desire to weep
with our Sauiour, and with this cõ-
sideration refraine and moderate thy
ouermuch mirth, reioycing only in
the seruice of God, and of our Sauiour, whome if thou imitate in weeping, thou shalt obtaine comfort in
those very thinges for which thou
weepest: if thou weepest for thy sins
thou shalt obtaine pardon of them:
if for the sinnes of others, thou shalt
also obtayne pardon for them; if by
reason of the exile and banishment
of this life, thou shalt obtayne ioy
& comfort, with certaine hope of thy
saluation.

THE 4. BEATITVDE.

CONSIDER, how our Sauiour
calleth Blessed those, who hungar and thirst after Iustice (that is.)
after vertue and holynesse of life, endeauouring euer to increase therein,
not after an ordinary manner, but

M 6   in

in the highest degree; and as one that
hath a great hungar, and most ardent
thirst after any thing, who ceaseth
not, votill he be satisfyed, and his ne-
cellity fully supplyed : for so our Sauiour did hungar and thirst, and was
neuer satiated with doing and enduring euills for our sake: wherfore he
sayd on the Crosse, I thirst. And so
to satisfy our thirst, he hath giuen vs
his most precious bloud to drinke,
& to satiate our hungar he hath giuen
vs his most sacred body to eate.

Ponder how much it importeth
thee to haue this hungar and thirst of
iustice and sanctity, and not of the
temporall goods of the world; least
that malediction of Christ light vpon
thee, when he sayd : Woe to you
that are filled, because you shallbe
hungry : as it happened to that rich
glutton, who doth and shall for euer
endure an eternall & vnquenchable
thirst, and not be releeued with so
much as the least drop of water.

Gather hence great confusion
and shame for thy negligence and
sloth in the seruice of God, and obserue

ferue how they that hungar after
vertue & fanctity (I meane the luſt)
Go wil repleniſh them with eternal
goods, as the moſt B Virgin ſavd in
her Canticle, and the ſloathfull and
negligent ſhallbe deuoyd thereof.

THE ſ. BEATITVDE.

TO conſider that our Sauiour calleth Mercifull, not only thoſe t at
haue a certaine feiing and compaſſion of the corporal and ſpirituall afflictions and miſeryes of their neighbours, not excluding any though
their enemies, as Chriſt our Lord had
of all: but alſo thoſe who according
to their ability endeauour to help o-
thers in their miſeries.

Ponder how mercifull our B.
Sauiour was, and how he exerciſed
himſelfe al the tyme of his peaching,
in doing good to all curing the ſicke,
releeuing the hungry, reuiuing the
dead, pardoning ſinners, inſtructing
the ignorant, praying for all, and giuing them whatſoeuer he had for
remedy of their neceſſityes: that is,
his honour, his life, his body, & his
ſacred bloud.

Gather

Gather hence how expedient it is for thee to be mercifull towards thy neighbours, imitating as much as thou canst thy Lord and Sauiour, who is the Father of mercies: for if thou be hard towards them, God wil be hard towards thee: for he hath sayd, In what measure you meat, it shallbe measured to you againe; as it may be seene in the example of the naughty seruant that had not compassion of his fellow seruant. Wherfore feare, least thou fall into the hands of Gods iustice, if thou forgoe mercy towards others: For iudgment without mercy shallbe done to him that hath not done mercy.

THE 6. BEATITVDE.

TO consider how our Blessed Sauiour calleth Blessed the cleane of hart, to wit, those whose affection is not intangled or addicted to any earthly thing, and who do not defile themselues with sinnes: and to such as these Almighty God doth promise his sight, and the knowledge of his diuine Mysteries and secrets.

Ponder

Ponder how Christ Iesus our
Lord was most eminent in this purity and cleannesse of hart : for neither did he euer sinne, nor could he
sinne, in so much that his greatest e-
nemies could not argue him of the
least sinne : neither was guilt found
in his mouth And as this our Lord
is the highest purity it selfe, so also
his holy will is, that those who serue
him, be pure, not contenting themselues with exteriour purity alone as
the foolish virgins and Pharisies did,
but much more procuring the interiour : Because all the glory of the
daughter of the king (which is euery
pure soule, as the Holy Ghost sayth)
is within.

Gather hence a desire (if thou
desire to ascend vp to the mount of
God, and enioy his blessed sight) to
obtaine not only corporall but also
much more spirituall purity : for it is
not fit that the Temple of God should
be polluted or not pure : seeing therfore thou art his Temple (as S. Paul
sayth) and the Holy Ghost hath his
aboad in thee, endeauour and striue
all-

alwayes to be pure and cleane, both
in body and soul, that in thee the
beames of the diuine light may appeare and shine, as in a very clean &
pure christall glasse : for it thou loue
this clearnesse and purity of hart, thou
shalt haue the king and Lord of heauen for thy friend, and enioy his
sight.

The 7. Beatitvde.

TO consider how God calleth the
peace-makers the children of God
for not only those who haue peace in
their soules with Almighty God, but
those chiefly who also procure to
haue the same with their neighbours
shallbe the children of God and of
our Sauiour, who with special prero-
gatiue is called the peaceable King,
and ordained that when he came into the world, his Angells should salute men with this peace : and made
so much reckoning thereof, that he
vsually saluted his Disciples with this
peace, saying vnto them : Peace be
with you.

Ponder the innumerable persecutions & afflictions which Christ
Iesus

Iesus our Lord suftayned to make
peace betweene his Eternall Father
and vs, purchasing for vs true peace,
and shewing himselfe peaceable euen
with those who did hate him.

Gather hence how behoofull it
is for thee, to haue peace with thy self
and with thy neighbours. Thou shalt
haue it with thy selfe, if thou be carefull to breake and to subdue thyne
inordinate appetits, attending to the
continuall exercise of mortification,
and waging continuall warre with
vice : for peace it gotten by warre.
With thy neighbours thou mayst
haue peace, if thou endeauour neuer
to giue them occasion of offence or
trouble, but rather to agree & make
peace with euery one, and so doing
thou shalt be the beloued child of
Almighty God.

THE 8. BEATITVDE.

TO consider how Christ our Lord
calleth those Blessed which suffer
persecution for iustice, that is for vertue and sanctity sake; which persecution is not vnderstood to be suffered in one or two things only, but in
all

all kind of iniuryes, to wit, in lands,
liuings, honour, content, life and
death &c.

Ponder how our Sauiour Christ
from his very cradle till his dying
day, suffered for iustice and sanctity
the greatest persecutions and afflictions which were euer endured, and
with the greatest patience that euer
any had, and for the most iust and
innocent cause that could be, to wit,
for reprehending vice and sinne, and
for the saluation of soules.

Gather hence a great desire to
suffer persecution in imitation of
Christ: neither esteem it any wonder
sith his enemies persecute him, that
thyne also persecute thee, but reme-
bring, that if it was necessary that
Christ our Lord shold passe through
innumerable tribulations and afflictions, and so enter into his owne
glory; it is euident that neither thou
nor any other shal enter into the glory which is not thine, but only by
this way of persecution. Wherefore
animate thy selfe to suffer persecutiõ
and affliction, because our present
tribu-

tribulation which is momentary and light (as also our life is) worketh aboue measure(as the Apostle sayth) an eternall weight of glory in vs.

THE XXIII. MEDITATION.
Of the tempest at sea.
THE 1. POINT.

TO consider that our Blessed Sauiour being entred with his Disciples into a little boat : he fell asleep, and forthwith a great tempest arose on the sea.

Ponder two things · first , that if the ship wherein Christ sayleth be tossed and couered with waues, what will become of that wherein the Diuell is Pilot (that is) if the soule of a iust and holy person be persecuted & afflicted with temptations : the soule of a wicked man & of a sinner what shall it endure ? what will become of such a one?

Secondly, ponder how that al those that betake themselues to the seruice of God, ordinarily sustaine tempests

tempests and tentations, for so the
Holy Ghost sayth: Sonne comming
to the seruice of God, stand in iustice
and feare, and prepare thy soule to
temptation. Wherfore many tymes
Almighty God permitteth great tempestuous stormes of temptations and
persecutions to be raysed against vs,
and he seemeth to vs as if he were a
sleep, and neglected vs.

Gather hence purposes to resist
the fury of thy temptations, for God
will assist thee, and releeue thee in
time of thy greatest need, and deliuer
thee out of danger as he deliuered
his Apostles when they came vnto
him, and craued his help and assistance.

THE 2. POINT.

TO consider how the Apostles seeing all their labour to be in vaine,
went presently to our Sauiour for
help, and awaking him sayd: Lord
saue vs, we perish.

Ponder how our Sauiour made
as though he slept, and did not presently deliuer his Apostles, albeit he
saw the danger in which they were,
partly

partly that they migh t know and vnderstand, how litle they could doe
without his help, and partly becaufe
he would they fhould call vpon him
in time of their greateft neceffity.

Ponder furthermore, how negligent thou haft beene in ftormes of
temptations, wherein thou haft byn
often toffed, and how floathfull thou
haft beene in hauing fpeedy recourfe
to Chrift our Lord, & in befeeching
him to fauour and ayd thee And
hence it hath come to paffe, that the
little boat of thy foule hath beene
often plunged, and ouerwhelmed
with the waues.

Gather hence purpofes to run
to God at all times for his help, but
efpecially in tyme of temptation and
affliction, faying vnto him : O Lord
deliuer me from this temptation that
caufeth this tempeft in my foule, deliuer me from this vice, from this perill and affliction. For if thou call
vpon him with fayth and confidence
he will ayd and fuccour thee as he
did his Apoftles. And will command
by the vertue of his diuine word the
blustering

blustering winds of thy temptations & tribulations (which are those that raise these stormes in thy soule) to cease and be quiet, & presently great tranquility and peace of mind will follow.

THE 3. POINT.

TO consider how Christ our Saviour awaking, reprehended his disciples, and sayd vnto them: Why are you fearefull, ô ye of little fayth? as if he should say. I being in your company, you need not feare.

Ponder the loue that Christ sheweth to his Disciples, and how he requireth the like loue of them againe, and that they trust in him, and fasten the anker of their hope in him, for they shallbe secure in the middest of the raging and tempestuous sea of this life, though the waues should rise to the very clouds.

Gather hence a great desire to be a faithfull disciple of Iesus Christ our Lord, and to follow him whithersoeuer he shall go, by sea and by land, mountaines or valleys, and that no perill or paynes may be able to

to make thee forsake his holy company, nor trouble or dismay thee,
though thou shouldst behold thy self
(as Susanna did) compassed round
about with the waters of tribulation,
euen vp to thy necke, least thou be
reprehended by Christ our Lord as
his Disciples were. For if they had
reflected and considered, that they
were in the company of Iesus Christ,
they would not haue feared, nor
doubted of his power, will and wisedome. Euen so thou, if thou be Religious, and in his house & company,
in the boate of Religion, cast thy selfe
at all tymes into his hands, but especially when thou shalt be tempted or
afflicted, trusting in him that he will
deliuer thee when it shall please him
and shallbe most for thy good.

THE 4. POINT.

TO consider how Christ our Lord
commanded the winds and the sea
and there ensued a great calme, the
windes and the sea obeying with
great punctuality. And those that
were present meruailing at such
power, demanded of one another:

What

What a one is this, for the windes
and the sea obey him?

Ponder the dominion ard rule
which our Lord hath ouer his creatures, and their punctuall obedience
towards him in whatsoeuer he commandeth them. He ruleth ouer the
power of the sea, and doth mitigate
the mouing of the waues therof, he
bringeth forth the winds out of his
treasures, and when he pleaseth in a
moment, he calleth them in againe.
He gouerneth the whole world, and
without his disposition there is not
moued the least leafe of a tree.

Gather hence great confusion
and shame, that being a creature of
his, a reasonable creature, and a
Christian, and perhaps Religious,
created to obey him & to serue him,
thou dost the same so poorely, and
dost so litle obey his comandments,
yea dost so often and dayly disobey
him, and offend him, not performing those thinges which he commandeth thee, as if he were not thy
Creatour, and he who hath giuen
thee all the being which thou hast.

THE

THE XXIIII. MEDITATION.
How Chrift our Lord walked on the fea.

The 1. Point.

TO confider how our Sauiour commanded his Difciples to go into a boate, and to go before him ouer the water, and he afcended vp to a mountaine alone to pray.

Ponder firft the great efteeme, thou oughteft to haue of prayer, fith our Lord that had no neceffity thereof, only to giue thee example, retyred himfelfe for many houres from all company to pray, giuing thee to vnderftand the neceffity thou haft of prayer, therby to arme thy felfe againft fuch temptations, as dayly hang ouer thy head.

Ponder fecondly the griefe the Difciples felt at the abfence of their Maifter, for they knew and did forefee how dangerous a matter it was & full of perill to enter into the boate & commit themfelues to the waters

N   withous

without him, and had rather haue
borne him company in his prayer,
but the vertue of obedience preuailed: for God is to be obeyed in all
thinges, although it were to vndergo some great danger, and to intermit thy recollection and prayer: for
this is to leaue God for God.

Gather hence a great desire to
exercise thy selfe in these two vertues
in which our Lord did proue his disciples, to wit, obedience and prayer,
highly esteeming them, and making
great account of them, specially seeing our Sauiour is thy example and
thy guide in them both, for he liued
and dyed in prayer and obedience.
And his will & pleasure is that those
that be his, do the like, thou especially, if thou desire to be his disciple.

THE 1. POINT.

TO consider how that Christ our
Lord being absent from his Disciples that were at sea, there arose a
great tempest, and held them till it
was almost day, and then their Lord
& Maister shewed himselfe vnto thē.

Ponder first, how that if Christ
our

our Lord abfent himfelfe from thy
foule, it is forth with toffed , plunged
and ouerwhelmed with the furious
waues of temptations.

Secondly, our Lord doth fome-
times prolonge and deferre his cōming vntill the morning , as heere he
did, that thou mayft fight valiantly
againft thy temptations: for as they
do increafe, fo much more doth vertue and fanctity increafe by them.

Hence thou mayft gather a defire alwayes to walke in the prefence
of God : befeeching him not to forfake thee , though it be his pleafure
fometymes to proue thee by temptations: nor long to deferre his fauour
and ayde , but to returne as he did
to S. Antony, and S. Catherine.

THE 3. POINT.

TO confider how our Bleffed Sauiour from the mountaine beheld
the affliction wherein his Difciples
were, & the need they had of his help
and affiftance in that danger, and hauing compaffion of them , came
downe to ayd and fuccour them, and
walking vpon the fea, he made himfelfe

selfe knowne vnto them, saying:
Haue confidence, it is I, feare yee
not.

Ponder first, how Christ our
Lord walking on the sea, did not
sincke, because he was Lord of both
sea and land, whome all creatures do
obey and serue, man only excepted.

Secondly, ponder how he sayd
to his Disciples: It is I, feare yee not,
that is to say, I your Father, your
ayd, your repose, your ioy and comfort in all your trauails, I your way,
truth & life. For so he is to those that
be good: but to the wicked, who
will he say he is? I am the iudge that
am to iudge you, I the God of reuenge that will chastice you, finally
I am the Almighty that shall condemne you.

Gather hence a desire that our
Lord will vouchsafe to visit thee
with his heauenly presence, & speake
in such manner to thy hart, whenso-
euer thou shalt be troubled and afflicted, that when he shall say: It is I,
feare not, thou mayst forthwith
know

know him, reuerence him, and serue
him, loue him, and haue full confidence in him .

THE 4. POINT.

TO consider how S. Peter seeing
Christ our Lord walking vpon
the sea, besought him, that he would
bid him come to him vpon the waters : and our Lord, seeing that his
petition proceeded from true loue,
gaue him leaue, and the Holy Apostle walked vpon the water, as if it
had beene firme land, and beginning
to doubt and to faile in his fayth, he
presently began to sincke .

Ponder, that if thou hast fayth
and confidence, thou shalt walke v-
pon the waters of tribulations and
temptations without feare, as if thou
shouldst walke vpon firme land, but
if thou begin to doubt presently thou
shalt sincke .

Ponder secondly, how it behooueth thee not to enter into the
occasions of temptations vpon thy
owne head : sith S. Peter entred not
into the sea, nor cast himselfe into the
water without the commandement
of

of God.

Learne to call vpon God when thou seest thy selfe plunged in perills and afflictions, because heerein consisteth all thy good and remedy; and he will giue thee his potent hand, as he did to S. Peter, & will bring thee safe to the happy port of euerlasting blisse.

THE XXV. MEDITATION.

Of the Conuersion of S. Mary Magdalen.

THE I. POINT.

TO consider the course of the life of S. Mary Magdalen. Before her conuersion she was of light behauiour, giuen to company keeping, and to worldly meetings; esteeming only that which was agreable to her owne gust and pleasure. She had neither shame, nor feare of God, nor of men : she regarded not her fame & reputation, nor what people did say of her, but was held for a publicke sinner.

Ponder

Ponder, that although this woman was so bad as hath beene sayd, yet her hart being once touched with the inspiration of Almighty God, she presently withdrew herselfe from all occasions, and retyred her selfe from company, betooke her selfe to repentance, and shedding tears of sorrow from her eyes, began to teare & cast away her gay attyre and her iewells, which were the snares wherwith the Diuell held her entangled.

Purpose not to deferre thy conuersion when God shall call thee; learne of this holy penitent to reiect and abhorre those things which were instruments of offending him, and labour for two things: first alwayes to haue a holy feare and distrust of thy owne frailty, learning to beware by the example of this Magdalen, who from little euills came to fal into many and grieuous sinnes.

Secondly, to haue great confidence in the mercy of God at whose hands this sinner found remedy, and thou also mayst find the like, if as thou hast followed her in sinning,

N 4   thou

thou imitate her in repenting.

THE 2. POINT.

TO confider how S. Mary Magdalen vnderftanding that her Lord and Maifter dined in the houfe of Simon the Pharify, tooke an alabafter box of oyntment, & putting on meane apparell repayred thither to feeke the health of her foule.

Ponder, how fhe that was a finner came to the iuft and holy: fhe that was ficke and infirme came to the Phifitian: the defiled to the Sanctificr: the loft fheep to the good fhepheard. And approching vnto him caft her felfe at his feet, and began to water them with teares, and wiped them with the haire of her head, and kiffed them, & anoynted them with a precious oyntment, with fighes & feruent defires of her hart, crauing that fhe might be reconciled vnto him, and receaue the kiffe of peace.

Gather out of all this, how neceffary it is for remedy of thy finnes, to haue fpeedy recourfe to Chrift our Lord, and proftrating thy felfe at his feet, and cleauing faft vnto them by
humble

humble & feruent affection, to powre
out teares of compunction, proceeding from the very bottome of a
contrite hart . And as S. Mary Magdalen conuerted thoſe thinges which
had beene the occaſion of her perdition to be inſtruments of her ſatisfa-
ction, imploying her eyes, haire, lips
and pretious ointments and odours,
and her ſelfe wholy in the ſeruice of
God : ſo thou oughteſt to turne to
his ſeruice, whatſoeuer heeretofore
thou haſt imployd in offending him,
caſting all thy honour & reputation
at the feet of Chriſt : for there is nothing greater, nor better thē to cleaue
faſt to the feet of thy Lord God and
Maiſter .

The 3. Point.

TO conſider, what opinion the
Phariſy had concerning B. Mary
Magdalen, eſteeming her a ſinner, &
Chriſt himſelfe leſſe pure, becauſe
he permitted himſelfe to be touched
by her.

Ponder how that thoſe who
conuert themſelues to God, haue
preſently ſome that murmur againſt
them

them and censure their actions, but
God himselfe hath care to defend thē
as he did S. Mary Magdalen, when
he demanded of the Pharisie, if he
did see that woman, and her teares,
sighes, humiliation and confusion;
that considering them well, he might
blush and be ashamed of the little he
did towards our Sauiour, and thereby obtaine pardon of God.

Thou mayst gather hence a desire to serue & loue God very much,
because these things moue his diuine
Maiesty to piety, and clemency and
to pardon thy sinnes, be they neuer
so great and enormous, as he did
pardon this holy penitent, and of a
captiue of the Diuell, set her free and
deliuered her out of his chaines, and
exalted her to the happy and blessed
estate of the children of God.

THE 4. POINT.

TO consider, how that albeit S.
Mary Magdalen had heard from
the mouth of Christ Iesus that all her
sinnes were forgiuen her, and that
she was absolued from all, both
guilt and payne, through the abundant

dant grace which was communicated
vnto her, fhe notwithftanding remayned ftill fixed at her Redeemers
feet, and would not depart from
thence vntill her maifter fayd to her:
Go in peace. And fhe began prefently
to punifh her body and did great and
rigorous pennance all her life time,
which endured the fpace of two and
thirty yeares after.

Ponder, what an one fhe was
when fhe came to the feet of Chrift,
& what an one fhe departeth thence:
fhe came dead, but fhe departed aliue
fhe cam a finner, but departed holy:
fhe came the flaue of the Diuell and
enemy of God, but departed the
daughter and Efpoufe of Chrift.

Gather hence a defire to do pennance for thy finnes, for thefe be the
fruits which this vertue bringeth: do
not prefently forget them againe,
making account that they are already
forgiuen thee: becaufe this happy
woman and Bleffed Saint did not fo.
Imitate her, and although thy finnes
fhould haue beene many more and
much greater then hers were, though

N 6   thou

thou haſt loſt the grace of God far
oftener, thou mayſt recouer it , and
attayne vnto a great degree of ſancti-
ty, aboue many iuſt which neuer loſt
it .

THE XXVI. MEDITATION.
Of the miracle of the fiue Loaues.

THE I. POINT.

TO conſider how different the
piety and mercy of the Apoſtls
is from that of our B. Sauiour,
for they beſought him , ſeeing there
was not therewith to feed ſo great a
multitude, to diſmiſſe them, that going into the towne, they might buy
themſelues victualls . But our Sauiour perceauing the ſlendernes of
their mercy and charity, ſhewed the
greatnes of his owne moſt bountifull
mercy, and ſought by himſelfe effe-
ctually to remedy that neceſſity, as
he did .

Ponder the care which Chriſt
hath to ſupply the wants of thoſe
which ſerue him, and how that his
                                will,

will, defire and pleafure is fuch, and
it pleafeth him greatly that thy mercy be not fcant or fparing, but great
and free : Teaching thee to lift vp
thyne eyes to heauen and acknowledging that from thence all good is
to be expected.

Gather hence defires to place
thy confidence, not in money (albeit al things obey it) neither in the
world, or humane forces, but in the
bounty and infinite goodnes of thy
Creatour, whofe hand (as the Apoftle fayth) is alwayes open to releeue
and giue his bleffing to the hungry
and needy, not only of corporall,
but alfo much more of fpirituall
food.

THE 2. POINT.

TO confider how the Apoftles being demanded by our Bleffed Sauiour of the fiue loaues which they
had, forthwith and without repug-
nance, and with a very good wil they
prefented them vnto him, togeather
with the two filhes they had in ftore.

Ponder the great pouerty of
our B. Lord and of his Difciples, &
the

the small care they had of their owne
comfort and corporall sustenance,
seeing for thirteen persons, & others
which might ioyne themselus vnto
them, they had only fiue loaues, &
those also made of barley, which
was the most vnsauery bread that
then was in vse, and peculiar vnto
poore people; hauing fed in the desert that vngratefull Nation with
bread from heauen, whereas him
selfe and his Blessed Apostles were
fed with barly bread.

Purpose firmely to choose for
thy selfe such thinges as Christ our
Lord did choose for himselfe, intrea-
ting thy body with like seuerity and
rigour wherwith he treated his, being ashamed from this day forward
of thy ouermuch sollicitude in seeking after superfluities and daintes
in meate and drinke, otherwise then
is pleasing to our Lord, who repro-
ueth these things.

THE 3. POINT.

TO consider how that our Sauiour
and Lord of all things taking the
bread into his holy and powerfull
hands,

hands, blessed it and gaue it vertue to
be multiplyed and become better, so
that though euery one did eat therof,
it was not consumed, but rather did
multiply and increase.

Ponder first, the omnipoten-
cy of God, which so easily could conuert a few vnsauory loaues into thousands, and those most sauory and
tooth-some bread.

Ponder secondly, the prouidence of God resplendent and manifest in this miracle: For whereas
those which did eate of this bread
were many thousands, & of different
ages and complexions, yet all of the
eating thereof, and of the selfe same
kind of bread, were notwithstanding satisfyed, & as wel content with
a small portion, as with a great quá-
tity thereof.

Gather hence a great desire wholy to rely & trust on the omnipotent
hand of God: for they can neuer
want, but will increase and prosper
alwayes whose Lord & God is Christ
our Sauiour.

THE

THE 4. POINT.

TO confider how, this heauenly
banquet being ended, our Sauiour
commanded his Apoftls to gather vp
the leauings: they therfore gathered
them, and filled twelue bafkets with
the fragments of thofe fiue barly
loaues, which remayned after all had
eaten.

Ponder the goodnes & boun-
tifulnes of our Lord in rewarding the
liberality and free hart wherwith his
difcipls offered him their fiue loaues:
for he reftored them twelue bafkets
full of moft delicate bread; that they
might vnderftand, that as they were
twelue, fo he would that the bafkets
of the remaynès fhould be twelue, as
it were to beftow vpon euery one of
them a whole bafket full for the fmall
part which each of them had renoun-
ced in the fiue loaues they had before
prefented him.

Gather hence a defire to be mercifull and bountifull towards the
poore of Chrift, becaufe al thofe who
offer him any thing for his feruice,
he rendreth them much more then
they

they gaue him: as it is manifeft in the
mercy he vfed with that widdow
which fed Elias the Prophet, who for
a litle meale which fhe had freely and
liberally beftowed vpon him in the
name of God, multiplyed the fame,
making it to fuffice for many dayes.
And for one glaffe of bad wine which
was giuen vnto Chrift our Lord at
the marriage, whereunto he was
inuited, he bountifully rendred fix
veffells full of moft excellent wine.
And if this our Lord deale fo liberally in this life with finners giuing
a hundred fold for one, what will he
giue in the eternall to the iuft? Good
meafure (fayth S. Luke) and preffed
downe, and fhaken togeather, and
running ouer fhallbe giuen in their
bofome, infinitely furpaffing that
which is, or can be done for him in
this life.

THE

THE XXVII. MEDITATION.

Of the Transfiguration of our Lord.

THE I. POINT.

TO confider, that when Chrift our Lord transfigured himfelfe and vouchfafed as it were to make a heauen heere vpon earth, manifefting his glory and heauenly beauty vnto men, he retyred himfelfe vnto an high mountaine, taking with him only three of his beft beloued and moft familiar difciples, to a place where no body but only they might enioy thofe diuine comforts and fauours, which in the night of his transfiguration he was to impart vnto them. Wheras to fhew himfelfe disfigured in Mount Caluary, there to fuffer a moft painefull and opprobrious death , he would it fhould be at midday, and in the fight of the w hole world.

Ponder how that God doth not beftow thefe graces & fauours (fuch as was to be prefét at the glory of his
                                   tranffi-

tranffiguration) vpon all thofe that
are iuft and holy , but only to the
moft feruourous and his beft beloued : and peraduenture hetooke not
the reft with him (not becaufe they
were leffe feruent in his loue, neither
were they fo, but)becaufe Iudas was
amongft them, who deferued not to
enioy fo great a fauour, neither wold
he exclude him alone, not to defame
him .

Whence thou mayft gather,
how much it importeth thee to be
feruorous in the loue of God , and
how much harme one bad member
doth vnto a whole community of
good men, being the caufe why they
are depriued of fuch fauours and benefits which Almighty God would
do them , if fuch a one were not in
their houfe and company .

THE 2. POINT.

TO confider , how that Chrift our
Lord tranffigured himfelfe in
prayer , permitting the glory of his
foule (which was hidden then and
reftrained) to communicate it felfe
to the body, though for a fmal tyme.

Ponder

Ponder how that thy sinnes were the cause why that most holy body of thy Redeemer, was depriued al the time he liued in this world of that glory which he made known in this his trāsfiguration, as also why it was passible and mortall : & albeit now he admitted that glory, it was but for a very short space, choosing rather to prosecute the worke of our Redemption, and to suffer and dye with great ignominy and shame for men, then heere to haue rest & enioy his glory .

Gather hence two things first a desire and loue rather of payns and trauells, and to suffer with Christ in mount Caluary, then to enioy the quiet of mount Tabor. Secondly how it importeth thee to be a great louer of prayer, and to profit therein if thou desire to be transfigured into the image of the Sonne of God, for by prayer our life is transformed & changed from terrene and worldly into a celestiall and diuine consolation .

THE

THE 3. POINT.

TO confider how our B. Sauiour
being in fo great glory and Maiefty, there appeared Moyfes & Elias,
and fpake of his death that he was to
fuffer in Hierufalem.

Ponder how that the reafon,
why Chrift our Lord made choice of
thofe two Prophets before many o-
thers, and to honour himfelfe and
them by this communication, was,
becaufe they were eminent in fanctity, and zealous of the obferuance
of the Law, and withall very much
giuen to fafting and prayer.

Gather from hence two things:
firft a great defire of thofe vertues,
which thefe Saints had, thereby to be
fo inward & familiar with our Lord
as they were. Secondly how our Sauiour in the middeft of his ioy and
comfort, did interpofe and mingle
fpeeches of forrow, of his death and
paffion, becaufe whileft he liued on
earth he would not haue one iote of
reft, but all his delights and pa-
ftimes were to treat of fuffering and
dying. And all this to the end thou
fhouldft

shouldst haue euer in thy mind his
passion, & delight to thinke theron,
speaking very frequently & willingly
of the same, and be ashamed if thou
dost not so.

THE 4. POINT.

TO consider, how the three Apostles enioying the glory of the
Transfiguration, S. Peter desired to
remayne there for euer: whereupon
he sayd to our Sauiour: Lord it is
good for vs to be heere: as if he should
say, Let vs exchange, ô Lord, all
whatsoeuer for this montaine, let vs
change all the goods and pleasures of
the world for the delights of this desert.

Ponder how that when S. Peter
saw his Maister transfigured & glorious, he was willing to accompany &
abide with him, but at the tyme of
his passion and of affliction, when he
saw him apprehended & reproachful-
ly delt withall, he fled with the rest.
The like happeneth to thee: for thou
continuest no longer in the seruice of
God, then he doth cherish and comfort thee: then thou sayest as S. Peter

Though

Though I should dye with thee, I wil
not deny thee, but perceauing perill
and paynes to be taken, forthwith
thou forsakest him and turnest thy
backe saying: I know not this man.
And as S. Peter knew not what he
sayd, so neither dost thou, seeing that
before thou hast taken vp thy Crosse
& taken paynes, thou desirest glory
and ease.

Gather hence a great loue of
the Crosse and mortification, that
thereby thou mayst come to enioy
eternally that passing & infinite comfort which is in heauen : seeing that
S. Peter tasting heere one only drop
of that sea of delights which maketh
the Citty of God ioyfull, absorpt, and
as it were out of himselfe, and vnmindfull of whatsoeuer els, to wit,
beholding the sacred body of our Redeemer with that so great splendour
& beauty, was so fully satisfyed, that
he could haue been content to haue
taken vp his rest foreuer. But our
Lord depriued him of that transitory
glory, to giue him the eternall in
heauen.

THE

THE XXVIII. MEDITATION.

Of the raising of Lazarus, who had beene foure dayes dead.

THE 1. POINT.

TO consider how that Martha & Mary seeing their brother Lazarus sicke, sent vnto our B. Sauiour a briefe and discreet letter, contayning these words: Lord, behould whome thou louest, is sicke.

Ponder, how that to treat and negotiate with almighty God, many preambles and florishing phrases are not necessary: for to him who knoweth and penetrateth our harts few words suffice, and the common saying is, that a short prayer penetrateth heauen, and commeth to the hearing of God, as the prayer of these two holy sisters did, whome thou must imitate to negotiate and obtaine that which thou desirest, saying vnto God: Behold ô Lord, he whome thou louest is sicke, and seeing thou art the heauenly Phisitian, cure me. Behold

hold, o Lord, that I am comfortles, luke warme, dry, vndeuout, tempted with anger, pride, and impatience, and sith thou art omnipotent and most mercifull, haue mercy on me.

Gather hence a great desire that that this soueraigne Phisitian cure & heale thy soule, and visit & comfort it with his diuine presence, because it sustaineth many sorts of euills and infirmityes.

THE 2. POINT.

TO consider how that Christ our Lord comming out of Iewry, entred into the house of these two sisters where Martha meeting him sayd vnto him: Lord if thou haddst beene heere, my brother had not dved.

Ponder first, that if thy soule be dead in sinne, it is because thou didst absent thy selfe from Christ, for if thou haddst not withdrawne and separated thy selfe from him, no manner of temptations could haue beene able to ouerthrow thee.

Ponder secondly, that as Lazarus fell sicke and dyed in Christs absence, euen so when our Lord absenteth himselfe, and ceaseth to do thee his wonted fauours, the passions and infirmityes of tepedity and spirituall weaknes begin to bud and sprout forth, and are sometimes wont to end in deadly sinne.

Gather hence desires not to depart nor separate thy selfe from God, because with his sight and presence al euill vanisheth, and the health of thy soule is continually augmented and increased.

THE 3. POINT.

TO consider how before our Sauiour raysed Lazarus (as the Ghospell sayth) he wept: for it is the property of Charity (as the Apostle sayth) to weep with them that weep.

Ponder how that Christ weepeth & lamenteth, that therby thou mightst vnderstand how much thy sinnes grieue him, and how great the malice of them is, seeing he wept and suffered so often for them, and how great the hardnesse of thy hart is, & how litle thou feelest the malice and greatnes of thy sinnes, seeing thou doest shed so few teares for them.

Ponder

Ponder secondly, how stony-
harted thou art, yea and more then
stony: for the stones made as it were
shew of their feeling, & of their griefe
at the death of their Lord, but thou
feelest not, nor bewaylest, because he
suffereth for thee and for thy sinnes,
but when he weepeth for them thou
laughest, when he sorroweth for
them, thou art ioyfull and without
care.

Thou mayst gather hence a
great desire to bewayle thy sinnes
with a very inward griefe & feeling,
seeing they cost thy Sauiour so many
teares. If thou be dry and hardly
moued to any teares, annoynt thyn
eyes and hart with his teares, and by
their vertue thyne eyes will become
fountaines of teares, and be able to
wash away and cleane fetch out the
staynes of thy offences and sinnes,
restoring thee againe to the life of
grace which thou hadst lost by sinne.

THE 4. POINT.

TO consider how Christ our Lord
caused the stone which couered
the graue, to be taken away, and

O 2   lifting

lifting vp his eyes to heauen , cryed
with a loud voice , saying · Lazarus
come forth,& pretently obeying his
voyce, he came forth aliue, & whole
out of the caue , who a little before
lay therein dead, putryfied ,and stinking.

   Ponder the meruailous vertue
of the voyce of Christ, by the power
wherof he who was dead came aliue
out of the sepulcher : and it would
haue been sufficient to haue reuiued
al others that were deceased,if he had
not restrayned the force thereof to
Lazarus by name .

   Gather hence a great desire to
rise at the voyce & calling of Christ ,
and that all those who ar· spiritually
dead may also rise ,that so sinne being
banished out of the world , holynes
and iustice may raigne therein , and
our Lord be glorifyed in all his creatures.

                              THI

THE XXIX. MEDITATION.
Of the entrance of Christ into Hierusa-
lem vpon Palme-sunday.

THE 1. POINT.

TO consider the great charity of
thy Redeemer, the singuler ioy
and content where with he entreth the citty of Hierusalem to offer
himselfe to death for thee for this day
he would be receaued with so great
triumph, to declare vnto thee the
content and iubily which was in his
hart, for that the day of thy redemption did now approach.

Ponder, how Almighty God
disposeth & prepareth himselfe with
great longing and ioy of mind, to
vndergoe afflictions and paines for
thee, wheras when any thing is to be
done for his seruice, or to be suffered
for his loue, thou art presently afflicted and discomforted and flyest a-
way.

Ponder furthermore, how that
all the iniuries, persecutions, igno-
O 3   minies,

mintes, and reproaches which our Lord receaued in Hierusalem were not able to diminish his great loue & charity towards vs .

Gather hence an inflamed loue and desire to suffer something for thy Lord, thy eternall louer, seeing that all the tymes thou hast offended him with thy so grieuous sins (which haue not beene few) haue not beene able to extinguish in hisdiuine breast the loue he beareth thee, and his desire to do thee good , and to saue thee.

THE 2. POINT.

TO consider the humility and pouerty of the Sonne of God, who as alwayes before , was wont to make his iourney on foot, so this day being to enter in triumph into Hierusalem, he chose not to go in coach or in a chariot, but vpon a silly asse , which also was another mans : and albeit he enrred with so great humility , yet all the people receaued him with exceeding ioy , solemnity, and triumph .

Ponder that the cause why our
Lord

Lord would this day be so magnifyed
and receaued with so great honour
and applause of all, hauing euer fled
such honours before, was that his reproaches and ignominies might be
the greater, and his dishonour the
more notorious.

Gather hence a great desire to
condemne and abhorre all worldly
pompes and honours, and to loue &
imbrace the pouerty, humility and
meeknes of thy Sauiour, because if
these be the armes & ensignes of thy
King and God, they ought also to be
theirs, who esteeme themselues his
vassals and seruants.

THE 3. POINT.

TO consider, how our B. Sauiour
and Lord of the Angells being
mounted vpon the asse, innumerable
people by diuine inspiration came to
receaue him with boughes & palmes
in their hands, & with voices of laud
and praise sayd: Hosanna to the Son
of God: Blessed is he that commeth
in the name of God, hosanna in the
highest.

Ponder how the Eternall Fa-

O 4   ther

ther did honour his most B . Sonne ,
not only when he entred first into the
world and was borne poore in B-th-
leem, sending hosts of Angells to so-
lemnize his entrance , and to bring
those happy tidinges of glory to God
and peace to men . But this day also
when he entred humble and meeke ,
multitude of people came to solem-
nize and celebrate his entrance into
Hierusalem , and his departure out
of the world, giuing God many
thanks and praises for so great a benefit .

Gather hence a desire to imitate
the great deuotion wherewith this
people receaueth their God, and be
ashamed that thou commest so often
to receaue thy Lord and God, in the
most Blessed Sacrament with so great
indeuotion and coldnes .

The 4. Point.

TO consider the deuotion and loue
wherewith all did spread their
clothes and garments on the ground
to adorne the way by which our Sauiour passed, accounting it a great
happynes to cast themselues, and
what-

whatsoeuer they had at the feet of
this our Lord, that he might dispose
of it all according to his most holy
will; acknowledging that vnto him,
as to the owner and Lord of all, all
subiection & seruice was most due.

Ponder the little regard and e-
steem which is to be had of the glory
of this world, seeing it receaued our
Sauiour to day with so great honor,
& within few dayes after it held him
for worse then Barabbas, and sought
his death, crying out against him :
Crucify, crucify him. And whome
to day it extolled & termed the Son
of Dauid (that is the Holy of Holyes
and the most holy amongst Saints) to
morrow it reckoneth the most vile
of all men, and treateth him as a malefactour , loading his sacred shoulders with a heauy Crosse , on which
he was to be crucifyed and dye.

Gather hence great compassion
and griefe to see the Lord of Angells
so much neglected and despised
by men , and to seeke their honour
at so great charge and cost of his .
Desire thou to serue & honour him

O 5   much

much more heereafter, and say vnto
him: Behold ô my King & my Lord
I cast at thy most holy feet, not only
all my goods and wealth, but my honour also, my content, my life, my
selfe, and all; tread vpon me, and do
with me what thou wilt: for thou art
my God, my King, and Lord, the
head of Angels and men, better, and
exalted aboue them all.

THE XXX. MEDITATION.

Of the supper which Christ our Lord made with his Disciples.

THE 1. POINT.

TO consider how Christ our Sauiour sent S. Peter and S. Iohn
his Apostles, to prepare for the
legall supper of the Lambe, and how
that forthwith the good man of the
house to whome they were sent, in-
spired by the Holy Ghost gaue them
the best, and best accommodated
roome of the whole house.

Ponder the fauour which Almighty God vouchsafeth to do thee
in

in particuler, whē he entreth into thy houfe, that is, into thy foule, to celebrate therein his feaft and Pafch, and make thee thereby partaker of the merits of his moft precious bloud & paffion.

Gather hence great forrow and repentance for that thou haft behaued thy felfe fo ill towards fo louing a Lord, feeing not once but many tymes thou haft fhut the dore of thy foule vpon him, & fhutting it againft his diuine infpirations, thou haft opened it to the perfwafions of thy enemy the Diuell, whom thou baft receaued and intertayned, as if he and not God had beene the owner, and Lord of thy foule. And therefore that which thou oughteft to do is to offer him, not only the beft roome in thy houfe, that is, thy foule, but alfo to giue it him wholy: for it is all wholy his. And would to God it were better then it is, that it might pleafe his diuine Maiefty to come and dwell in it for euer.

THE 2. POINT.

TO consider how that Christ our Lord, the day being come whē the Paschal lambe was to be eaten, would fullfill that ceremony of the Law, & for the accomplishing of the shadows and figures of the old law , be sacrificed as the true lambe which taketh away the sinnes of the world , at the same tyme and in the same place that the mysticall lambe was wont to be sacrificed. Wherfore our Lord being at the table with his disciples, and all things being prepared and ready, he sayd vnto them: With desire I haue desired to eat this Pasch with you, to giue you to vnderstand how much I loue you, as if he should say : Very long haue I greatly desired this day and this houre, wherein you shal see nothing in me but ignominies , reproaches, blowes, stripes, wounds &c.

Ponder the great and earnest desire which God had to suffer and to giue his life for thee, longing to be plunged in the bitter sea of his passion, and to encounter with death, expecting

pecting it as a thing after which he
much hungred, & tooke much pleasure and delight in. And this was that
which he desired (as he sayd) with
a great desire, becaufe it was very
pleasing to him, and a thing wherein
he receaued speciall guft.

Gather hence great confusion
and shame, considering that thy desires are not like vnto those of thy
Lord and God, to suffer and endure
something for his honour and glory,
thou being so worthy of all reproach
and contempt, but rather thy desires
are to follow thyne owne pleasure &
contentment, not to serue his diuine
maiesty, but to fullfill thy owne will
and disordered appetite.

THE 3. POINT.

TO consider how Christ our Lord
did behold and contemplate that
lambe which he had before him on
the table, layd there dead, flayed &
rosted. In it no question he saw himselfe represented more innocent then
a lambe, and how without any his
deserts he was to be flayed with
stripes, and embrued with his owne
most

most precious bloud through most
cruell torments , and finally to be
put as it were vpon the spit and
stretched on the table of the Crosse,
where, with the hote burning coales
of loue, he was to be rosted to death.

Ponder how bitter this supper
was vnto thy Redeemer, being min-
gled with sauce of so distastfull a representation, as was that of his death
and passion .

Purpose, when thou sittest at
table, to mingle thy meat with this
sauce, to wit , with the consideration
of the passion and paynes of thy Sauiour, that thou be not carryed a-
way with the gust and sauour of the
meat: and that if thy meat be not
good or not so well dressed or seasoned, or not in such due tyme prepared as thou wouldst, thou mayst haue
patience, and haue some what to offer
vnto God , and make thy spirituall
profit thereof.

THE 4. POINT.

TO consider how the legall supper
being ended , Christ our Lord
gaue thanks to his eternall Father; &
did

did offer himselfe perfectly & intier-
ly to accomplish his holy will, as hauing taken vpon him our mortall
flesh to be sacrificed and dye vpon
the Crosse.

Ponder how pleasing this offering and sacrifice of the Sonne of
God, was to the heauenly Father, in
which he offered himselfe to fulfill in
all things the diuine will : for where
this perfect resignation is wanting,
whatsoeuer other sacrifices and holo-
caufts are not of any value, because
we offer not our selues.

Gather hence an inflamed and
effectuall desire to offer thy selfe vnto
God with an humble and prompt
will, to performe whatsoeuer he shal
command thee, how paynefull and
difficult soeuer it be.

THE

THE XXXI. MEDITATION.
Of washing the Apostles feet.

THE 1. POINT.

TO confider that fupper being ended, Chrift Iefus our Lord arofe from table, and putting of and as it were defpoyling his royall Maiefty of his authority & greatnes humbled himfelfe to be the feruant of his feruants : and laying afide his vpper garment, himfelfe alone, not admitting the help of any, girded himfelfe with a towell, tooke the tankerd in his hand, and put water into the bafon, and wafhed, not the hands, but the foule and dirty feet of thofe poore and filly fifhermen his difciples, and louingly and tenderly did bath them, wipe them, and make them cleane.

Ponder the excellency of the perfon that performeth this fo meane and fo bafe an office, and humbleth himfelfto thefe things. The Creatour of the world, the beauty of the heauens,

uens, the splendour and brightnes of
the glory of the Father, the fountaine
of wisedom, in whose hand God hath
put heauen, earth, hell, life, death,
Angels and men, power and authority to pardon sinnes, the saluation
and iustification of soules, the glory
of the iust, and al the treasurs of God:
this same our Lord so great in Maiesty, abased himselfe to this act of so
great humility and charity.

Gather out of all this, great confusion to see thy selfe so proud notwithstanding that thou art so base a
creature. Admire thy haughtinesse of
mind, yea thy foolishnes that being
most ignorant and most poore and
vile, canst be so proud, seeing Christ
who is Lord of infinite power and
wisedome hath so humbled himselfe.
Our Lord Iesus himselfe teacheth vs
to exercise workes of humility and
charity, choosing rather to practise
these acts, then to comand: why then
wilt not thou do the like, & seriously
set vpon that worke, from which so
great profit and abundant fruit is to
be reaped.

THE

THE 2. POINT.

TO consider, how Christ our Lord being now ready to performe this so humble and base an office, came first to S. Peter to wash his feet: but the Apostle was so amazed and confounded, considering with liuely fayth the greatnes of his Lord and Maister, & togeather his owne basenes, that he sayd with admiration: Lord dost thou wash my feet! Thou being the infi ite God and Lord of all thinges! And I the most vile and basest of them all! Thou the Creatour of heauen & earth, Lord of the Angells and Seraphims, and I thy creature, thy slaue, a most vile sinner, and yet wilt thou wash with those hands, which giue sight to the blind, health to the sicke, & life to the dead, not my head or my hands, but my filthy and abominable feet! This ô Lord I may not endure, but I shall fall dismayd at thy blessed feet. But our Lord saying vnto him: Peter know for certaine, that if I wash thee not, thou shalt not haue part withme: this threat was so terrible vnto him,

that

that forthwith he yelded, not only to
haue his feet washed, but also his
hands and head.

Ponder what so high and soueraigne a God doth for so low & base
a creature, and what his diuine Maiesty vndertaketh himselfe to do, to
make vs humble: esteeming highly
of this which Christ doth, and mean-
ly of thy selfe.

Gather affections of admiration,
of thanks giuing, and imitation. propose vnto him the necessity which
thou hast, that his diuine Maiesty
wash & purify thee from thy sinnes,
seeing he is so humble & do desirous
to do thee this fauour, to the end
thou mayst haue part with him : for
no creature hath this power and authority of himselfe but the only Son
of God alone.

THE 3. POINT.

TO consider how Christ Iesus our
Lord prosecuting this act of humility and charity, vouchsafed also to
do the same to Iudas. And prostrating himselfe at his feet, as if he had
beene the Lord and Maister, and
                              Christ

Chrift Iefus the feruant, he wafhed &
wiped his feet, with fignes of more
fpeciall loue, to mollify that his hard
rebellious, and obftinate hart, and to
win him (if it had beene poffible) to
fome good, with this infpeakable humility and charity.

Ponder, and behold Chrift our
Lord proftrate at the feet of fo wicked a fellow as Iudas. And we may
picufly thinke that our Bleffed Sauiour, being thus humbled and proftrate at the feet of this traitour and
wretched difciple, would with tears
failing from his eyes for his impiety
and hardnes of hart, fay vnto him:
Come Iudas, my deere Apoftle, giue
me thy feet, for I will wafh them and
bath them, and wipe them, euen now
it being the eue of that day in which
my feet are to be nailed vpon the
Croff, and wafhed in my bloud for
thy finnes, and by occafion of thy
treachery And if thou haft any com-
plaint againft me, behould I am heer
at thy feet, do with me what thou
wilt, vpon condition that thou betray me not, nor offend me no more.

Gather

Gather out of this so remarkable an example of humilitv, two things: First, motiues of loue towards him, who humbled himselfe so much for thee, and learne to humble thy selfe that thou mayst doe good to thy neighbours although in regard of their vnworthinesse they deserue it not.

Secondly, learne out of the obstinacy of Iudas, to be wiser by others harmes. Beseeching Almighty God to take away thy stony hart, & to change it into a hart of flesh, that thou mayst feele his diuine inspirations, and imbrace his louing examples.

THE 4. POINT.

TO consider how that Christ our Lord, hauing finished this worke of so rare humility and charity, tooke his garments & sitting downe againe at the table, sayd to his Apostles: Know you what I haue done to you?

Ponder this demand, as if our Lord would say: Know you the mystery which is comprehended in this

my

my deed? and the end wherefore I do it? Make account that God sayth vnto thee, Dost thou know what I haue don for thee? the benefits which I haue bestowed vpon thee? the euils & dangers from which I haue preserued thee? Knowest thou how much I haue humbled my selfe to exalt thee? Dost thou know that I made my selfe man, to make thee the sonne of God? If then I haue washed your feet, being your Lord & Maister (that is) if I haue humbled my selfe so much, with how much more reason ought you to humble your selues and exercise al works of humility and charity: specially I hauing spent my whole life in giuing you so rare and admirable exan ples of these and other vertues.

Gather a desire and firme purpose from this day forward to do that which our Lord Iesus doth counsaile and command thee. Because humbling thy selfe thou shalt euer find grace in the sight of God, and thereby be exalted to the dignity of the sonne of God.

THE

THE XXXII. MEDITATION.

Of the institution of the most Blessed Sacrament.

THE I. POINT.

TO confider the vnfpeakable greatnes of the loue which our Lord bare to mankind, feeing in the very felfe fame night of his paffion when men went about to kill him, and to deuour his facred flefh as it were by bits, and fucke his precious bloud with terrible torments difgraces and ignominies, he was preparing for them this foueraigne morfell, and celeftiall banquet, to make them partakers of euerlafting life.

Ponder how neither the contradictions of the wicked, nor the pefence of death, and of any torments were able to turne his mind, nor to diminifh his inflamed charity, and make him relent in his loue, and purpofe of comforting his elect with this foueraigne banquet.

From hence thou mayft gather purpo-

purposes, that no afflictions, contēpts or persecutions, notorments or pains shallbe able to separate thee from him, nor to make thee omit to serue him, or to receiue him often in this most B. Sacrament: for to this end he hath vouchsafed to stay heer with vs vnder the forme of bread, which is a meat that all eat of, great and little, poore and rich.

THE 2. POINT

TO consider the place, which Christ our Redeemer did choose, to institute this most Blessed Sacrament, which was a great hall, handsomely adorned, offered freely for his vse, by a man whose name is not known.

Ponder how this hall is thy soule into which Christ entreth and remayneth there, in this most diuine Sacrament, and it importeth thee very much to haue it adorned withall kind of vertues, which be the hangings of the house wherein God dwelleth.

Ponder secondly, how Christ our Lord esteemeth greatly of a ready and prompt will to receaue him,

and

and maketh no account of the state &
titles of the world. And therefore he
would, that this mans name that gaue
him this house or Hall should not be
knowne, to signify that he regardeth
not whether he be poore or rich, noble or ignoble, learned or vnlearned,
that is to receaue him into his soule,
but only that he offer what he hath
vnto him with a prompt and deuout
will.

Gather hence a great affection
and longing desire to giue thy selfe
wholy vnto this thy Lord, offering
thy selfe willingly vnto his seruice,
seeing though thou be so miserable,
and so vile and base, yet he vseth so
great mercy towards thee, that he
vouchsafeth to make thee his house
and aboad, and to celebrate his sacred and diuine Mysteries in thee.

THE 3. POINT.

TO consider how Christ Iesus our
Lord, whiles he was at supper
tooke bread in his Blessed hands, saying : This is my body &c. by vertue
of which wordes he conuerted the
substance of the bread into his owne

P   most

most sacred body and bloud.

Ponder the omnipotency of this our Lord: for in an instant he conuerted the bread into his sacred flesh, in such a sort that both God and man entierly & wholy, is vnder that small quantity of the host, & in euery part or parcell therof, without any diuision of the body, although the host be broken and deuided.

Ponder secondly, that Christ our Lord sayd not, this is part of my body or of my flesh, but this is my body wholy and perfectly: for albeit euery least particle of his Blessed flesh would haue sufficed to sanctify vs, he would neuertheles be there wholy & euery part of him, that is, his head, eyes, eares, breast and hart, to giue thee to vnderstand, by the participation of his most holy members, he would sanctify all those that would duely receaue him, and perfectly cure and heale them.

Gather hence a desire to giue thy selfe wholy vnto our Lord, imploying all thy members and sences in his diuine seruice, that thou mayst wholy

wholy be a perfect reprefentation of
him.

The 4. Point.

TO confider how Chrift Iefus our
Lord communicated all his A-
poftles, and Iudas amongft the reft
(albeit he knew what an one he was)
becaufe as yet his finne was not notorious ; wherefore to him as to all
the reft, he gaue in this diuine Sacrament, all he had, to wit, his moft
holy body and bloud, his foule, diui-
nity and humanity, that they might
euer haue in mind his great loue
towards them, and what he had fuffered for their fake.

Ponder the reuerence and deuotion wherewith thofe B. Apoftles
(Iudas only excepted, who was in
mortall finne) did take and receiue
into their breafts that moft Bleffed
bread. There S. Peter did ftir vp his
fayth, and turning his fpeech to him
that he beleeued to be co aine & to
lye hidden in that facred bread, faid:
Thou art Chrift the Sonne of the liuing God. To whome we may imagine that our Lord would anfwere:

Bleffed

Blessed art thou Simon Bariona, because flesh and bloud hath not reuealed it to thee, but my Father which is inheauen. S. Iohn likewise would enkindle in himselfe affections of loue: seeing his soueraigne Maister not only to vnite himself so vnto him, as to permit him to leane on his breast, but also to do him so great a fauour as to enter into his soule & body for more perfect coniunction.

Learne when thou commest to receaue our Lord, to bring with thee these vertues, to wit, fayth, purity, and loue, as these holy Apostles did, that thou mayst reap such profit as they did: & follow our Lord as they did follow him.

¶ It is to be noted, that in the end of the third booke, a few meditations are added, for preparation before, & thankes-giuing after we haue receaued this most B. Sacrament: where he that is desirous to know how to prepare himselfe, and to giue due thanks after vnto our Lord for the benefit receaued, may find them.

THE

THE XXXIII. MEDITATION
Of our Blessed Sauiours prayer in the Garden, and agony there.

THE 1. POINT.

TO consider the great desire that Christ had to suffer for our sake, and because the tyme seemed long till he should be deliuered into the tormétors hands, that they might see, that he did not shrinke nor yet fly, supper being ended, he went to the garden to pray, that being a place well knowne to the traytor Iudas, to shew that of his owne freewil he offered himselfe to prison, and to death it selfe.

Ponder how our Lord for no manner of afflictions or perils would leaue his good and laudable exercise of prayer and meditation : for supper being ended he betooke himselfe forthwith to a solitary place to pray, before he was to enter vpon his passion.

Be confounded, because through

P 3   thy

thy tepidity and negligence for euery light occasion thou leauest thy prayer and forgettest thy laudable customes, whereas thou shouldst do quite contrary, because in tyme of greater perills, afflictions and temptations we ought to haue more particuler recourse vnto Almighty God, prayer being the only meanes to strengthen our selues in them.

THE 2. POINT.

TO consider how our Redeemer, being come to the garden, went aside from his disciples, and began to wax sorrowfull, and to be sad.

Ponder what is that which maketh our Lord to grieue and to be sad and afflicted, he being the ioy of Angells, whom when they behold, they are exceedingly reioyced: thou shalt find that the cause of this affliction was the feare of the torments and of the death which he was to sustaine, the remembrance and liuely apprehension of the sinnes of all men, present, past, and future, the multitude and grieuousnes of them both was the cause of this his trouble & griefe,

as

as also the vnspeakable domage
which by sinne commeth to man, in
that by it they deserue to be condemned to the euerlasting torments of
hell. out of all this arose his so incredible sorrow.

Gather hence affections of griefe
and sorrow for the torments & death
which is euen now to come vpon thy
Lord: for thou hast beene the cause
of his paynes and afflictions. Endeauour from this day forward to abhorre and detest, and fly from sinne,
sith thou seest in what case thy Lord
is, to deliuer thee from it, and from
the eternal damnation which for thy
sinnes thou deseruest.

THE 3. POINT.
TO consider the perseuerance of
our Sauiour in his prayer, many
times crauing of his Eternall Father
one and the selfe same thing, to wit,
that the bitter chalice of his passion
might passe.

Ponder the deuotion & inward
feeling, the teares and sorrow of thy
Lord, how solitary, destitute & comfortles he is in this his so great affli-
P 4   ction

ction : his difciples were a loofe of faft
a fleep, his Eternall Father gaue him
no anfwere, neither graunted him
his petition : his moft holy Mother
was alfo abfent, his enemies now ready to come vpon him, and notwithftanding all thefe afflictions and dif-
comforts he remayned conftant and
perfeuered in his prayer.

Gather hence the great efteeme
thou oughtft to haue of prayer, feeing
Chrift teacheth thee that the only remedy of thy afflictions and forrows,
is not to talke, or conuerfe with men,
but to treat with God and continue
in prayer : confiding that though in
beginning he deny that which thou
afkeft, yet at laft he will graunt it, if
it be a thing conuenient for thee.

THE 4. POINT.

TO confider how the Sonne of God
feeing his Eternall Father gaue
uim no anfwere the firft nor fecond
tyme, he had recourfe vnto him the
third tyme, and repeating the fame
prayer with great loue and confidence, fayd: Father if thou wilt, tranf-
fer this Chalice from me : But yet
not

not my will, but thyne be done.

Ponder that the cause why the Eternall Father did defer so long to make answere vnto the prayer of his most holy Sonne, was to let thee know the great necessity thou and all haue of the passion and death of our Sauiour.

Learne, not to complaine, nor to be weary when thou prayest, if God do not heare thee: for certainely he heareth thee. But if vnto Christ our Lord (who deserued to be heard at the first opening of his mouth) answere was not made til he had prayed the third tyme, what wonder is it if thy petitions be deferred, who in regard of thy sinnes, deseruest not to be heard at all.

Gather secondly how God many tymes will not comfort nor remedy thy necessity in prayer, that thou mayst perceiue and know the need thou hast to haue recourse vnto him with patience and perseuerance.

P 5   THE

THE XXXIIII. MEDITATION.

Of the apparition of the Angell, and the sweating of bloud.

THE 1. POINT.

TO consider how the Eternall Father seeing his most Blessed Sonne in so great affliction and anguish of mind, and that according to the inferiour part, he feared to suffer and dye, he sent him an Angell from heauen, to comfort and strengthen him, and to propose vnto him the glory of God which thence would arise, and the benefit which would follow to all mankind by meanes of his passion, and that for humiliation and ignominy of the Crosse, his Name should be exalted and adored of all creaturs.

Ponder how the Lord of Angells (as if he had forgotten his owne soueraigne Maiesty) vouchsafed to receaue comfort by one of his creatures, and being the fortitude of the Father, and he who with power and

might

might gouerneth and sufteineth the
world, receaueth comfort and reliefe
from an Angell, hauing made himfelf
by reafon of humane nature which
he affumpted, inferiour to the Angells.

Gather hence that the office of
the Angells is to affift vs in our prayers, to comfort and animate vs, and
to prefent our prayers in the fight of
God, which if they be performed as
they ought, they haue their effect:
for God doth either deliuer vs out of
tribulation, or giueth vs forces to endure it with patience and ioy. Truft
in God that thou fhalt reap the like
comfort and benefit by thy paynes &
afflictions, if in them thou haue recourfe to prayer, as our B. Sauiour
had in his.

The 2. Point.

TO confider, how the Sonne of
God praying with more force and
earneftneffe, the anguifh, forrow, &
feare of death, and of the manifold
torments which he was to fuffer, did
fo wonderfully increafe, that his
fweat became as drops of bloud trick-

ling

ling downe vpon the earth.

Ponder first the greatnes of the tormerts which our Sauiour suffered: for if the only representation of them wrought so strange an effect in him who is the vertue and fortitude of God, what may we thinke it was to endure them.

Ponder secondly the example which our Lord giueth thee to striue strongly with thy passions and bad inclinations, withstanding them all valiantly euen to the shedding of thy bloud, if it be needfull, for the ouercomming of them.

Gather hence desires to fight against them, proposing to thy selfe all those thinges which may terrify thee or cause thee any way to shrinke in the way of vertue, or in the accomplishment of the diuine will, whether it be feare of pouerty, dishonour, sicknes, griefe, torment or whatsoeuer other difficulty, that thus preparing thy selfe thou mayst preuaile and get victory ouer them.

THE

THE 3. POINT.

TO confider the immenfity of the loue of Chrift our Lord, and the great liberality which he fheweth thee in fhedding voluntarily his precious bloud for thy fake, and not ftaying till the tormentors fhould do it with their ftripes, thornes & nayls.

Ponder how great the agony & forrow of our Lord was through the apprehenfion of all the torments which he was to fuffer in euery part of his body, fith it was of force to make a bloudy fweat to fall downe from his face, neck, breaft, & fhoulders, leauing him wholy bathed and embrued in his owne bloud.

Gather from hence defires that all the parts of thy body might become as fo many tongues to praife & magnify the loue and mercies of thy Lord, or fo many eyes to weep tears of bloud for thy finnes, or fo many hands to chaftice & reuenge thee on thy flefh by rigorous and tharp pennance, it hauing beene the caufe why thy Sauiour fuffered fo much, efpecially at that tyme, all at once, and

vpon

vpon a heap, al that he was to sustaine
after at seuerall tymes.

THE 4. POINT.

TO consider the vigour and force
which the most holy flesh of
Christ receaued by prayer to encou-
ter with the many griefs & torments
of his passion, it being strengthned to
vndergo that which before it did naturally fly from and abhorre

Ponder that the causes of courage and strength of mind and body which our Lord shewed heere,
were two. First, because he saw that
by his death and passion he was to
heale all the mortall soars & wounds
of the mysticall body of the Church,
which are the faythfull. Secondly to
giue vigour, force and courage to his
elect to vanquish and subdue their
spirituall and corporall enemies, vndergoing for him and for his honour
and glory, afflictions, persecutions,
reproaches, torments, crosses and
death, as S. Peter, and S. Paul, S.
Andrew, S. Steuen, S. Laurence &
many others did, imitating like faithfull souldiers their valiant Captaine,
                                    who

who went before and gaue them a liuely example of fuffering patiently
and conftantly .

Gather hence a defire to arme
thy felfe like a true fouldier of Chrift
with the armour of prayer , which is
the armour of light, that in all thy labours and affli&ions thou mayft
fight, and get the vi&tory ouer thyne
enemies, the world, the flefh, and the
Diuell .

THE XXXV. MEDITATION.

*Of the comming of Iudas, and of the in-
iuries done vnto our Sauiour .*

THE 1. POINT.

TO confider, how that our Sauiour hauing ended his prayer
that falfe traitor & fainedfriend
Iudas approached with a greatmul-
titude of armed men , making himfelfe the leader and captaine of them
to apprehend Chrift our Lord .

Ponder the extremity of euills
wherinto this wretch isfallen, becaufe
he did not refift his couetoufnesat the
beginning

beginning : and what may be expe-
&ed from thee, if thou resist not that
which thou feel-stin thy selfe, especially hauing got so good meanes of
vertue as he had : for thou dost not
learne in such a schoole , thou seest
not such miracles , neither conuersest
with such a maister , nor with such
schoole-fellowes. Yet all this was not
inough to restrain this accursed companion , and keep him from falling
like another Lucifer from the highest
degree in the Church , to the deepest
bottome of all wickednes, to wit, to
become the head conspirer of the
death of Christ .

Gather out of all this a great
feare of the iudgements of God , beseeching him, not to leaue thee, least
thy impiety proceed so far as to thyne
worke owne ruine , by the benefits
which he bestoweth vpon thee .

THE 2. POINT.

TO consider that the signe which
this traytor had giuen to the Ministers of Sathan, to betray his Maister was this : Whome soeuer I shall
kisse, that is he, hold him fast .

Ponder

Ponder that the enemyes of the author of life, could entrap him by no other wile then by shew of loue. And he accepted this cruell kisse, that with the sweetnes thereof, and of his meeknes he might soften the rebellious and obstinate hart of Iudas.

From hence thou mayst gather a great confidence in the mercy of this our Lord, that he will not refuse nor disdaine thy kisse, nor of those sinners which desire to reconcile thēselues to him, & renew their friendship with him which they haue lost, seeing he did not reiect the kisse of him who so cruelly betrayed him, & sold him as Iudas did.

THE 3. POINT.

TO consider how Christ our Lord encountred those impious officers of iniustice, and demanding of them : Whome seeke yee? they answered him, Iesus of Nazareth, and our Lord sayd vnto them : I am he.

Ponder first that word of Christ, whome seeke yee as if he should say: Take heed, you seek a iust & innocēt man, who doth good to al, & hurteth
no

no man You seeke him who descended from heauen to earth, for your eternall weale and saluation, and you seeke him to depriue him of his life.

Gather from hence desires to seeke this thy Lord, but after a far different manner, to wit, for thy saluation and remedy, & for his honour and glory, and thou mayst be assured, that seeking him after this manner, thou shalt find him.

Ponder secondly that word, I am he. A word which vnto his good Disciples was alwayes a great comfort in their trauails and afflictions, but vnto the bad, it is of so great feruour and dread, that it alone did fall them flat to the ground, neither could they haue risen againe if the same our Lord, who ouerthrew them with one only word, had not giuen them leaue to rise.

Gather hence desires to seeke God: & note by the way, that vnto the good who seeke him in prayer he is a father and protectour, he is their repose and ioy: But vnto the euill who seeke him to offend him, and

kill

kill him, he is a iudge that shal iudge
and condemne them. Finally he is
he, which is to their losse and eternall griefe.

THE 4. POINT.

TO consider how Christ our Lord
the most innocent Lambe (himselfe giuing place to the fury of his
enemyes) was deliuered vp to the rauenous wolues and princes of darknes (which are the infernal spirits)
by meanes of their seruants and ministers, to be put to al manner of torments and crueltyes, his life not excepted (as in holy Iob it was, when
he was deliuered to the power of Sathan) but without any limitation at
all, that they might wreake their fury vpon his most sacred humanity.

Ponder the malepertnes & ru-
denes of those sauadge furyes, making their sport and pastime to iniure
and torment the Sonne of God, of
whome they had receaued so great
benefits, and whome a little before
they had iudged worthy of highest
honour: but forgetting all this they
stroke him on the face, they spurned
and

and buffeted him with their firfts, they plucked him by the haire & , by the beard.

Hence thou mayft ftir vp in thy felfe fhame and confufion, for that thou haft beene fo bold, as to handle thy Sauiour as ill as thefe traitors did, laying thy facrilegious and violent hands vpon him, if not in outward fhew, at leaft through thy manifold finnes and wicked deeds, perfecuting him with them, as his enemies did, not once only, as they did, but many tymes.

THE XXXVI. MEDITATION.

How Chrift our Lord was apprehended.

THE 1. POINT.

TO confider how our Lord being Innocency it felfe was reckoned and treated as a theefe, and for fuch his enemies came to apprehend him with chaines and cordes, with fwords and clubbs: and our Sauiour gaue them power ouer his body, to fpurne & torment it at their pleafure.

Ponder

Ponder the surpaſſing great humility of our Lord, and how he is caſt at the feet of moſt vile ſinners, whoſe ſeat and throne is aboue the Seraphims: how he is kicked at and trodden vnder foot as a malefactour, who is the mirrour of innocency & the vnſpotted Lambe. Admire the rare ſubmiſſion & humiliation of ſo great a God, who did not only proſtrate himſelfe at the feet of his Apoſtles and of Iudas, and waſhed them and kiſſed them, but alſo ſuffered this traytor and his accurſed company, to ſet their abominable feet vpon him, to tread vpon him, and ſpurne him.

Gather hence an earneſt deſire to yeld and humble thy ſelfe to thy inferiours, beholding Chriſt thy Rędeemer ſo humble and meeke, and conſidering of whom and for whom he receaueth ſuch iniuries and reproaches.

THE 2. POINT.

TO conſider how that wicked band of ſouldiers, after they had ſtriken and abuſed Chriſt our Lord, tying
him

him by the wrests with strong cords
like a theefe , they brought him
bound vnto Annas the High Priests
house .

Ponder how far our Lord was
from being a theefe and robber of
other mens goods · for he gaue all he
had, and that which was particuler to
himselfe alone for thy good ,& tooke
vpon him the forme of a seruant,
concealing the dignity of Lord and
Maister . But if to rescue and deliuer
soules out of the thraldom of Sathan,
and to draw our harts to his loue
(which he hath euer done) be to be a
theefe , beseech him to take thy hart
and all that which thou hast besides.

And with earnest affection say
vnto him: Bind ô Lord I beseech thee
my hands with the fetters of thy loue
that my works may be gratefull vnto
thee . Bind my memory , that it forget not so many fauours and benefits
which thou dayly bestowest vpon
me . Bind my eyes , that they may
not behold vnlawfull things . Bind
my torgue , that it detr. & not , nor
murmure against my neighbour.
Bind

Bind my feet, that they may only walke the pathes of thy diuine Commandements. Bind finally, o Lord, this nature of myne and all my senses and powers from all that which is sin and offence, and set me free to all that which is vertue.

THE 3. POINT.

TO consider that the Apostls, seeing their Lord and Maister apprehended by the Iewes and fast bound, much affrighted, fleu away and forsooke him.

Ponder how thy Sauiour in this exigent is all alone and forsaken of his friends, & enuironed with cruell and mercilesse enemies how he was well accompanyed at his supper and in time of prosperity, but now abandoned of all in tyme of aduersity.

From hence thou mayst gather confusion and shame, for hauing often forsaken & left thy Father, Lord and Maister, and omitted to accomplish his holy will to fullfill thyne owne. And our Sauiour here being forsaken of his heauenly Father and of his disciples, giueth thee a rare example

ample of patience, that if thou be
destitute and left by thy friends and
kinsfolke, thou endure it patiently,
for it is not much that the disciple suffer that which his Maister hath suffered before him. Beseech him humbly
that seeing he is a true and faythfull
friend, he will neuer forsake thee, although al others should forsake thee;
but especially that he will not leaue
thee in the houre of thy death.

THE 4. POINT.

TO consider who this Lord is vpon
　whome so many iniuries are dis-
charged, who he is that sustayneth so
many reproaches and indignityes, &
at whose hands he taketh them.

Ponder first that he is the eternall Word of the Father, of infinite
vertue, innumerable goodnes, true
glory, and the cleare fountaine of all
beauty. He it is that is bound, manacled, buffited, haled, spurned, and
trodden vnder foot. He it is that is
handled in so vnhumane and rude
manner.

Ponder secondly the griefe
which our Sauiour felt seing himself
so

so much abused by so base a people, and so vngratefull, that for so many benefits, returned him so many & so greeuous iniuries. And if God tooke it so heauily to be so delt with all by his enemyes, how heauily did he take it suffering the like from his friends, seeing himselfe all alone and desolate, and in so great affliction, hauing beene betrayed and sould by one of them, denyed by another, and forsaken of all.

Gather from hence desires to become a true disciple of our Lord, indeauouring neuer to leaue him, but to accompany him, and follow him euen to the Crosse, that so thou mayst enioy him in his glory.

THE XXXVII. MEDITATION.

How Christ our Lord was presented before Annas the high Priest.

THE I. POINT.

TO consider what thy God and Lord suffered in that long way between the garden and Annas

Q   his

his house, vnto whome his enemies
carryed him, buffeting him, & spur-
ning him, and forcing him to go a-
pace, halfe running, and trayling him
on the ground, as it is wontto happen
to them that are led like theeues and
malefactours, and are fettered and
chained.

Ponder the meeknes & silence
wherewith our Lord suffered so many affronts, not hauing deserued the
least of them, for he neuer had nor
could haue committed any fault,
though his aduersaryes pretended
that he was guilty of many.

Gather hence a great desire to i-
mitate the example of thy Lord in
being silent, and suffering patiently
when occasion shallbe offered thee,
seeing thou hast so many imperfections and sinnes, as thou hast, is it
much that thou beare and be silent
for the loue of God, who being free
from all fault gaue thee so great an
example of inuincible patience & suf-
ferance.

THE

THE 2. POINT.

TO consider the shouts & outcryes of those wicked ministers, when they entred the citty with our Blessed Sauiour, proclayming and vanting theselus of the prey they had gotten.

Ponder how different this entrance into Hierusalem was, from that which the same our Lord made on Palme-sunday, when many went with him with boughes of palmes in their hands in token of the victory which he had atcheiued ouer his enemies. But now they bring him in with swordes and launces, as if they had gotten the victory ouer him. In that entrance all cryed out in his prayse: Blessed is he that commeth in the name of our Lord; in this they cry out in derision of him, making him their laughing-stock, and calling him by a thousand vnworthy names. In that they spread their garméts on the ground, that he might passe vpon them: In this they haled, rent and tore his garments from him, yea and pulled the haire from his beard and sacred head.

From

From hence thou mayst gather
a certaine equality of mind, and conformity with the diuine will in all
things, being mindfull of aduersity
in tyme of prosperity, of disgraces &
reproches in tyme of honour, and of
a bad day in the good : for it is cleare
that of little pleasure much sorrow
followeth.

THE 3. POINT.

TO consider in what plight those
sacred feet of thy Sauiour were
being embrued with bloud, the skin
flayed of them with often stumbling
and with being trodden on and spurned at, by those hellish ministers.

Ponder first, how those diuine
feet begin to pay for the sins which
thy feet haue committed in the rath
and crooked wayes by which they
haue walked, to fullfill thy desirs &
inordinate appetits.

Secondly the spirit and affection
wherewith our Lord goeth along
that way, and the vertues he exerci-
seth of humility & patience, offering
those painefull steps vnto his Eternal
Father in satisfaction of those which
thou

thou makest to offend him .

And gathering hence desires of
thankefullnesse vnto so good a Lord,
who hath walked such wayes for thy
saluation and remedy, beseech him
to giue thee grace to ordaine thyne
to his holy seruice, and to the per-
formance of his holy Law and Commandments.

The 4. Point.

TO consider in what manner thy
Sauiour was receaued, when he
arriued at Annas his Pallace and was
brought in before him, and before
the Scribes or Interpreters of the
Law: with what arrogancy they began to examine our Lord, causing
that diuine Maiesty to stand before
them as one that was esteemed guilty
and they in the meane tyme remayning sitting as Iudges: they in state,
and in their Doctorall robs, and the
Lord and Maister of the Wisedome
of heauen, manacled and bound before them, as if he had beene a theef
and malefactour.

Ponder how differently God
our Lord is now among the doctors

and Lawyers from that he was when being twelue yeares of age, he sate among them, hearing them and asking them : all being astonished vpon his wisedome and answers. Then he was seated in the midst of them, hearing and answearing, to the esteeme and admiration of all : but now he standeth, and if he make answere to the questiõs they aske him, he is scorned and mocked, being the Doctor of al Nations.

Gather hence a desire to humble thy selfe, and to beare patiently (in imitation of our Lord) when thou shalt be accounted by others as vnwise, and ignorant, & perswade thy selfe, that thou art so indeed, and be glad to imitate in something, and to be like thy Sauiour.

THE

THE XXXVIII. MEDITATION.

Of the blow giuen to our Sauiour vpon the face: and how he was sent bound vnto Caiphas.

THE I. POINT.

TO consider how that Lord (of whome it is sayd in S. Iohn: Neuer did there man speake so as this man) giuing now a mild and gentle answere to the high Priest, is stroken and buffited by a base fellow.

Ponder how the face of our Sauiour remayned sorely brused and disfigured with this cruell blow, & was exceeding red, partly with it, and partly through his natural bashfulnes & modesty hauing receaued so great an affront. And albeit the buffets, blowes, aud spurnes which were heaped vpon thy Lord by his enemies, when he was apprehended, were many, yet of none but only of this, mention is made in particuler in holy Scripture, because it was more re-

Q 4   proach-

368 A MANUALL of spirituall

proachfull & iniurious then the rest,
and because it was giuen in presence
of the high Priest, & of many nobles
and of the chiefe of the people.

Gather from hence compassion
& sorrow beholding that soueraigne
countenance of thy Redeemer so
buffeted and wounded : On whome
the Angells desire to looke. And be
ashamed to greeue and complaine,
not for that thou art buffeted (for
thou art not arriued so high as to in-
dure so much) but because others do
not honour and countenance thee,
when thou art in presence with them
desiring heerein to be better then thy
Lord God who was so much reuiled,
scoffed at, and despised for thy sake.

THE 2. POINT.

TO consider the great patience,
meeknes, cheerfulnes, and sere-
nity of mind which our Lord kept
in his most holy soule, receauing such
a wrong & neuer reuenging it, either
by word or deed.

Ponder that wheras Christ our
Lord could haue caused fire to come
from heauen, or the earth to haue o-
pened

pened and to swallow and consume
that wicked fellow, he did it not, but
in all patience shewed that he was
ready to turne the other cheek, if he
would haue stroken it.

Gather and take example heerby not to be angry or offended for
any thing whatsoeuer may be befall
thee, be it neuer so weighty, nor to
render euill for euill. Beseeching him
in this mystery to giue thee in all occasions which shalbe offered thee
that constancy of mind and meeknes
which he had and shewed heere, that
thou mayst be meeke and humble of
hart, as he was.

THE 3. POINT.

TO consider the mild answere
which Christ Iesus our Lord gaue
vnto him, who had thus abused, and
wronged him, to wit: If I haue spoken euill, giue testimony of euill, but
if well, why strikest thou me? and
accusest me of vndutifullnesse, seeing
thou art no iudge, but only a wit-
nesse?

Ponder that albeit this reason
was good and conuincing, yet it was
Q 5   not

not admitted, neither did it auayle
him, nor any reckoning was made of
it, but rather all that were present
were glad and reioyced that, that
blow on the cheeke was giuen him:
and none was found that would take
his part, and reprehend the audacity
of that bold and barbarous companion.

From hence thou mayst gather
conformity with the diuine Will
when thy answers and reasons shall
not be heard, nor admitted, nor account made of them, seeing no account was made of the aswere which
the Sonne of God gaue, whose nature
it is euen to speake that which is reason: and therfore he is now stroken
and abused, to satisfy for thy faults,
which thou hast done and dost dayly
commit in euill speaking. Beseech
our good Lord that he will giue thee
grace alwayes to speake well of him,
and to do honour vnto all.

THE 4. POINT.

TO consider that the hatred & rancour of Annas, as of all the rest of
that wicked counsel against our Redeemer,

deemer, was fo great, that blinded
with the fplendour of fuch patience
and meeknes, they determined to
fend the moft meek lambe faft boúd
vnto Caiphas the high Prieft, that
beholding him brought in that manner he might vnderftand that they
thought him guilty and worthy of
death.

Ponder how different thefe
bands and fetters were, wherewith
the cruell tormétors bound the Lord
of Angells, from thofe with which
he bound them, to wit, the bands of
charity, but his charity is fo great,
that he delighted to be tyed with
new fetters and cords, to loofe thee
and them from the grieuous finnes
which thou haft committed againft
his diuine Maiefty.

From whence thou mayft ga-
ther defires to fuffer and to beare the
like croffes if in publike or in priuate
thou be held guilty or fauly (for in
truth thou art no leffe) feeing thy
Lord though he be fo much worthy
to be glorifyed, is notwithftanding fo
defpiled and fcoffed at.

THE XXXIX. MEDITATION.

Of the denyall of S. Peter.

THE 1. POINT.

TO confider how Peter hauing fled the night of the Paſſion of our Sauiour with the reſt of the Diſciples, entring into himſelfe againe, & deſiring to know the euent of the buſineſſe, and the ſucceſſe of the impriſonment of his Maiſter, he folloved him. And by S. Iohn Euangeliſt his meanes (who was knowne in the houſe of the high Prieſt) he entred in, & being known by thoſe which were there, to be our Sauiours diſciple, he denyed him thrice, ſwearing and forſwearing that he knew him not.

Ponder how deeply this ſinne, and greiuous offence of his Diſciple did pierce the very ſoule of our Lord, that his deere and tenderly beloued Apoſtle, and ſo much honoured aboue the reſt with the primacy of the Church, ſhould be aſhamed
to

to be accounted his Disciple.

Gather hence confusion and shame for that thou hast often times denyed thy Sauiour, if not in words at least in deeds, being ashamed to keep his holy Commandements, or to performe some actions of vertue, as to confesse and communicate, or to suffer some iniury. Al which what els is it then to be ashamed to seeme the disciple of Christ, and to deny him: wherefore thou mayst iustly feare, least that sentence of our Sauiour, and punishment fall vpon thee, where he sayth: He that denieth me before men, the Sonne of man shal deny him before the Angels of God: or he that shallbe ashamed to seeme my disciple before men, the Sonne of the Virgin willbe ashamed to acknowledge him for his, before the holy Angels.

THE 2. POINT.

TO consider how dangerous a thing it is to continue in the occasion of sinne, and not to learne to bew are by the first fall: for the present occasion, and the presuming too much of him-
selfe

selfe and his owne vertue, and also
euill company were the causes of his
fall: Almighty God permitting that
a silly woman, Portresse in Pilates
house, should preuaile against him
who had the keyes of the house of
God: so doth he chastice pride and
presumption.

Ponder that he who was the
fundamentall stone of the Church,
and so much fauoured by our Lord,
he that confessed Iesus Christ for the
Sonne of the liuing God, he that of-
red himselfe to dye for him, rather then to be scandalized & to fly,
now findeth himselfe so weake and
fearfull, that being demanded by a
poore girle whether he be the disciple of Christ, is ashamed to cofesse it,
feareth and trembleth, & at last flatly
denyeth it, not once or twice, but
three times.

Gather out of this weaknes and
frailty of Peter how neer he is to a fal
who confideth much and presumeth
of himselfe. And seeing thou art not
a Rocke, but dust and ashes, and all
the gould and siluer of thy weake
vertue

vertue is founded vpon feet of clay,
and the least stone of contradiction is
sufficient to ouerthrow it, and bring
the whole tower to ground: therfore
boast nor bragge of any thing; for
thou hast not any stronger hold, nor
greater strength then with humble
acknowledgment of thyne owne nothing and weaknes wholy to rely on
the goodnes and mercy of our Lord.
Wherefore not to fall, it behooueth
thee to fly bad company, and al occasions of danger, arrogancy, pride
and presumption.

The 3. Point.

TO consider that as soone as S.
Peter had denyed his Maister,
Christ our Lord moued with compassion, and greeuing to see the Pastour of his flocke, and that sheep
which was head of all the rest, now
fallen into so great calamity and misery, looking on him, reclaimed and
conuerted him.

Ponder the infinite mercy and
charity of Christ our Lord, who albeit he be enuironed with his enemies, and loaden with afflictions,

is

is mindfull of his disciple, and insteed of chastising him, hath pitty on him, & turning his eyes of mercy towards him, illuminateth his blindnes with heauenly light, that he may know & see his errours: for the eyes of God haue this property, that they open, and awake the drowsy, and reuiue the dead.

Gather hence affections of loue towards this our Lord, because when thou gost about to offend him, he inuenteth means and findeth out wayes to pardon thee, he hath compassion on thee, he beholdeth thee with the eyes of his mercy, he toucheth thy hart, and all to the end that thou mightest know, feele & lament thy sinnes and offences.

THE 4. POITN:

TO consider, how our Lord inlightning & penetrating the wounded soule of Peter with that his silent and louing looke, that remembring himselfe and being sory for his sinne he might bitterly bewayle the same, he presently returned to himselfe and wept bitterly, and for more effectual

redresse of his offence, he departed
the house and Pallace of the high
Priest, where he had found so bad
intertainement, and shut himselfe vp
into one of those caues; which were
towards the fountaine of Siloe, and
lamented his sin with deep sorrow, &
said: O trecherous old age, ò yeares
ill spent, ò life naughtily imployed,
ô blasphemous tongue, ô wretched
sinner, coward, lyer, what hast thou
done? Oughtst thou so to haue denyed thy Maister, hauing receiued so
many fauours and benefits of him?

Ponder how Peter because he
had denyed his Maister thrice in one
night, wept and repented himselfe of
his sinne all his life tyme, and did very sharp and rigorous pennance, albeit he knew that God had already
pardoned him.

From hence thou mayst gather
desires to do the like for thy sinnes,
seeing that not one night alone, but
all thy life tyme, and not thrice, but
innumerable times, thou hast denyed
and abandoned thy God. Wherfore
it behooueth thee, if thou desire to
haue

haue pardon , very seriously to bewayle and hartily to repent for thy
sinnes, and do pennance for them.

THE XL. MEDITATION.

VVhat happened vnto our Saviour in
Caiphas his house, and of the things
he suffered that night.

THE I. POINT.

TO consider the answere which
our Lord gaue vnto the demaund of Caiphas the high
Priest : I adiure thee by the liuing
God , that thou tell vs if thou be
Christ the Sonne of God. And our
Lord although he knew right well
the great iniuryes , reproaches, and
torments, which his confession would
cost him, yea death it selfe, he plainely answered and told the truth , and
savd what was befitting his person.
The high Priest blinded with splendour of so great light, and being in
passion iudged that he had blasphemed , and so he and all the rest of his
counsell condemned our Lord to
death

death. And hauing no respect to the
innocency of his life, nor to their
owne state and quality intreated him
most vildly.

Ponder the meeknes wherwith
our Lord suffered these affronts and
iniuryes and heard that vninst sentence: He is guilty of death. O how
that immaculate lambe, hearing this
sentence would offer himselfe willin-
ly to death, to giue life vnto them,
who gaue sentence against him, and
condemned him to death.

Gather hence desires alwayes to
say of our Sauiour the contrary to
that which these his enemies pronounced of him, to wit, such innocency, such a Lord, such a benefactor,
such a Sauiour and Maister deserueth
life: Such a God and Redeemer is
most worthy to liue, and all those
which condemne him or offend him,
or accurse him are worthy of euerlasting death.

THE 2. POINT.

TO consider that it being now late
and tyme for the high Priest and
his fellowers to rest, they deliuered
VP

vp our Lord to the fouldiers to watch him, & they to keep themfelues from fleeping, did deride, fcoffe, & mocke at our Lord, and couering his eyes with a fhameful ragge, fmote his diuine face, faying vnto him : Prophefy vnto vs, o Chrift, who is he that ftroke thee ?

Heere thou mayft ponder Chrift our Lord full of payne and affliction, reiected, defpifed and contemned of all, great and little: neither was it the leaft caufe of griefe to haue his diuine eyes couered, that his enemies might the more freely ftrike him on the face, perfwading themfelues that fo he could not fee them : for it is the property of great finners to defire not to be feene, that they may finne more freely and without reftraint. But he faw them notwithftanding with the eyes of his foule, and of his God-head, becaufe he was God : whofe eyes, fayth the Wifeman, behold in euery place the good and the euill, whicheuery one continually doth.

Hence thou mayft gather, that
when

when thou sinnest, forgetting that
God doth see thee, thou art as it were
hoodwincked and deceauest thy self,
couering thyne owne eyes with this
false and blacke veile: for Gods eyes
are most cleare and open vpon thee,
beholding thy thoughts, words and
deeds. Wherfore from this day forward be affraid to offend our Lord,
carrying euer in thy memory this
admirable saying: Behold, God beholdeth thee.

The 3. Point.

TO consider how that after this
iniury those cruel fellows deuoyd
of all humanity, did vnto our Sauiour
another no lesse affront, spitting in
his face, and couering it with their
loathsome and stinking spittle: for
all of them (and they were many)
striuing who shold do worst, did cast
their spittle vpon him, wonderfully
defiling and obscuring that beauty,
which reioyceth the heauenly court
and company.

Ponder whose face it is that is
thus defiled & spit vpon, as if it were
the most vile & contemptible corner

of

of the world; and thou shalt find that
it is the face of the God of Maiesty, of
whome the Prophet sayd : Shew thy
face and we shallbe saued . It is the
face before whom the Seraphims out
of due respect & reuerence do couer
theirs . It is his face wherewith his
diuine spitle gaue sight to the blind,
hearing to the deafe , and speach to
the dumbe. It is his face , whom the
Angells of heauen continually beholding and adoring are neuer satiated.

From hence thou mayst gather
abundant motiues and affections of
compassion and sorrow , grieuing
to behold the face of such a Lord,
defaced and spit vpon by such and so
base miscreants , to see the Creatour
so abused by so vile creatures, his
diuine maiesty permitting himselfe
to be obscured and defiled, that thou
mightst become pure and cleane .

THE 4. POINT.

TO consider , the iniurious & dis-
graceful words, that euen the very
Kitchen scullians of that pallace ,
gaue vnto Christ our Lord , and also
how they layd lead vpon him with
blows,

blowes, buffets, and spurnes, and
asked him: Ghesse who stroke thee?
seeing thou sayest that thou art chist
and a Prophet, who gaue thee this
blow on the eare? who this spurne
with his foot? who this kicke, & who
this cuffe in the necke? And laughing
aloud, and iesting at him they mani-
festly declared that they held him for
a fayne Christ and a false Prophet.

Ponder the inuincible patience,
the inestimable meeknes, & the most
louing hart, wherwith God our Lord
suffered all this, as also that patience
with which he supporteth thee, seeing that as much as lyeth in thee thou
hast far oftener scoffed at thy Redeemer, offending him with thy manifold sinnes, and yet his mercy is so
great that he greeueth more at thy
offences, and at the harme which
commeth to them that torment him,
then at the paines which he himselfe
sustayneth.

Gather hence affections and desires to suffer something for this thy
Lord, who endureth so much for
thee, louing him with all thy hart,

with

who gaue thee such & so many signes of loue, ioyning with côtinual thanks giuing, continuall seruices for them.

THE XLI. MEDITATION,

Of the presentation of our Lord before Pilate, and what questions he asketh him.

THE I. POINT.

TO consider how much Christ Iesus our Lord, and also his enemies desired the comming of the morning, but for very different ends : Our Lord to suffer and dye, and they to put in execution their damnable intent, which was to murther him : and forthwith in the morning the high Priest Caiphas and the whole counsell assembled togeather, & calling our Lord Iesus the second tyme, he asked him : Art thou Christ the Son of the blessed God? but our Lord answered him not to his demand.

Ponder how much it importeth thee, to aske our Lord this question, but with a different meaning and desire

fire from that which his enemies had,
saying: O my Lord, if thou art Chrift,
if thou art the promifed Meſſias, if
thou art the Sonne of the liuing God,
and the fplendour of the glory of
the Eternall Father, as it is moft true
that thou art, how commeth it to
paſſe that thy diuine face is fo disfigured? how is it defiled with fpitle?
how is it bruifed with buffets? And
framing hence affections of tender
loue and compaſſion, acknowledge
that thy finnes haue beene the caufe,
why thy Sauiour Chrift and Lord is
in that plight, in which thou feeft
him, and his vnfpeakable charity giueth teftimony of him that he is the
Son of the liuing God: for no other
then he could haue vndergone fo
many torments for the finnes which
he neuer committed. And adoring
him with all thy hart, thou ſhalt fay:
Thou ô Lord art my Chrift, and my
God, my Sauiour, and my Redeemer
and he, who thirty and three yeares
hadſt fo great and earneft defire and
longing to fee this day of paine and
affliction once come, to deliuer me

R   from

from the eternall affliction , and
payne.

THE 2. POINT.

TO confider how the high Prieft
bearing the anfweare which our
Lord gaue afterward to hisdemaund,
he and all the reft that were prefent
being vnworthy to heare that which
they deferued not to vnderftand,
they treated him as a flaue . And
thinking any punifhment that they
could inflict vpon him by their law,
too little, they yeilded him vp to the
fecular power of the prefident Pilate,
that he might fentence and torment
him more cruelly .

Ponder the prouidence and
wifedome of our Lord God , who
would that the Iewes , and Gentils
fhould concurre to the death of him
who dyed for the faluation of all : for
his death is our life, and his condem-
nation is our faluation .

Gather hence compaffion and
greefe to behold thy Lord, and thy
God hated of all , as well of thofe of
his owne nation as of ftrangers. And
lament ,for that many Chriftians do
the

the like through their sinnes: and if
those who haue obligation to serue
and honour him do this, what wonder is it if the Turkes and Gentiles,
who know him not, do offend him.

THE 3. POINT.

TO consider, the presentation and
accusation of Christ before Pilate,
as if he had beene a malefactour and
a seditious person, being accused as
one who prohibited Tribute to be giuen to Cæsar, making himselfe the
Messias promised of God.

Ponder how Christ our Lord in
all these accusations and calumnia-
tions answered not a word in his
owne defence, shewing heerein his
great meeknes and patience, and declaring in fact how earnest a desire he
had to dy for our saluation, seeing he
would not by speaking for himselfe,
cause his death to be one iote delayed.

From hence thou mayst gather
that the strongest armour to resist
thy enemies, in the midst of the tempests of aduersity and persecutions,
is confidence in God, such as our

Lord had, whose name is Admirable:
for he is not only admirable in perfections and miracles but also in humiliations and afflictions. Admirable in
meeknes, admirable in patience, and
in suffering, admirable in silence, giuing thee example how thou oughtst
to keep silence, and not excuse thy
selfe when thou art reprehended for
thy misdeeds & sins, albeit thou find
not thy selfe in conscience guilty of
any thing.

THE 4. POINT.

TO consider how Pilate hauing
heard all these accusations, entred
with Christ our Lord into the Pallace to examine and enquire of him
concerning all that which was layd
to his charge, and hauing heard al his
diuine answeres from the mouth of
God, in whome neuer was found de-
ceit, perceiuing his vprightnes & integrity, iudged him to be an innocent
man.

Ponder the desire our Lord
had, that, that miserable iudge would
open the eyes of his soule, to receaue
the beame of his diuine light. But the
vnhappy

vnhappy wretch, although he began to haue a defire to know the truth, yet he did not expect an anfwere, becaufe he deferued not to heare it from the mouth of the true God.

Gather from hence defires to know the truth, and that God, as the Father and author therof, will teach it thee, beleeuing that his life is truth, his miracls truth, his Sacramēts truth, truth all that he taught & preached. Wherfore feeing this is the moft certaine truth, althou h the defence thereof coft thee thy life, as it coft thy God his life, be glad to loofe it for him : neither loofing it fhalt thou loofe it, but gayne it euerlaftingly.

THE XLII. MEDITATION.

Of the prefentation of Chrift our Lord before Herod.

THE 1. POINT.

TO confider how Pilate vnderftanding that our Sauiour was borne in Galilee, and vnder Herods iurifdiction (who was come to
R 3   Hierufalem

Hierusalem in those days to celebrate the feast of the Paschall lambe) sent him vnto him, that he might iudge & discusse the processe of that prisoner, whome he held as his subiect .

Ponder the paynes and ignominy our God endured betweene Pilats house and King Herods pallace, those his cruell enemies carrying him with great violence, tumult and noise, through the midst of the market place and streets of Hierusalem, that he might be seene and noted of all, and esteemed guilty .

Haue compassion to see the Son of God haled to so many Tribunals and Iudges , euery one worse then the other , his diuine maiesty ordayning it so , that he might haue abundant matter wherein to shew his inuincible patience , humility and longanimity , giuing thee an example , that thou mayst know wherein to imitate him , and follow this vertues.

THE 2. POINT.

TO consider how glad King Herod was when he saw our Sauiour, because

cause he had heard many thinges of
him, the wonders he wrought, and
the miracles he did: and so desired that he would do some before
him.

Ponder how Christ our Lord to
eschew death or any other torment,
would not do any miracle before
Herod, and also because he knew that
he was moued to desire it through
pride and vaine curiosity, and not of
a desire of his owne spirituall benfit,
neither would our Lord speake one
word in defence of himselfe, or to
that he asked him: all which redoun-
ded to his greater reproach.

Gather from hence a desire that
God would vouchsafe to graunt thee
the vertue of silence, and make answere for thee in all thy doubts and
difficultyes, for the benefit of thy
soule, thou being full of darknes &
ignorance, and of thy selfe art not
able to giue any answere to the purpose, nor to rid thy selfe of the questions and impugnations of others.

R 4　　　　The

THE 3. POINT.

TO consider how that Herod, seeing our Lord not to yield to his desire, nor to satisfy his curious leuity did contemne him, and with all thoie of his court held him for a simple and foolish fellow, and therefore not so much worthy of death as to be mocked and scorned at, and so in derision and mockage put on him a white & homely garment.

Ponder how Christ our Lord is heere mocked and disgraced by the King and all his courtiers, who made a foole of him, & stood plucking him and pinching him, and iesting at him in most rude & vnciuill manner. And when they had done, the King sent him backe to the President Pilate, as if he should haue sayd vnto him: Loe I send you backe this foole and idiot.

From whence thou mayst gather desirs to accompany in spirit thy true King and Lord, who suffered al these opprobrious dealings with adm rable patience, teaching thee to make smal reckoning of the iudgements and o-
pinions

pinions of this world which are meer
folly, and what people fay or do : defire to fuffer for iuftice and piety that
thou mayft be affured of the kingdome of heauen : for there is no greater wifedome then to reioyce in contempt for the loue of God, nor greater
folly, then to feeke to be honoured
without him.

THE 4. POITN.

TO confider how that amongft fo
many garments which our Lord
changed that night of his paffion, his
Eternall Father neuer permitted his
enemies to inueft him with a blacke
one (it being the vfe and cuftome a-
mong the Iewes, that he who went to
the tribunal to be arraygned, fhould
be clad in blacke, which was a figne
of a condemned perfon) but would
that it fhould be white in token of
innocency, or ruddy in token of
loue.

Ponder how that garment which
was giuen vnto Chrift our Lord in
derifion, was a figure of the witneffe
and purity of his moft bleffed foule,
and of the innocency of his life, as

R. 5   his

his enemies themselues were faine to
confesse, saying : I haue found no
cause in this man of those thinges,
wherein you accuse him .

Gather hence desires, that our
Lord inuest and adorne thy soule
with the white garment of innocency
& thy body with his reproachs, that
in all thou mayst imitate him, and so
thou shalt become more white and
purer then the snow.

THE XLIII. MEDITATION.

How *Barabbas was compared, and preferred before Christ.*

THE I. POINT.

TO consider that Pilate desirous
to deliuer Christ from death
and being to release some one
condemned person in honcur of the
Pasch, sayd vnto the Iewes : Whom
will you that I release, Barabbas or
Iesus that is called Christ? for (Barabas being so seditious & wicked a
fellow) he made no doubt, but that
rather then he should go vnpuni-
                                        shed,

shed, they would releafe our Sauiour
Iefus Chrift.

Ponder the wonderfull hu-
miliation of Chrift our Lord, who
being fo great, fo wife, fo holy, and
fo great a benefactour of all, is now
ballanced and compared with Barabbas an infamous companion, a thief,
a murderer, a feditions and publike
malefactour.

Gather hence defires not to
difdaine, grudge or repine when an
inferiour and worfe then thy felfe, is
preferred before thee, and more honoured and refpected, if account be
made of him, and not of thee, if a-
other be imployed in offices and bufines, & of thee no mention be made,
nor thou regarded, feeing thy Lord
and thy God endured all this and
much more.

The 2. Point.

TO confider, how the vngratefull
people and thofe blind and paffio-
nate Scribs & Pharifies, out of malice
brake into open iniuftice, and how
in their fight, Barabbas his life, notwithftanding al his murders, robbe-

R 6   ries,

ries, and abhominations weighed
more, and was thought more profitable, then the innocency of Chrisi our
Redeemer for all his vertues and miracles. Wherefore they besought the
iudge to release the man-ki'ler, the
wicked villaine, and to murder and
crucify the author of life.

Ponder how mutable men are,
& easy to be deceaued: for they who
'a few dayes before with common
consent and festiual acclamation, called Chrisi their King, now with a different note & tumultuous clamour,
say: Make Iesus away, and release vs
Barabbas.

Gather hence confusion for thy
pride, and endeauour from this day
forward to humble and submit thy
selfe, seeing that our Lord is held for
lesse then the lewdeit fellow in the
world. And heere thou mayst see lit-
terally fulsilled that which our Lord
sayd by his Prophet: I am a worme
and no man, a reproach of men, and
outcast of the people. And for such
he is now reputed of those who
ought to honour and respect him a-
boue

boue all men and Angells.

The 3. Point.

TO consider that the more the President Pilate desired to deliuer Christ our Lord, the more the Iewes were earnest to haue Barabbas released.

Ponder how often the like iudgement, strife and controuersy passeth betweene thy flesh & thy spirit, the one making choice of Christ, & the other of Barabbas, the one of God the other of a creature, the one seeketh after the vaine perishing glory of men, the other seeketh the glory of God, which is perpetuall and euerlasting. Finally the one enquireth after corruptible and transitory thinges, the other after things permanent and which endure for euer.

Whence thou mayst gather great sorrow for hauing left Christ thy only and chiefest good, for so vile and contemptible a thing as Barabbas: I meane, for hauing so often chosen & regarded more a creature, a little sensible delight and vaine honour, then Christ Iesus our Lord: In
whome

whome be all the goods and treasures
of the wisedome and infinite knowledge of God hidden. Be confounded in consideration of this thou miserable wretch, as thou art.

The 4. Point.

TO consider how Pilate did testify
vnto the people the innocency of
Christ saying: I find no cause in him,
why he should deserue death, but the
outragious people raising their voices
cryed aloud, saying: Crucify him,
crucify him.

Ponder how much those redou-
bled and often repeated clamours
grieued our Lord, seeing that they
did not only seeke his death, but that
he should dye so cruell a death, as
the death of the Crosse.

Gather hence sorrow for that
thy sinnes haue put our Lord to so
great straites: for they alone were
those that importuned and cryed
out that he should be crucifyed.
Wherefore it behooueth thee to abhorre them, and detest so cruell and
bloudy beasts, which with so great
cruelty murdered thy Sauiour.

                              THE

THE XLIIII. MEDITATION.
Of the stripes which our Lord receaued at the Pillar.

THE 1. POINT.

TO confider, how the Prefident Pilate feeing that his former proiect and deuife did not fucceed, and that all the people began to be in an vproare, he tooke another meanes and counfell to appeafe the fury of thofe cruell enemies, which was to giue fentence againft the Lord of Angells, that he fhould be whipped.

Ponder how vniuft, cruell, & reproachfull this fentence was which the Prefident gaue againft our Lord, notwithftanding he knew very well and was fure of his innocency. But our Lord Iefus lifting vp his eyes to his Eternall Father, fayd thofe words of the Prophet: I am ready o my Lord for fcourges, & defirous to pay the thinges that I tooke not. And without appellation or making any
other

other meanes to quit himselfe, he accepted that bloudy sentence, offering most willingly his sacred body to be scourged in satisfaction of our sinnes.

Gather hence desires not to complaine when by thy Superiours, equalls, or inferiours thou shalt be reprehended and chastised, although thou be without fault, seeing God most free from all fault, is not only reprehended, but also cruelly whipped, and handled like a theefe with so horrible a punishment, and yet not complayning, but as if he were dumme, not once opening his mouth.

The 2. Point.

TO consider, how the sentence of his whipping being pronounced, those cruell butchers layd hands on the Lord of heauen, the creatour of the world, and glory of Angels, and led him into the court to the place of punishment, where with barbarous inhumanity and fury they stripped him naked, and couered him with stripes from top to toe, as if he had beene a slaue.

Ponder how much our Lord, who

who inuesteth the heauens with
cloudes, beautifyeth the fields with
flowers, couereth the trees with leaus
the birdes with feathers, the beasts
with woll and haire, would be abashed, beholding himselfe so naked &
poore without any thing to couer
himselfe withall, and that before
such a multitude of people that were
there present, hauing none to take
compassion on him, nor so much as
to cast a cloake ouer him to couer his
nakednesse.

Gather hence affection of pitty
and compassion, seeing thy God and
Lord in such extreme need, abandoned, naked, and exposed to all ignominy, and shame, and compassed a-
bout with his enemies, who desired
to drinke his bloud.

THE 3. POINT.

TO consider how those cruell and
barbarous tormentors hauing that
chast and most delicate body now
naked amongst them, bound him
hand and foot fast to a pillar, that
that they might beate him more freely at their pleasure.

Ponder

Ponder the great barbarousnes, and cruelty wherwith they began to lay on load with thonges and rods, on that most tender backe of thy Sauiour, heaping stripes vpon stripes, and wounds vpon wouudes, vntill that most sacred body, al bruized, torne and flayed, the bloud bursting out and trickling downe drop after drop on euery side, became so disfigured and imbrued with bloud that his owne mother could hardly haue knowne him.

From hence thou mayst gather a great detestation of thy sinnes, for they were the cause of so outragious a punishment, and a great desire to chastise them with rigorouspennance and discipline.

The 4. Point.

TO consider how the torturers being weary of scourging that innocent body of Christ our Lord, already spent with stripes, which mounted (as some Saints affirme) to aboue fiue thousand, they vnloosed him, but he not being able to stand on his feet, fell downe vpon the cake of his

owne

owne bloud that lay at the foot of the
pillar.

Ponder the folicitude and defo-
lation of Chrift our only good, who
had not there any friend or acquaintance to help him vp, but his only e-
nemies who did tread, kick & fpurne
him, that gathering forces out of fee-
blenes he might get vp againe. Neither was there any who would go &
aduertife the moft Bleffed Virgin of
the extreme need and nakednes of
her beloued Sonne, that fhe might
with fpeed come to couer him with
her veile, who fo often had wrapped
him in cloths when he was a child.

Gather hence a great confidence
of the remiffion of thy finnes, feeing
this Lord endureth fo much to deliuer thee from them, and an earneft
defire to reft & cleaue faft to the feet
of Chrift, kifi.ng fometymes in fpirit
and deuotion the ground embrued
with his moft facred bloud: other
tymes that holy pillar bathed and e-
nameled with the precious bloud of
this holy lambe, which was fhed to
make thee ftrong as a piller, in the
Church

Church of God, that is, to make thee
haue a couragious & inuincible hart
to withstand thyne enemies, thy paf-
sions and temptations.

THE XLV. MEDITATION.

Of the purple Garment, and Crowne
of Thornes.

THE I. POINT.

TO consider how those cruell
soldiers hauing made an end of
whipping him, they inuented
another punishment to afflict him
withall: wherfore approaching vnto
our Lord Christ, they cloathed him
with an old scarlet cloake which was
a wearing for Kings, but they put it
on him in derision and scorne, to giue
the people to vnderstand that being a
vile and base fellow, he would haue
made himselfe a King.

Ponder how Christ our Lord
would be thus made a King in mockery, to declare vnto the world that
all the honours & kingdomes of this
life are but mockeries, and that therfore

fore little reckoning is to be made of
them, as our Lord himselfe did so
little esteem them : and so that which
the world accounteth an honour in
others, he would vndergo, therby to
be disgraced and abased by the same
world which scoffed and mocked at
him.

Gather hence great compassion
at the extreme dishonour which thy
Lord God suffered, and for this his
humiliation, being made the scorne
and mocking stocke of the people.
And humbly beseech him that thou
mayst not make so light of him as to
contemne him through thy sinnes, as
those souldiers did, but rather serue
and loue him, desiring that he would
vouchsafe to inuest and honour thee
with this his precious and costly liuery, that following him (albeit the
world despise thee therefore) thou
mayst deserue to see and enioy him
clad with the rich and precious robes
of grace and glory.

THE

THE 2. POINT.

TO confider how thofe cruell enemies forthwith brought a cruell
crowne of fea rufhes (which were certaine fharp and long thornes) and fa-
ftened it on his facred & tender head
by which on the one fide he fuftained
intollerable paine, and on the other
extreme difgrace.

Ponder how that this crowne
was not of gold nor filuer, not of
pearles nor precious ftones, of rofes
nor odoriferous flowers, albeit this
Lord right well deferued it, being
the true King of heauen and earth,
but that which inftead of thefe they
gaue him, was of ftrong & boifterous
brambles and thornes which pierced
his delicate head: our Lord permitting this becaufe thou haft often
bound and crowned thy head with
rofes and flowres of pleafure & delights.

Gather hence how great the
bounty & charity of God is towards
men, feeing that when they are bufy-
ed in preparing for him fo cruell and
terrible a crowne therwith to afflict
and

and torment him, he prepareth for
them a crowne of glory in heauen to
reward them. And seeing God teacheth thee by his exáple, that by the
crowne of thornes, the crowne of
glory in heauen is gayned: and that
the crowne of affliction which pric-
keth in this world, is better then that
of pleasures and delights which torment in the life to come. Procure to
crowne thy selfe, and make choice of
the first (as S. Catherine of Siena
did) to auoyd the second.

THE 3. POINT.

TO consider how that to increase
his confusion and reproach, they
after this put into the right hand of
thy soueraigne King & Lord a reed,
insteed of a Kingly scepter, & smoat
his head therewith, al to the end that
the world might know that his kingdome was hollow, vaine, and without substance, and he voyd of iudgement and wit, making himselfe a
King.

Ponder how our Lord Iesus
did not refuse to take the reed into
his hand, but rather willingly accepted

ted it and held it fast as an instrument
of his contempt.

From hence thou mayst gather
how much it importeth thee to resist
and reiect honour & selfe estimation
and to imbrace humility and submission of mind, in regard that by this
way and meanes our soueraigne King
entred into his kingdome: & by the
same, and no other, thou must enter
into the kingdome of heauen, which
is not thyn but anothers to giue thee,
if thou desirest it.

The 4. Point

TO consider how those fierce people
more cruel then Tygers, not contenting themselues with the former
iniuries, which they had done to that
meeke lambe, they add yet another
iniury: for bowing their knees before
him in mockery & scorne, they sayd
vnto him: Haile King of the Iewes,
and presently they stroke his diuine
face with a reed, deriding and making faces at him.

Ponder in how different a manner the celestiall spirits adore this
great King and Lord, from that men
adore

adore him on earth. The Angels reuerence him as God and King of all thinges, and men adore him as a false God and counterfaite king: they call him holy, holy, and men, wicked, sinner, possessed with a Diuell.

Gather hence desires throughly to feele and lament thy sinnes, and that which thy Lord and God suffereth: and as his louing child & true friend prostrating thy selfe on the ground, adore him as thy King and Lord after another māner then these do, and say from the bottome of thy hart: Hayle King of heauen & earth, King of Angells and men, saue me o Lord, and admit me into thy heauenly kingdome, when I shall depart this miserable life.

THE XLVI. MEDITATION.

Of the words, ECCE HOMO.

THE I. POINT.

TO consider how these cruell souldiers led thy Sauiour in this so lamentable a plight vnto the
S   President

Prefident Pilate, who wondering to
fee him fo ill handled, carryed him
vp to an eminent place, whence he
might be feene of all, to the end that
moued with compaffion they might
ceafe to feeke his death.

Ponder firft how much our
Lord was afhamed at this appearing
in fo reproachfull an habit, with the
crowne of thornes vpon his head, a
reed in his hand, a rope about his
necke, his body al bruized, rent, wearied & exhauft with fo many ftripes,
all goare bloud through the multitude of thofe blowes: and with the
drops of bloud which trickled down
his venerable face, thofe lights of
heauen were eclipfed and almoft
blinded.

Ponder fecondly the difference
betweene the figure wherein our Sauiour appeareth now, and that which
he fhewed in the glory of the mount
Thabor: that which was fo glorious
and pleafant, he difcouered only to
three of his difciples, this fo painefull
and ignominious he fheweth to all
the people of Hierufalem: that in a
                              mo untaine

mountaine all alone and retyred, this in the middest of a great & populous City.

Be confounded at thy pride seeing thy Lord so much humbled and despised for thy sake, and thou endeauourest not to be so handled of men, but rather with all honour and esteeme, & desirest that they should know the good which is in thee, that they may prayse thee.

THE 2. POINT.

TO consider how Pilate shewing Christ our Lord in presence of all the people, sayd aloud : Behold the Man.

Ponder these words in the sense and meaning with which Pilate did pronounce them, and thou shalt find that, moued with pitty to behold so wofull a spectacle, he desired to deliuer Christ our Lord, and therefore he sayd : Ecce Homo, Behold this man, and you shall perceaue him to be so punished that he hardly retayneth the shape of man, being so disfigured & misused: wherfore in regard that he his a man as you are, and no

beast,

beaſt, haue compaſſion of him . But
they would not affoard him a good
looke , nor haue any pitty on him .

Hence thou mayſt gather de-
ſirs that God would graunt thee eyes
of compaſſion , and a hart of fleſh,
that beholding him thou mayſt be
moued to compaſſion, ſeeing he ſuffered ſo much for thy ſake, and giue
thee grace to loue thē that hate thee ,
ſeeing that in this kind our ſoueraign
Lord, God and man hath giuen thee
ſo rare an example .

The 3. Point.

TO conſider vpon the ſayd words
of Ecce Homo , how much it behooueth thee to ſtir vp thy ſelfe, and
to behold with the eyes of liuely
fayth this our Lord, & ſay vnto thy
ſoule: Ecce homo, behold o my ſoule
this man : for albeit he is ſo wounded
with ſtripes, ſo defiled with ſpittle, ſo
bruized with buffets, crowned with
thornes, had a reed inſteed of a ſcep-
ter in his hand , and is clad with an
ignominious garment, yet he is more
then a man, he is alſo God .

Ponder the great deſire which
the

the Eternall Father hath that thou
wouldst behold this soueraigne Lord
God and man, with meeke & com-
passionate eyes, and make benefit of
the tyme he allotteth thee to do it,
and not mispend so great a iewell,
nor omit to reap profit by beholding
this man : for if thou marke it well,
thou shalt find that this is the man,
which that sicke man that lay at the
Pond stood in need of, and required
his help that he might rise and go into
the pond, and be cured of his diseases
& infirmities. This is the man who
is the head of Angels and men, and is
so much disgraced to honour them,
so defiled to beautify them, condemned to death to exempt men from a
greater death, and to saue them finally he is the man who is made the
outcast of men to make them the children of God.

Gather from hence how abominable a thing sinne is in the sight of
God, seeing it brought his only Son
to such a passe, and in what case thy
sinnes may haue left thy soule, when
the sinnes of others haue wrought so

S 3   strang

strang an effect in the fountaine of all beauty it selfe: and what confusion & shame will a sinner sustaine for his owne, seeing the Sonne of God hath sustained so much for the sinnes of other men.

THE 4. POITN.

TO consider the hatred and rancour of those cruell enemies against Christ our Lord, seeing that so lamentable and pittifull a spectacle was not able to mollify their harts, but rather railing their voices, they began to cry aloud : Away, away with him out of our sight, as who would say : seeing thou hast made so good a beginning, commanding him to be whipped, make an end of that which thou hast begun, and crucify him.

Ponder, that although such & so woful a spectacle could not asswage & pacify those raging minds, yet was it doubtles of force to appeale the wrath of the Eternall Father who had beene moued to iust indignation : for beholding his most Blessed Sonne so ill handled for to obey him, and for

our

our loue, he gracioufly pardoned all
thofe finners, who with forrow for
their finres, and with deuotion and
confidence beholding this figure of
their Sauiour, fhould reprefent it vnto him, faying: Ecce Homo: Thou
feeft, o Lord, the man which thou
haft giuen vs, the worke of thy right
hand, the man that is fo humble, fo
obedient, fo meeke, and fo louing.

From hence thou mayft gather
harty forrow and compaffion to fee
him fo much abhorred by his owne
people, who deferued to be loued
moft of all. Endeauour from this day
forward to be fo much the more feruent in the feruice of this Lord, by
how much his enemies did the deeper abhorre him: fo doing he wil giue
thee grace with pure and cleare eyes
to behold and imitate him.

S 4   THE

THE XLVII. MEDITATION.
How our Blessed Sauiour carryed his Crosse.

THE I. POINT.

TO consider how the President, seated in his tribunall seat, gaue finall sentence in his cause, and our Lord Iesus being condemned to the death of the Crosse, the soldiers forthwith pulled off the purple garment which they had put on him in scorne, & stripping him naked, they put him to that sham againe the secōd tyme, not only before the officers, but in presence of all the people also, and gaue him backe his owne garments embrued in bloud to put on.

Ponder how Christ our Lord, to carry his Crosse, layd aside the garments which others had put on him in Herods, and Pilats house, & cloathed himselfe with his owne, not without extreme great payne, for they cleaued fast to his sacred woūds & were dryed into them, they being

no w

now cold.

Gather hence defires to put off all
affections vnworthy the child of God
that is, all vicious cuftomes of the
world, and of the flefh, wherewith
thou haft gone clad, and affume thofe
which are befeeming and proper to
Chrift, to wit, humility, charity and
the like, by which thou muft be
knowne and held for his difciple for
this was euer more the liuery of the
Sonne of God.

THE 2. POINT.

TO confider how our Lord taking
the Croffe vpon his tender and
wearied fhoulders, becaufe there was
not any one found among fo many,
who would carry it for him to the
place of punifhment (for the Iewes
held it an accurfed thing, and the
Gentills efteemed it reproachfull) he
was forced himfelfe to go with it on
his backe towards mount Caluary.

Ponder how this meeke lambe
full willingly fpread forth his armes
to imbrace the Croffe, and notwithftanding it was fo heauy a burden, &
to his fo great difhonour and fhame-

full

full death, he carryed it with more loue then he did euer before any other crosse, because the vtility & fruit, the honour & glory, which through the weight of this Crosse was to be gathered, was thyne, & it is credible that he did wellcome it with kisses of peace, interiourly saluting it with a thousand sweet and louing acts, far better then S. Andrew did the crosse of his Martyrdome.

Hence thou mayst gather confusion and shame to be an enemy of the Crosse of Christ, flying so much taking of paines, and procuring to cast thy burden vpon another mens shoulders, imitating in this rather these wicked people: for if thou wert the seruant of Christ, thou wouldest be glad & reioyce to follow him with thy crosse, although it should cost thee thy life, and thou shoulast dye in the fact.

The 3. Point.

TO consider, how the obedient Isaac commeth cut of Pilate house with the burden of the wood of the Crosse vpon his backe. The trumpet

soundeth

foundeth, the common Cryer cryeth
aloud, clamour & outcryes are heard
on euery fide, an infinite multitude
of people approach, they behold cōming out of the pallace gate a lamentable, and such as was neuer seen before, a most afflicted creature, dou-
bled & ouercharged with the weight
of a Crosse of fifteen foot long, crowned with a crowne of thornes, scarce
able to stand on his feet, nor to sustaine the weight of the Crosse without crouching and falling vnder it.

Ponder the barbarousnes of
those mercilesse harts against our Sauiour, for insteed of helping him vp
to rise againe, and taking compassion
on him, as to make him go on that
bitter and paynefull iourney, they
gaue him a thousand blowes, kickes
and spurnes, saying vnto him: Arise
traitour, sorcerer, didst not thou say
that thou wert the Sonne of God, and
he who in three dayes couldst build
vp his holy Temple, why dost not
thou raise now thy selfe?

Gather hence comfort in thy
afflictions carrying with patience &
loue

loue in imitation of our Lord Iesus,
the crosse which shall fall to thy lot,
though it be very heauy and should
make thee stoop: for it is impossible
in this life to want crosses and afflictions. Trust in God and in his diuine mercy, who will prouide one to
assist thee to carry it, that thou mayst
not be ouerloaden and fall vnder
it.

THE 4. POINT

TO consider that the Blessed Virgin vnderstanding how they carryed her most holy Sonne to crucify
him, accompanied him in this last
iourney, and making hast, & finding
meanes to passe through the throng
of the people (according as some deuout contemplatiue persons obserue)
she came and met her deerest Sonne.

Ponder what may haue passed
betweene these two diuine harts,
where that Sunne and Moone so
sad & eclipsed behold one the other:
this was no doubt one of the greatest
sorrowes which Christ our Lord endured, to see that meeke Doue his
mother come out of the arke of her
retirement,

retirement, so much greeued & afflicted at the fight of him so disfigured,
and enuironed with his enemies that
defired to make a finall end of
him, and loaden with so heauy a
burden that it permitted him not to
go one ftep more forward : the B.
Virgin would haue holpen him, but
the cruell minifters would not permit her . And this forrow full encoū-
ter was so mouing and full of compaffion, that this p raduenture was
the tyme and place, where the women beholding it, burft out into
teares, bewayled and lamented him
so much , that they enforced our
Lord to fay vnto them, that they
fhould not weep vpon him, but vpon
themfelues, and for the finnes of the
people, and the punifhments which
for them were to befall that vngratefull Citty . For if in the greene wood
they do thefe thinges, in the dry what
fhallbe done? By which he would
fay : If the diuine iuftice chaftice me
fo terribly for other mens finnes,
who am a greene and fruitfull tree,
how will he, I pray you, punifh finners,

ners, who are dry and whithered ftocks and vnfruitfull trees, for their owne finnes? If I who am innocent, haue beene fcourged, buffeted, fpit vpon, reuiled, and (though I deferue nothing of all this) do notwitftanding now go with this croffe on my fhoulders to be nauled vpon it, what will become of the guilty, what ftripes, what thornes, what buffets, finally what torments wil befall them?

From hence thou mayft gather defires to bewayle thy finnes and offences: for they were that which ouercharged and weighed down the wearied fhoulders of thy Lord God, and made him ftoop and fall.

THE XLVIII. MEDITATION.

How our Sauiour was crucifyed.

THE 1. POINT.

TO confider that Chrift our Lord being arriued at mount Caluary, fore afflicted and tyred with going that long and painefull
iourney

iorney, was by thefe furious foldiers
with barbarous cru-lty defpoiled of
his facred garments, and becaufe the
bloud was now dry and cold, his garments ftucke faft to his body, and fo
they againe r:n & flayed that meeke
lambe, who did not open his mouth,
nor fpeake a word againft them that
thus tormented him

Ponder that of all the tyms that
they ftripped our Lord (which were
in all foure) this was the moft painefull, and moft ignominious, being
now ftripped and naked from top to
toe, not only of his garments, but of
his fkin alfo.

Gather hence patience & longanimity in iniuries and aduerfity,
and not to be angry, nor offended,
when thou fhalt fee thy felfe poorely
apparelled, and to want neceffaryes,
feeing fo rare an example, as Chrift
our Lord hath giuen thee, of fufferan-
ce, nakednes and pouerty in all his
life, and efpecially in his death: for
his nakednes muft be thy garment,
his difhonour, thy liuery, his pouerty, thy riches, his confufion, thy glory,

ry, and his death thy life of grace &
glory.

The 2. Point

TO consider how Christ our Lord
being now naked, & the soldiers
laying the Crosse on the ground, they
commanded him to lye downe vpon
it on his backe, that he might be nailed to it, and so he did.

Ponder first the most excellent
obedience of thy Sauiour, which
shined most in hearing and obaying,
in whatsoeuer hard & difficult matters those cruell tormentors proposed
vnto him, giuing thee an example, to
subiect thy selfe to euery humane
creature for his loue, where there is
no sinne.

Ponder secondly how our Sauiour, lying vpon that bed of the
Crosse, which thy sinnes had prepared for him, lifted vp his eyes to heauen, and rendred thanks to his Eternall Father, for hauing brought him
to that point, wherein he beheld himselfe so poore, so dishonoured, and
misused for his loue.

Gather hence, when thou shalt
see

see thy selfe in aduersity and distresse, to be resigned to the diuine will in them, giuing Almighty God due thankes for them : for once giuing thanks to God in aduersity is more worth, and of more merit, then many tymes in prosperity .

THE 3. POINT.

TO consider how Christ our Lord was nayled on the Crosse, and the excessiue paynes which he felt when those rough and boisterous nails entred, breaking the veines, piercing the sinewes, and renting the most tender parts of the most delicate body of all bodyes, enduring with great patience and loue to see himselfe so loaden with paines, & full of vnspeakable sorrowes.

Ponder how our Lord permitted the nayles to pierce his sacred hands, and diuine feet, to shew thee that he would haue thee alwayes imprinted in his hands and feet, so great was the loue and holy zeale which he had of the saluation of soules, and of thyne in particuler .

Gather hence desires of thyne owne

owne saluation, and of thy neighbours, setting light by whatsoeuer
difficultyes, paynes and trauels,
which to deliuer them out of sinne,
may befall thee, that by this meanes,
as a souldier of this spirituall warfare,
thou mayst imitate in some sort thy
Captaine Iesus, who with so great
loue gaue his life for them, hanging
on the Crosse.

THE 4. POINT.

TO cõsider, that after Christ our
Lord was nayled on the Crosse,
his enemies lifted it vp on high, with
that true lambe of God vpon it, who
taketh away the sinnes of the world,
letting it fall downe violently into
the pit which they had made for the
purpose.

Ponder the payne, and confusion, and shame which Christ our
Lord had whan he saw himselfe on
high naked in the middest of an open
field full of innumerable people, and
as another Noe, exposed shamefully
to the sight of all, without any thing,
to couer his nakednes withall, not
hauing any to affoard him any thing,
but

but many who were ready to take
from him al that might be giuen him.

Gather hence a great shame and
confusion at the small griefe, sense
and feeling thou hast of the paynes of
our Lord, not shedding so much as
one teare of compassion, whereas
he powreth out all his bloud. And
seeing the insensible creatures which
want both reason and feeling made
so wonderfull demonstration of sorrow at the death of this our Lord,
that they were torne and rent in
peeces for euery griefe; it is good
reason that thou, who art his creature, and the cause why he endured
that which he did, shouldst acknowledge and be thankefull for it, and
haue a speciall and inward feeling
thereof, seeing he suffered it in benefit of thee.

THE

THE XLIX. MEDITATION.

Of the seauen wordes which our Lord
spake hanging on the Crosse.

THE 1. WORD.

TO consider the great charity of
our Lord, which was such, that
before he would comfort his
Mother, before he would prouide
for his friends, before he would cō-
mend his spirit to his Father, he
prouideth his enemies of remedy.
Wherfore the first word he spake on
the Crosse, was to excuse his enemies, who crucified, blaſphemed, and
murdered him.

Ponder, how Christ Iesus our
Lord being ful of grieuousdolours &
paynes in euery part of his body, not
finding any place of rest in that hard
bed of the Crosse, euen then did lift
vp his diuine eyes to heauen & shedding teares of most tender loue and
compaſſion, opening his diuine
mouth, not to commaund that fire
should come from heauen, as Elias
prayed,

prayed, but to beseech his Eternall
Father to pardon those which were
there, and the sinne they committed
in crucifying him.

Gather hence how exactly our
Lord God fullfilleth the precept he
hath giuen thee. To loue thyne e-
nemies, and to pray for them that persecute thee, that by this example thou
mayst learne and know to do the
like.

THE 2. WORD.

TO consider how that the second
Word, which thy Redeemer spa-
ke, from the chaire of the Crosse, was
to pardon the theef, and graunt him
heauen. Because he confessed his fault
and declared the innocency of Christ
our Lord, and freely, and plainely
calling him King, craued fauour at
his hands, saying: Lord, remember
me, when thou shalt come into thy
kingdome. And so our Lord Iesus
did, honouring this theefe before his
Eternall Father, as he confessed him
before men, enduing him with so
exceeding great graces and priuiledges, that being the last, he made him
of

of all mortall men the first, who departing this life should presently receaue the reward of glory.

Ponder that if God rewarded him with so great liberality, who did only follow him, not fully three houres, how will he reward those who shal serue and follow him with perfection, all the houres and dayes of their life? And if our Lord shewed himselfe so gratefull to this sinner, who had iniuried him innumerable tymes, for one only tyme that he confessed and honoured him, what manner of gratitude will he shew to him who shall spend his whole life in seruing and honouring him?

Gather hence desires to serue him alwayes, that securely and with confidence thou mayst haue accesse vnto him, and aske him that which this good theefe did aske him saying: Remember me o Lord (that is) remember not my sinnes, nor the robberies which I haue done, but that I am a fraile man, and infirme, that I am thy creature made to thy image and likenesse, wherfore I beseech thee

to

to remember me.

THE 3. WORD.

TO confider, that the third word which Chrift our Lord fpake from the Altar of the Croffe, was to recõmend his B. Mother to S. Iohn and S. Iohn vnto his Mother: And from that houre the difciple tooke her to his owne, and loued her with fpeciall loue.

Ponder the exceeding great greefe with which this word of recommendation pierced the hart of the Bleffed Virgin: for fhe throughly weighed the inequality of the change which was made, receiuing for the fonne of the liuing God, the fonne of a poore filher man: for the Maifter of heauē, an earthly difciple, for the Lord, a feruant, and for him that can do althings, him that can do nothing without his grace.

Gather hence a great and earneft defire to take this Bleffed Lady for thy mother, & to loue and ferue her with fpeciall care: And a firme purpofe to obey the diuine will, learning to reuerence, as in place of

God

God, his creature (that is to say)
thy Superiour, Father, or Maister,
which he shall assigne thee, whosoeuer he be, and to serue, and obey
him as God himselfe, as our B. Lady
did, who tooke S. Iohn for her Son,
and he tooke her for his mother.

THE 4. WORD.

TO consider the fourth word,
which Christ Iesus our Lord spake
to his Eternall Father, representing
him the affliction which he felt by
reason of his internall desolation of
mind: for he cryed with a loud voyce
and sayd : My God, my God, why
hast thou forsaken me?

Ponder how the Eternall Father permitted the most sacred humanity of his Eternall Son, to suffer,
and to continue in torment, and released him not out of those terrible
paynes & sorrowes which he had vn-
dertaken for our good and remedy,
neither in them did he giue him any
comfort or ease at al, nor in the crosse
it selfe. He could not leane his head
on any side without increase of payne
and greefe, the thornes thrusting in
deeper

deeper thereby: of his hands he had
no help, becaufe he could not wipe
away the drops of bloud which ran
downe from his head vpon his face,
nor the tears which he did fhed from
his eyes, they being nailed faft to the
Croffe. Neither of his feet, for they
were not able to fuftaine the poyfe of
his body, but rent themfelues with
greater payne. Wherfore our Lord
feeing himfelfe fo afflicted, cryed vnto his Eternall Father and fayd: My
God, why haft thou forfaken me ?

Gather hence forrow and compaffion to fee that there is fcarce any
that make benefit of his paffion, or
that accompany our Lord in his hard
and painefnll trauels: for bis difciples had forfaken him, his people a-
bandoned him, and many men loft
their fayth which before they had in
him. Hartily befeech him that he wil
not forfake thee now, nor at the
houre of thy death.

T   THE

THE 5. WORD.

TO consider how that our Sauiour being now quite and cleane exhauft, and his body through the abundáce of bloud which he had fhed, being dryed vp, and all the condu its of his veines emptied, he had naturaly a moft greeiuous thirft, and therefore he fayd : I thirft.

Ponder how great griefe pierced the foule of the B Virgin, feeing her beloued Sonne, and her God fo abandoned and deftitute of all manner of eafe and comfort for afking a little water to coole his thirft withal, there was no body that would giue it him: and albeit fhe could haue gone for water, fhe durft not leaue him, fearing leaft in the meane time he fhould depart this life, feeing him now at the point of death.

Ponder fecondly that befides al corporall thirft which our Lord Iefus had, he had a much greater thirft of other three thinges. Firft he had an infatiable thirft to obey his eternall Father in al things, without omitting any thing how painefull foeuer it
                                                                                        fhould

should be. And because he knew it to
be the will of God, that they should
giue him vinegar and gall, he would
not omit to fullfill his will in accepting that also. His second thirst was
an inflamed desire to suffer for our
sakes, far more then he had yet suffered. The third thirst was of the saluation of soules, and in particuler of
thyne, and that thou wouldst serue
him with perfection.

    Gather hence confusion and
shame seeing that thy thirst is not to
suffer for Christ our Lord, nor to be
obedient, patient, humble and poore
as he was, but to haue plenty of all
thinges, and that nothing be wanting euen for superfluous expences.
Beseech him to graunt thee some
practicall knowledge of the thirst
which he had, that thou mayst become his disciple in something.

    T H E 6. W O R D.

TO consider that the sixt word, that
  Christ our Lord spake from the
chaire of the Crosse was: Consuma-
tum est, It is consumate, all whatsoeuer my Father commanded me to
      T 2   suffer

suffer from the cribbe vnto the Croſſe
is accompliſhed and ended.

Ponder how thy Lord who is
now in this chaire of ignominy ready to giue vp the Ghoſt, will come at
the day of iudgment in another very
different throne of glory and maiesty
to iudge, and will ſay in like manner
this word: Conſummatum eſt: now
the world is at an end, and the vaine
pompe and glory thereof, now the
delights of the wicked are paſt, and
alſo the trauels of the iuſt.

From hence thou mayſt gather
deſires to liue in ſuch ſort that at the
houre of thy death, thou mayſt ſay
with S. Paul: I haue conſumated my
courſe, I haue ended my life, wherin as a good Chriſtian, or as a good
Religious man, I haue fullfilled the
obligations of my ſtate. But if thou
haſt beene ſlacke and remiſſe in this,
thou mayſt not ſay, it is conſumated,
but now my paine and eternall woe
beginneth. Beſeech our Lord to giue
thee grace, that thou mayſt begin
from this day forward, and continue
to the end in his holy ſeruice.

THE

THE 7. WORD

TO confider that the laft word which our Lord fpake on the Croffe, being now ready to giue vp the Ghoft, was to commend his fpirit into the hands of his Eternal Father.

Ponder firft that he fayth not, I commend vnto thee my liuings or poffeffions, for he hath none: not my honour, for he is not much follicitous thereof: not my body, for that is not that which he regardeth moft, but his fpirit, which is the principall and ought moft to be reckoned of by man.

Ponder fecondly, that our Lord doth not only commend vnto his Father his owne fpirit alone, but alfo the fpirit of his elect, which he efteemeth as his.

Gather hence defires in thy life time and in the houre of thy death to commend thy fpirit into the hands of God, for theron dependeth the eternall weale of thy foule.

THE

THE L. MEDITATION.

Of the taking downe from the Crosse, &
of the buriall of our Lord.

THE I. POINT.

TO consider, that the euening of that sad and dolefull day being now come, the Blessed Virgin being poore, and besides destitute of all help, knew not which way to turne her selfe : for there was no body that would bring her a ladder to take downe the body of her beloued Son, neither had she any body to assist her disciple S. John, and the night drew on, and euery one betooke himselfe to his home At last she saw two principall men comming, Ioseph, and Nicodemus, who brought necessaries for the buriall.

Ponder how our Sauiour ordained, that because his most Holy Sonne had a poore and reproachfull death, he should haue a rich & glorious sepulcher, and that wheras his disgraces had been such and so great, his

his honour alſo & exaltation ſhould
begin euen from the Croſſe, many
of his enemies euen then confeſſing
him to haue beene the Sonn of God.
And therefore he ordayned that Ioſeph ſhould ioyne with Nicodemus,
and that both togeather ſhould ſtout-
ly and without reſpeēt or feare of the
Iewes vndertake that enterpriſe.

Gather hence deſires that God
would vouchſafe to touch thy hart
with the vertue and force of his diuine inſpiration, that making no account of human feare, nor of the ſay-
ings of men, thou mayſt with great
fortitude and zeale ſet vpon whatſoeuer ſhallbe for the ſeruice, honour,
and glory of his diuine Maieſty, as
theſe Saints did.

The 2. Point.

TO conſider that theſe holy men,
hauing firſt obtained leaue of the
Preſident Pilate, to bury the body of
their Maiſter, came to the place where
our Lord Ieſus remayned hanging
on the Croſſe, and hauing comforted
the afflicēted and ſorrow full Mother,
and craued her licence to mount vp

to the Croſſe, ſhe willingly graunted them.

Ponder firſt how they kneeled downe vpon their knees, and with exceeding great deuotion made their prayers to Chriſt crucifyed, ſaying: O good Lord thou didſt permit that thoſe ſacrilegious hands, which haue intreated thee in this manner and put thee vpon the croſſe, ſhould hale and pull thee ſo irreuerently: graunt that the hands of theſe thy deuout ſeruants may with reuerence touch thy ſacred body & take it downe from the Croſſe. When they had ſayd theſe or the like words with many teares rearing the ladders they mounted vp with great ſilence to the Croſſe, and tooke downe the holy body, & placed it in the armes of his moſt Bleſſed Mother, who to receaue it, & to waſh it with her tears ſate her ſelfe downe, hauing euer before ſtood conſtant at this rufull and ſorrowfull tragedy.

Ponder ſecondly the anguiſh and greefe of mind, that the Bleſſed Virgin felt when ſhe beheld and imbraced

braced that sacred body of her Sonne
and our Lord so mangled, how she
held him fast in her armes, and layd
her face betweene the thornes of his
sacred head, and ioyned her face to
the face of her Beloued Sonne. O
how would this soueraigne Lady
then remēber how far different kisses
& imbracings were these from those
which she had giuen him in his natiuity and childhood, and what difference there was between these dayes
and those which she had spent with
him in Bethleem and in Hierusalem.
How cleare was that night of his natiuity, and how darke and obscure
is this day of his passion? How rich
was she in the stable, and how poore
at the Crosse? And if when she lost
him whiles he was yet aliue, she was
so much greeued and afflicted for his
absence: how great was her sorrow
heere, seeing him dead in her armes,
and in so wofull a shape? without
doubt it was a sword of so excessiue
griefe vnto her, that it pierced her
very soule and hart.

Gather hence desires that our

Blessed

Blessed Lady would vouchsafe to
giue thee licence, to adore him in spirit, and to kisse and haue in thy arms
her most holy Sonne, as she held him
in hers: and obtaine for thee some inward griefe and feeling of the Passion & death of her God & thy Lord,
to the end that thou mayst be partaker of his trauels, seeing thou hopest
to haue part of his ioyes and Resurrection.

THE 3. POINT.

TO consider how that after the
most B. Virgin had held the dead
body of her Blessed Sonne for some
time in her lap, Ioseph and Nicodemus, fearing least she should dye
with griefe, besought her with all humility and respect, she would moderate her sorrow, and giue them leaue
to bury him; she yielded to their re-
quest: and forthwith those holy men
annoynted him with Myrrhe, and
wrapt him in a cleane syndon, and
couered his face with a napkin.

Ponder the loue which Christ
our Lord had to pouerty : for he
would not that the Myrrhe wherewith

with they annoynted him, the nap-
din, and sheet in which they foulded
him, should be his owne, but anothers, his sepulcher borrowed, and as
it were lent him of almes.

Hence thou mayst gather to
loue pouerty, which this our Lord
loued so much, exercising thy selfe
in this verue, in life and death, as he
did; because if thou renounce not all
that thou possessest in imitation of
him, thou canst not be his disciple.

THE 4. POINT

TO consider how the body of our
Lord being annoynted & bound
in a white syndon, they found means
to carry him, and bury him in a new
monument which was in a new garden hardby the place where he was
crucifyed, and there they layd the
holy body of our Saviour. And when
the B. Virgin saw that there she was
to leaue him, whome her soule loued
so much, and the treasure of her hart,
then her griefe began a fresh, and she
fell to lament her solitude.

Ponder how he, who is the
splendour & brightnes of the Father,
the

the glory of Angells, the saluation &
life of men, refuseth not to be straitned and prest togeather as it were, &
enclosed euery day in the loathsome
& stincking sepulcher of our brests,
couering his sacred body with the
white vaile of the accidents or forme
of bread.

Gather from hence desires to
beseech this Lord, that seeing he
vouchsafeth to straiten, as it were,
himselfe, and to enclose himselfe so
often in thy sepulcher, to the end
thou mayst receaue and eate him,
being as thou art a silly and vile wormes he would also renew thee with
vertues, that so thy sepulcher may
become and remaine cleane and pure
as if no dead thing had euer come in
it.

T HE

THE
THIRD BOOKE
OF MEDITATIONS,

Appertayning to the
Vnitiue Way.

VVhat is the Vnitiue VVay.

THE end of the Vnitiue Way, is to vnite & ioyne our soule with God by perfect vnion of loue, being glad when we consider his innumerable and infinite riches and perfections, reioycing at his infinite glory, power, and wisdome, desiring that he be knowne of all

all the world, and that his holy and
diuine will be done and performed
in all creatures. For this is the way by
which those who arriue to the perfect
state of vertue, do walke, exercisi g
themselues in the contemplation of
the impatlible and glorious life of
Christ our Lord.

THE I. MEDITATION.

*How our Lord descended into Limbo,
and of his glorious Resurrection.*

THE I. POINT.

TO consider how our Lord Iesus
Christ, hauing fini ned the com-
bate of his Passion, to accomplish fully the businesse of our saluation, as soone as he had giuen vp his
sacred Ghost, leauing his body dead
on the Crosse, in soule he descended
to the lowest parts of the earth, into
Limbus, to deluer the soules of those
holy Fathers that were there, and to
carry them with him to heauen.

Ponder how our Lord, though
he were so mighty and powerfull,
that

that he could with one only word haue deliuered out of Limbo those holy soules, without descending thither personally (as he did with Lazarus when he called him out of his sepulcher) he would notwithstanding descend thither, to discouer by this heroicall act of humility the loue he bare vnto them.

From hence thou mayst gather to performe by thy selfe the busines which God commendeth vnto thee of helping of soules, how meane soeuer they seeme, humbling thy selfe as Christ our Lord humbled himselfe on earth, that thou mayst be exalted in heauen.

The 2. Point

TO consider the great ioy which the soule of Christ our Lord had, seeing it selfe to vanquish death, to triumph ouer hel, and to glorify such a multitude of soules as were there in Limbo. How well would he then thinke the labours of the Crosse imployed seeing the fruit which that sacred tree began now to yield.

Ponder the wondefull ioy and

exulta-

exultation which those holy Fathers receaued (who for so many thousand of yeares, with such patience, confidence and expectation, had looked for that happy houre of their ransome and liberty) when they saw that Blessed soule of Christ their Redeemer triumphant in those bottomles pits, and obscure dungeons of hell, destroying with his diuine vertue & power the gates of brasse, and iron barres of that dungeon, and turning that obscure and mornefull place into a ioyiull and pleasant Paradise.

Gather hence a firme confidence in God, when thou shalt find thy selfe assaulted with sundry sorrowes and afflictions, & be not wearied, afflicting thy selfe for continuance of them, seeing there is no time that commeth not at last, nor any euill that hath not an end, as the imprisonement of those Saintes had an happy end

THE 3. POINT.

TO consider how that most Blessed soule of thy Sauiour, accompanied with that resplendent & bright shining

shining army of holy Fathers, came
with them to the sepulcher, where
his body lay disioynted, disfigured &
wrapt vp in a winding sheet.

Ponder that the first thing
which our Lord did, was to discouer
vnto them the lamentable shap of his
sacred body, that they might vnderstand how deere their ransome had
cost him : and when they beheld that
holy body all blacke and blew, out
of ioynt, and so bruized & mangled
on euery side, they yeilded againe
vnto their deliuerer infinite thankes
for hauing redeemed them with so
great labours and paynes.

Ponder secondly, how that as
soone as that Blessed soule entred a-
gaine into that body which was more
disfigured then any body euer was,
it transformed it into a far more excellent shape then it had in the mount
Thabor, & made it a thousand times
more beautifull & resplendent then
the Sunne. And with a ioyfull countenance he arose out of the sepulcher,
immortall and glorious, without re-
mouing the stone from the place
which

which was layd vpon the sepulcher,
as he issued out of the sacred bowels
of the most Blessed Virgin, without
domage of her integrity and purity.

Out of all this thou mayst gather affections of thanks giuing, of
laud and prayse to the Eternall Father: for that he hath conuerted the
sorrow of his most Blessed Sonne into so vnspeakable ioy, and so incomparable beauty, communicating vnto
his body the prerogatiues of immortality and glory.

The 4. Poitn.

TO consider that Christ our Lord,
when he was risen againe, did not
forthwith mount vp to heaué, which
is the seat due to glorified bodyes,
but remayned in the world for the
space of forty dayes to comfort and
animate his discipls, enforming them
of many things concerning the kingdome of God, that being eye witnes-
ses of his resurrection they might
preach it more confidertly to the
world: & it may piously be thought
that at that tyme all the quiers of the
Angels came downe to gratulate this
his

his victory, and to celebrate the feast
of his glorious triumph: for it they
descended to celebrate his Nativity,
when he came to liue heere a mortall
and passible life, with great reason
may we thinke they came at his Resurrection, when he began to liue an
immortall and glorious life.

Ponder how the heauenly spirits with angelicall harmony renewed that canticle of the Natiuity: Glory
in the highest to God, and in earth
peace to men of good will, and with
great reason, seeing that by meanes
of this peace, of enemies we were
made friends, of slaues of sinne and
the Diuell, we were made children &
heires of his glory.

Gather hence desires to reioyce
and to say with the holy Prophet:
This is the day which our Lord hath
made: let vs reioyce, and be glad
therein. Desiring that all may do the
like, and adore him for that he hath
gotten so glorious a triumph and victory ouer all his enemies.

                    THE

THE II. MEDITATION.
Of our Sauiours apparition vnto his most Blessed Mother.

THE 1. POINT.

TO consider that the first visit, & apparition which Christ Iesus our Lord made, is thought to haue been to the most Blessed Virgin his Mother, to cleare that Heauen darkened and ouercast with sorrow, and to dry the floud of teares from those virginall eyes, which had wept so much, and aboue al others had felt the sorrowes and afflictions of his Passion, and of his absence.

Ponder how the Blessed Virgin being in her retirement, not a sleep, but in prayer, expected this new light, with liuely fayth, and assured hope of the Resurrection of her Sonne, meditating those wordes of the Royal Prophet: Arise my glory, arise my psalter and harp, and reioyce with thy musicke those that are sad and lament thy absence. And if Dauid

uid contemplating his God and Lord
so far off, had such a thirst & longing
desire to be partaker of his Resurrection, how great desires had the most
Blessed Virgin (louing him and desiring him much more then Dauid)
being so nigh to the tyme, and euery
moment expecting to see and enioy
againe her beloued Sonne, now glorious in his Resurrection.

Gather hence like affections &
desires. And beseech this our Lord
that he will vouchsafe to rise in thy
soule, to visit and comfort it, as he
did his most holy Mother, that thou
mayst deserue to see and enioy him
in his glory at the generall Resurrection.

The 2. Point.

TO consider how the Blessed Virgin our Lady being in this contemplation and these longing desires,
her most holy Sonne entred in, and
manifested himselfe vnto her withall
the glory and brightnes which his sacred body had, strengthning her corporall sight to be able to behold him
and enioy him.

Ponder

Ponder how great the ioy of the Blessed Virgin was, when she saw the body of her most sweet Sonne not now hanging amidest the cues, but enuironed with Angells and Saints: not recomending her from the crosse to the beloued disciple, but himselfe giuing her a louing kisse of peace, not disfignred as he was at his death, but resplendent & beautifull. O how fully content and satisfied did she remaine with this comfortable sight, how sweetly did they imbrace one another, what tender speach and inward feelings would there passe betweene those two blessed harts!

From hence thou mayst gather desires to giue thankes vnto this Lord, who is so certaine a friend and so ready to comfort those who suffer for his loue, for according to the measure of his Mothers sorrowes he gaue her consolation and ioy : so if thou accompaniest Christ crucifyed in his paynes and Passion, thou shalt also be partaker of his rest, and shalt rise as he did, to a new life of glory.

T H E

THE 3. POINT.

TO contemplate the moſt Bleſſed
Virgin enioying thoſe graces and
fauours which her moſt Bleſſed Son
had done her, and what tender, pleaſant and louing diſcourſes he held
with her , perchance theſe or ſuch
like : Mother behold thy Sonne , I
do not now recommend thee from
the Croſſe to my diſciple Iohn ; I do
not call thee woman , thou doſt not
hold me dead in thyne arms, but behold I am aliue and riſen againe, and
am come to beſtow on thee a thouſand imbraces , and to ſhew thee the
ſpeciall loue and affection which I
beare thee .

Ponder the ioy that wholy poſ-
ſeſſed the ſoule of this moſt bleſſed
Lady, when ſhe ſaw her ſelfe ſo fauo-
red , honoured and cheriſhed , and
with ſuch loue, wiping away the
teares from her virginall eyes , full of
deuotion doubtles , and proſtrating
her ſelfe vpon the ground, ſhe would
adore him, and ſay : O my Sonne &
my God, I giue thee infinit thankes ,
for that according to the multitude

of

of my sorrowes, my consolations haue abounded. And making no end of kissing those Blessed signes of the sacred wounds which yet remayned in his glorious body, and had caused vnto him so great paine in his passion, and seeing them now so beautifull and shining, they were a cause of great comfort vnto her.

Gather hence desires to giue thanks vnto this Lord for so speciall, and singular fauours done vnto his B. Mother, as to one most worthy thereof: for disposing thy selfe to a good life, holy desires and works, he will do thee the like fauours and graces, albeit thou be vnworthy thereof.

THE 4. POINT.

TO consider how wel accompanied Christ our Lord was, when he came to visit his beloued Mother with that most bright shining squadron and troupe of so many Saints which he had deliuered from Limbo, where diuers of them had, for so many thousands of yeares, expected to enioy him in heauen.

Ponder

Ponder how that when al thofe Saints faw themfelues in prefence of the B. Virgin our Lady , acknowledging her for the Mother of their Redeemer, and bruizer of the infernal ferpents head, they would kneele downe and proftrate themfelues vpon the ground, yielding her a thoufand thankes and congratulations , for fuch a Sonne as fhe had there, and for the paynes fhe had taken in the worke of their Redemption.

Ponder fecondly how glad and ioyfull the Bleffed Virgin was to fee the fruit of the Paffion which now the facred tree of the holy Croffe began to yield, in fo many foules ranfomed therewith . O how wel imployed did this Bleffed Lady then account all thofe afflictions , forrowes , labours trauailes and paynes which pierced her foule all her life tyme, feeing that which then fhe faw , & enioying that which then fhe enioyed .

Hence thou mayft gather defires to affociate and ioyne thy felfe with this holy company, to adore & reuerence this moft Holy Virgin: for

V   the

the Mother of such a Redeemer, acknowledging that by her meanes, if
thou take her for thy Patronesse, and
become truly deuout vnto her, thou
mayst (by the grace of God) be partaker of the glory and eternall blisse,
which thou hopest to enioy in heauen.

THE III. MEDITATION.

Of the apparition of Christ to S. Mary Magdalen.

THE 1. POINT.

TO consider how S. Mary Magdalen vpon Sunday very early
came to the monument, bringing with her odoriferous oyntmēts
and aromaticall spices to anoynt her
maisters body : and not finding him,
she thought that he had been stollen,
which occasioned in her soule new
griefe and sorrow: for before she wept
because her Lord was dead, and now
because they had taken him away, &
put him she knew not where. And so
she stood at the monument, & could

not

not depart thence, but sayd : O maister, where art thou ? where shall I seeke thee my ioy ? my life ? where haue they put thee ? O Lord whither shall I go ? where may I seeke thee ? whome shall I aske for thee ?

Ponder how much the earnest and longing desire, the abundant and feruent teares of this holy sinner , wrought in the louing breast of God: for by her tears she obtayned pardon of her sinnes , by teares she obtayned the resurrection of her deceased brother , by her teares she deserued to haue Angells for her comforters, yea and the Lord of Angells himselfe, & to be the first vnto whome our Sauiour did appeare .

Gather hence a great shame and confusion for that thou so little feelest and lamentest thy sinnes , hauing by them so often lost God and his grace. But if thou desire to find and not to loose him , imitate this holy and feruent woman , not taking comfort in any thing vntil thou find and possesse thy Creatour : for if thou seeke in this sort, thou shalt find him , and he
will

will comfort thee with his sight and presence.

THE 2. POINT.

TO consider how that our Sauiour seeing the holy desires of his disciple, would now without further delay fullfill them, appearing vnto her yet disguised, so that she might not know him: and speaking vnto her in a different voyce from that he was wont to vse vnto her, he sayd : Woman, why weepest thou? whome seekest thou? And she answered him : Because they haue taken away my Lord, and I know not where they haue put him.

Ponder that when this sinner before wept at the feet of Christ, & washed them with the teares of her eyes, our Lord sayd not to her: Why weepest thou? nor whome seekest thou? because those tears proceeded from the selfe knowledge of her sinnes, and from a liuely fayth and loue of our Lord, whome she had present, who knew and approued them: but in regard these tears proceeded out of ignorance, and want of fayth, bewaylling

ling him as dead who liued, and seeking the liuing among the dead, he
sayth: Why weepest thou? whome
seekest thou? For doubtles thou
knowest not, because knowing thou
wouldst not lament for me in this
manner, neither wouldst thou seeke
him as absent, whome thou hast present with thee.

Gather hence desires to examine and discusse wel the cause of thy
tears, because many tymes thou wilt
perswade thy selfe that thou weepest
for thy sinnes, and thou dost not,
but for the temporall losse which they
haue caused thee. And other whiles
thou wilt thinke that thou lamentest
with desire to see and enioy God, yet
thou dost not, but only to fly the tra-
uel which thou endurest. And in like
manner thou wilt thinke that thou
seekest God and his glory, & in very
deed thou seekest thy selfe, & thyne
owne honour and commodity. And
seeing God in this sort, with good
reason he will aske thee: Whome seekest thou? Seeke therefore God in
such sort, that he may approue thy
teares,

teares and say vnto thee and vnto all:
Blessed are they that mourne, for they
shallbe comforted.

The 3. Point.

TO consider the mercy of our Lord
who would not long conceale
himselfe, but forthwith meekly and
louingly discouered himself vnto his
disciple calling her as he accustomed,
Mary. And she presently acknowledging his voice, answeared, Maister: and seeing her Lord and her
God glorious and risen to life, she
adored him.

Ponder how far the ioy, admiration, deuotion and astonishment
she conceiued of so great a wonder,
might extend it selfe, finding so much
more then she desired: for seeking a
dead body she found her Lord aliue
and victorious ouer death. And casting her selfe at his feet she would
haue adored and kissed the most sacred signes of his wounds that were
so beautifull and resplendent: but our
Lord would not permit her as then,
saying: Do not touch me: for I haue
not yet ascended to my Father, as
thou

thou thinkeſt, I am not to leaue thee
ſo ſoone, neither ſhall this be the laſt
tyme that thou ſhalt ſee me : for he
fullfilled her deſires when he appeared to the women, with whome ſhe
alſo was.

From hence thou mayſt ga-
ther feruent deſires to ſeeke God : for
if thou exerciſe thy ſelfe in the vertues of loue, and deuotion, patience
and perſeuerance in which this holy
ſinner exerciſed her ſelfe ſeeking our
Lord, be aſſured that (albeit thou haſt
been as great a ſinner as this his diſciple was) he will ſhew thee his mercy,
graunting thee that which he gaue
vnto her, to wit, to ſee her Lord and
Maiſter riſen and glorious.

THE 4. POINT.

TO conſider the infinite charity of
thy Redeemer in honouring ſinners truly penitent, ſith that he choſe
for an eye witnes of his Reſurrection
a woman, a notorious ſinner, & that
ſhe ſhould deſerue this viſitation before the Apoſtles, yea before the
Prince of the Apoſtles, & before the
diſciple ſingularly beloued aboue the

reſt

reſt of the Apoſtles, becauſe with ſo many teares and ſuch perſeuerance ſhe had ſought the Bleſſed body of her Lord.

Ponder how that the multitude of ſinnes paſt, do not preiudice, when they are recompenced with greater feruour preſent. Wherefore in regard that Magdalen was eminēt in performing many thinges that others did not for the loue of Chriſt (as we haue ſayd in her 15. Meditation of the ſecond booke) and was preſent, and accompanied him at mount Caluary, and aſſiſted at his buryall: euen ſo ſhe was moſt fauoured & cheriſhed of all.

Gather hence courage & confidence that thou be not diſmayd at the multitude of thy ſinnes : for if thou come in tyme and art dilgent in the ſeruice of God, excelling therin through particuler ſeruices, he will beſtow on thee ſpeciall graces and fauours, that thou mayſt deſerue to ſee and enioy him for euer in his glory.

THE

THE IIII. MEDITATION.

Of Christ his apparition to the Apostle Saint Peter.

THE I. POINT.

TO consider how S. Peter and S. Iohn went to the monument, and entring in, saw only the linnen clothes wherein his holy body had beene wrapt, and the napkin lying at one side, which they tooke for a certaine signe of his Resurrection, as the women had told them.

Ponder how that amongst the disciples of Christ, Peter and Iohn were the most feruent, and they who excelled most in the loue of Christ our Lord: for although these Apopostles knew right well of the persecution that the Iews raised against the disciples of Christ, keeping watchmen at the monument; they resolued neuertheles to go & see how matters passed.

Gather hence how the loue of God maketh all thinges easy, ouer-

V 5   maistereth

maistereth and preuaileth against difficultyes, be they neuer so great. Beseech him to graunt thee that loue &
charity which he gaue to his Apostls,
that laying aside humane feare, thou
mayst seeke him, and enter whersoeuer he shall be.

THE 2. POINT.

TO consider how these Apostles
returning to their lodging, Saint
Peter retired himselfe to pray al alone
and to ruminate vpon this mistery,
and meruayling with himselfe at that
which he had seene and done, our
Lord appeared vnto him risen and
glorious.

Ponder first the singular content and ioy that bathed the hart of
the holy Apostle, when he perceiued
him present, whome his soule loued
and desired. With how liuely a fayth
of the Resurrection would he say:
I verily beleeue o Lord that thou art
Christ, the Sonne of the liuing God,
with what deuotion and tears would
he cast himself at the feet of his Lord
and Maister, who had done the same
vnto him the night of his Passion, &
deeming

deeming himfelfe vnworthy of fuch a
fight and prefence , would repeate
thofe wordes which he had fpoken
vpon another occafion , to wit: Go
forth from me o Lord , becaufe I am
a finnefull man . But by how much
the more he humbled and debafed
himfelfe, the greater were the prerogatiues & fauours he beftowed vpon
him .

Ponder fecondly what it was
whereby S . Peter made himfelfe
worthy of his apparition , and thou
fhalt find, that it was the prayer and
meditation of the thing he had feene
in the monument .

Gather hence defires to be a louer of prayer, becaufe that, & a good
life , repentance of our finnes , and
purpofe of amendmēt are the means
and remedy to find , fee , and enioy
Chrift rifen and glorious .

THE 3, POINT.

TO confider how that the holy A-
poftle enioying that foueraigne
fight and prefence of Chrift rifen,
our Lord would fay vnto him: Peace
be to thee, it is I, feare not, thy finnes

are forgiuen thee.

Ponder how much S. Peter would be abashed, and blush to see himself in the presence of his maister calling to mind how he had denyed and offended him· and it is credible, that he would abundantly renew his teares, weeping bitterly and lamenting his sinne, & crauing againe pardon thereof.

From hence thou mayst gather how meruailous great the diuine mercy is towards all those who hartily bewayle their sinnes & do pennance for them. Wherefore if thou lamentest thy synnes, although thou be a greater sinner then this Apostle was, and so vnwcrthy to receaue fauours and benefits; yet cōming in tyme, thou shalt make thy se'fe worthy of his soueraigne apparition in the kingdome of his glory.

THE 4. POITN.

TO consider how Christ our Lord, hauing visited S. Peter, sayd vnto him : Go, and confirme thy brethren in the fayth of this mistery: and so he, our Lord vanishing out of his sight,
                              betooke

betooke himſelfe preſently with great
ioy and content to the place where
his companions were, to confirme
them in fayth, as his Maiſter had giuen him in charge . And the teſtimo-
ny he gaue of the Reſurrection of our
Lord was ſo effectual and ſtrong that
many beleeued in him .

    Ponder the great deſire God
hath of thy ſaluation, and that thou
ſhouldſt know the miſtery of his Reſurrection, giuing thee maiſters to
inſtruct and declare it vnto thee, and
that thou ſhouldſt beleeue in him
thereby to obtaine eternall life .

    And gathering hence deſires
to be gratefull vnto our Lord endeauour to make benefit of the fauours
thou ſhalt receaue at his diuine hand,
to confirme thy brethren in vertue
with thy examples and wordes, that
they may glorify and prayſe him .

                              THE

THE V. MEDITATION.

Of Christ his apparition vnto the two disciples that went to Emmaus.

THE I. POINT.

TO consider, the desolation and sorrow wherewith the two disciples going to a towne called Emmaus, talked and reasoned with themselues of the paynes and Passion of Christ our Lord : who approaching went with them, and vouchsafed to accompany them in this voyage, but their eyes were held they might not know him : meaning to discouer vnto them, in the end of the iorney, his glorious Resurrection.

Ponder the loue of Christ towards these two discipls, sith the smal and slender fayth they had of his Resurrection, was not a cause to withdraw him from their company, because he is infinitly delighted to be with them who speake and discourse of holy thinges, who sayd : Where there

there be two or three gathered in my
name, there am I in the middeſt of
them.

Gather hence how fit and be-
ſeeming a thing it is euer to talke of
God, and to entertaine thy ſelfe in
like diſcourſes with thy companions,
eſpecially in tyme of affliction : ſith
our Lord is at hand to comfort them
conuerting their ſorrow and deſola-
tion into ioy and content. And contrarywiſe how ill it is to ſpeake of
prophane and bad matters, becauſe
ſuch do baniſh and exclude Chriſt Ieſus from their company, & he flyeth
from them.

THE 2. POINT.

TO conſider how Chriſt our Lord
encountred theſe his two ſeruants in a pilgrims weed, and (as if
he had not known) ſayd vnto them:
What are theſe communications that
you conferre one with another walking, and are ſad?

Ponder that our Lord is not
only glad and recreated for that he
hath endured ſo much as he hath, yea
and death it ſelfe, being ſo reproach-
                              full

full and ignominious, but defireth
that all fhould heare it recounted and
spoken of. And therfore he afked his
difciples (which he, as an eye witneffe, knew right well) of what they
only by hear-fay treated off, for their
feare and cowardlineffe had caufed
them to flv.

Gather hence confufion and
fhame confidering how forgetfull
thou art of what our Lord fuffered
for thee, whereas thou hauing done
and fuftained fo little for him, art
notwithftanding moft mindful therof, expecting that he reward and
crowne thy flender feruices, & defirous to be efteemed as one who hath
trauelled and endured much for the
loue of God, yea and art difcontented
to be otherwife reputed.

The 3. Point.

TO confider how our Lord hauing heard them, forthwith began to rid & deliuer them from their
ignorance, and reprehending them
for their incredulity and hardnes of
hart, proued vnto them by authority
out of the Prophets, how Chrift
ought

ought to haue suffered, & so to enter
into his glory.

Ponder that if it were necessary that Iesus Christ should suffer such
& so greiuous iniuryes & reproaches
thereby to enter into glory, which
was his by inheritance, as being the
naturall Sonne of God; how will it be
possible that thou, who art a seruant
and spendest all thy life in contentments, pleasures & vanityes, shouldst
enter into glory, which is not thyne,
but that it must cost thee a Crosse,
mortifications and afflictions: for
costing God all this, shouldst thou
enioy it at free cost? that is, for nothing?

From hence thou mayst gather
desires to imitate in some thing thy
Captayne Iesus, with a great feare
least thy want of fayth be a iust cause
why thou deseruest to be reprehended of his diuine maiesty, and held as
foolish and slow of hart to beleeue &
vnderstand his diuine Misteryes.

T HE

THE 4. POINT.

TO consider that as these holy pilgrimes drew neere to the towne whither they went, our Lord made semblance to go further : but they with much instance and intreaty forced him, saying : Tarry, because it is towards night, and the day is now far spent.

Ponder that howsoeuer Christ our Lord made semblance to go further, his intention and desire was to remaine with them, to impart vnto them that toothsome repast, and to open their eyes and manifest Himselfe vnto them, as he did in this occasion, refreshing and feeding them with his sacred body : for his delights are to be, and conuerse with the children of men.

Hence thou mayst gather confusion and shame, that thy delights are not to be with God, nor to draw nigh and conuerse with him, but to withdraw thy selfe from him, and not to discourse and treat of him, but of the vaine, transitory, and perishing things of this world ; not reflecting
how

how that the day of thy life passeth
on, and hasteneth to an end, and the
night of thy death approcheth, wherin thou art to giue an account to
God of all .

THE VI. MEDITATION.
Of his apparition to the Apostles vpon
Easter day .

THE I. POINT.

TO consider how Christ our
Lord appeared to his Apostles,
being gathered togeather , v-
pon the day of his Resurrection .

Ponder the great care our Sauiour hath to visit his beloued disciples.: forgetting the small fidelity
they shewed him in his Passiō, when
as leauing him in the hands of his
enemyes, they all fled, and forsooke
him .

Gather hence desires of gratitude to this Lord, who many times
affordeth thee spiritually , that which
he did to his Apostles visibly & corporally : for albeit thou hast beene so
vngrate-

vngratefull and disloyall vnto him,
shunned, forsaken & fled from him
many tymes, he neuertheles omit-
teth not oftentymes to visit thee
with his diuine inspirations, giuing
himselfe also vnto thee with great
loue corporally, as often as thou
commest to receaue him in the most
B. Sacrament.

The 2. Point.

TO consider how our Lord entred into his disciples, hauing
the dores of the house shut, where
they were retyred for feare of the
Iewes, our Lord entring in far better
then the Sunne entreth through the
chinks of the windows, to awake the
sleepy, and to rid the fearefull of
their dread.

Ponder that the causes, why our
Lord entred to visit his disciples the
dores being shut, amongst others
were these: The first was to manifest
vnto them, that his body being glorifyed, he could enter and penetrate
by the grace of subtility, whither
soeuer he would, without any obsta-
cle or let at all. The second, to make
knowne

knowne vnto them the efficacy of
his omnipotency . The third , and
that which maketh moſt for thy purpoſe , is to teach thee, that Gods holy will and pleaſure is thou ſhouldſt
keep ſhut the gates and windows of
thy hart , which are thy ſenſes , that
theeues may not enter thereat, which
are the Diuells, to robbe and ſpoyle
the fruit of a good conſcience .

Gather hence liuely and effectual deſires, from this day forwards
to be very vigilant and circumſpect
ouer the guard and cuſtody of thy
ſoule, powers and ſenſes, not permitting them to wander without bridle
in purſuit of creatures . And ſo doing
the Lord and owner thereof will enter to repleniſh her with true ioy &
comfort.

The 3. Point.

TO conſider how our Lord, the
diſciples being thus gathered togeather, came with a cherful countenance , and placing himſelfe in the
middeſt of them (which is the place
of him who maketh peace , to inſi-
nuate hereby , that for this effect he
had

had come into the world , and that
this was which he had negotiated &
brought to paſſe by his death) ſayd
vnto them : Peace be with you.

Ponder how great a friend
Chriſt our Lord is of peace , ſith the
firſt word he vttered, by the miniſte-
ry of his Angells, when he came into
the world was giuing peace to men.
And being in the world he ſayd to
his Apoſtles: My peace I giue vnto
you . And being to depart out of
the world: My peace I leaue to you
purchaſed by my death and Paſſion.
Whence it followeth by good conſequence that our Lord recommen-
ded vnto vs in life & death, nothing
ſo much as peace : and becauſe ſinne
had beene cauſe of ſo great emnity
betweene God and man, Chriſt our
Lord vouchſafed (thereby to reconcile and ſet vs at peace with his Eternall Father) to receaue the blowes of
his rigorous iuſtice vpon that ſacred
humanity , rent and torne in a thouſand places , and ſetting himſelfe in
the middeſt , to ſay : Peace be with
you.

Hence

Hence thou mayſt gather two thinges: the firſt, how often thou being at emnity with God, he hath inuited thee to peace, and thou baſt not admitted it, neuer ceaſing to warre againſt him with thy ſinnes. The ſecond, how little peace thou haſt kept with thy neighbour, falling out with him for matters of ſmall importance and trifles. Beſeech this Lord who is God of peace, to come into thy ſoule & graunt thee that which the world cannot giue, eſtabliſhing peace betweene thy ſoule and thy ſpirit, betweene thy powers and ſenſes, betweene his Eternall Father and thy brethren.

THE 4. POINT.

TO conſider how Chriſt our Lord entring, the diſciples were troubled and affrighted, imagining that they ſaw a ſpirit, and our Lord ſayd to them: Why are you troubled, and cogitations ariſe into your harts? See my handes and feet, that it is I: handle and ſee, for a ſpirit hath not fleſh and bones, as you ſee me to haue.

Ponder

Ponder the sweetnes of his
voice, which was sufficient to ap-
pease them, and rid them of all
feare, and to make them to know
him, as who should say : My deerest
disciples, I am the same I was wont
to be, in my nature, in person, and
in quality : I am your Sauiour, your
Maister, your brother, & your God,
feare not the fury of the Iewes, nor
the indignation of the Gentils, nor
the cruelty of Kings & Princes who
haue risen against me, nor those who
oppose themselues & persecute you:
for I being in your company you
are secure and in safegard .

Gather hence security & con-
dence for thy soule, timerous and
fearefull through the manifold sinnes
thou hast committed, saying to her:
O my soule feare not, for although
thy sinnes be many, this Lord promiseth and assureth thee of the pardon
of them all. This lambe is he that taketh away the sinnes of the world, &
he who will take away thyne : and if
he be the protectour of thy life, of
whome shouldst thou be afraid ?

                              T H E

THE VII. MEDITATION.
Of Christ his apparition to the Apostles,
Saint Thomas being present.

THE I. POINT.

TO confider how our Lord, the difciples being gathered togea- ther, entred and fayd to his difciple that had not beleeued the Miftery of his Refurrection: Put in thy finger hither, and fee my hands, and bring hither thy hand, and put it into my fide, and be not incredu- lous, but faithfull.

Ponder the infinite charity of God in being follicitous for the well- fare of his fheep, for hauing expected eight dayes to fee if Thomas would recall himfelfe and acknowledge the hardnes of his hart, he would not deferre the remedy any longer, but came in perfon to cure this his Apo- ftle and loft fheep, and taking him by the hand, defired to put & place him in his hart.

Gather hence how great the
X   mercy

mercy of God is, granting thee by infallible promise and assurance, that he will not conceale himselfe from thee if thou seeke him, yea albeit thou hast beene as incredulons as S. Thomas · & confessing him for thy Lord and thy God as he did, he will graunt thee that which he affoarded him, that is his body, not only to touch him, but also to receaue and enioy him in thy brest.

THE 2. POINT.

TO consider how that our Lord, who permitted not himselfe to be touched by Mary Magdalen, leuing him so deerely and seeking him so earnestly, taketh Thomas (as we see) being incredulous, by the cold and frozen hand, maketh it warme and cherisheth it, and putteth it into his bosome, heaping vpon him so many benefits.

Ponder, how that whatsoeuer S. Thomas desired and asked, our Lord graunted him, as if by his be-leeuing, some profit were to ensue to Christ, whome loue made to reckon for gaynes, as his owne, yea and to
procure

procure them euen with his loſſe.

Gather hence an exceeding deſire to beare with the defects of thy brother, & not to be ſlacke nor wearyed with ſeeking his redreſſe, but euen leauing thy owne right, to go vnto him if he will not come to thee, and with breach of thyne owne will to condeſcend vntohis, perfectly imitating Ieſus Chriſt our Lord, who albeit he was triumphant and glorious yet did he not omit to come, and do S. Thomas ſo great and ſpeciall fauours and priuiledges. And as he did with him, ſo doth he alſo dayly with thee when thou commeſt to receaue him corporally and ſpiritually: learne to be gratefull and ſeruiceable therefore.

THE 3. POINT.

TO conſider S. Thomas his worthy confeſſion: for as ſoone as he touched (as piouſly we may beleeue) the precious wounds of his Sauiour, & had his eyes enlightned with that diuine Sunne, he became ſo illuminated with the rayes & beames of his diuine light and ſplendour, that he

confeſſed

confessed plainely and clearly the article of his Resurrectiō, which he had not beleeued before.

Ponder the loue which Christ our Lord hath to sinners, and which himselfe shewed to haue to this his incredulous and sinnefull Apostle, sith the sinne of his small fayth, was not inough to make him leaue to bestow such fauours and benefits vpon him, as being impassible & glorious, to vouchsafe him his diuine handes and feet, bowels and hart, to touch and handle.

Ponder secondly how the Apostle seeing himselfe so honoured and fauoured of our Lord, brake out into those tender and deuout wordes, saying: My Lord, and my God. And with good reason he called him his, and not our Lord, because he loued him so tenderly, that for his good alone he appeared to all the Apostles: and forgetting as it were all the rest, vpon him alone bestowed the grace and benefit, to inflame him in his diuine loue.

From hence thou mayst gather
desires

defires to confeffe with S . Thomas
that Iefus is thy Lord and thy God :
for his loue is fo exceeding great, that
he is ready to do for thee alone, that
which he did for S . Thomas, fith
that, as well for thee, as for him, he
deliuered himfelfe vp to death, to
purchafe for thee eternall life.

THE 4. POINT.

TO confider the wordes which our
Lordfayd to his difciples. Becaufe
thou haft feene me Thomas, thou
haft beleeued. Bleffed are they that
haue not feene and haue beleeued.

Ponder that albeit our Lord
approued the confeffion of S . Thomas, yet would he not cal him Bleffed
as he did S . Peter when he confeffed
him for the Sonne of God , and the
reafon was, becaufe he had beene
flow in beleeuing: wherefore infteed
of prayfing him , he reprehendeth
him, faying : Becaufe thou haft feene
me, Thomas, thou haft beleeued; as
who would fay : Thankes be to thy
hands and eyes which I haue giuen
thee to beleeue, that I am thy Lord,
and thy God.

Endeauour

Endeauour to gather hence an earnest desire to see Christ thy Lord, if not corporally, as the disciples saw and enioyed him with their corporal eyes, at least spiritually, sith those, who beleeue his Resurrection not hauing seene him, Almighty God calleth Blessed.

THE VIII. MEDITATION.

Of his apparition to his Apostles vpcn Ascension day.

THE 1. POINT.

TO consider how our Sauiour appearing to his disciples, told them that the same day he was to goto his father, & that if they loued him, they should verily be glad, in regard that it was expedient for them that he went to heauen.

Ponder how desirous the disciples were, not to loose the corporall presence of their Maister, seing it was necessary with these and other like speaches to aduertise them, that it was not only expedient for his honour

nour to afcend to heauen, but alfo that
it imported them much , thereby to
make more perfect their fayth , to
raife their hope , and to purify their
charity . For if I go not to my Father (our fayd Lord vnto them) the
Holy Ghoft fhall not come to you .

Gather hence , that if to loue
the corporall prefence of their Lord
and Maifter, with a loue fomewhat
leffe pure, & in part intereffed, would
haue hindred the comming of the
Holy Ghoft to the difcipls, how much
more will it hinder thee to loue thy
felfe , or any other creature with an
inordinate loue .

THE 2. POINT.

TO confider that our Lord fayd
vnto his difcipls to comfort them:
Reioyce my beloued difciples at my
departure , becaufe I go to prepare
you a place .

Ponder how that thy Redeemer
directeth likewife the fame fpeech to
thee, as to his Apoftles: Reioyce,
becaufe I goe to heauen , that now
from this day forward thou mayft
haue entrance therin; reioyce for that
I

I afcend and go before, to open for thee thofe celeftiall gates, by which thou (albeit a wretched and finnefull creature) mayft haue franke & free entrance, which before I afcended was not graunted to the iuft and holy. Reioyce becaufe I afcend to day, that thou mayft afcend to morrow, and be feated by me in the place affigned thee by my Father.

Hence thou mayft receaue meruailous great ioy and content for that thy Lord and thy God afcendeth into heauen : becaufe for him principally it was created. Craue of him this diuine grace, that by meanes of a good & vertuouslife, thou mayft deferue to fee and enioy him in his glory.

THE 3. POINT.

TO confider how our Lord hauing comforted his difciples, fayd vnto them: Tarry in the Citty, till you be endued with power from aboue.

Ponder that word, Tarry, that they fhould abide, reft, and ftay, whereby he meant to fignify, that
they

they were to expect him with patience and perseuerance, with repose of body and mynd. Secondly God commanded them to keep in the Citty, to giue them to vnderstand that this fauour was not done to them alone, but was also ordayned for the good of the vniuersall world.

Gather hence desires to expect the coming of this diuine spirit with repose and quietnes, because God desireth that his, though they liue in the middest of the streets, and noyse of the world, may haue their mind quiet and peaceable, that they may pray and attend to him with such spirit and recollection as his diuine maiesty requireth, and to thee shallbe necessary.

THE 4. POINT.

TO consider how Christ our Lord, commanded his disciples forthwith to betake themselues to mount Oliuet, because from thence he was to ascend to heauen.

Ponder how these holy disciples would call to mind, that the place which their Lord and Maister
had

had chofen to fuffer iniuryes and reproaches on the Croffe , he now
chofe to mount thence vp to Heauen, there to enioy the immeafura-
ble greatnes of his glory : and that
the way to afcend to heauen is the
mount Oliuet , or of oliues , which
fignifyeth charity and mercy .

Gather hence defires to be cha-
ritable and mercifull towards thy
neighbours , and to extoll and magnify the wifedome and prouidence
of God , who is able to make that,
which is the beginning of thy humiliation and contempt , to be the origen and caufe of thy exaltation and
prayfe , as may be feene in Iofeph ,
whofe calamity, infamy and impri-
fonment , God vfed as a meanes to
make him foueraigne Lord & King
of Ægypt ,

THE

THE IX. MEDITATION.
Of the Ascension of Christ our Lord.

THE I. POINT.

TO confider that fourty dayes being paft after the Refurrection of Chrift our Lord, in which he had treated and conuerfed with his, the houre of his glorious afcenfion being come, hauing all his difciples prefent : he tooke his leaue of them with manifold fignes and demonftrations of loue, and as a moft louing Father who departeth, lifting vp his hands, he bleffed them, and fo departed from them.

Ponder how great the griefe & feeling of thefe moft louing children would be for the departure of their Father, when they fhould fee that Lord to leaue them, for whom they had left all thinges. It is to be beleeued that then fome would caft themfelues at his feet, others would kiffe his moft facred hands, others would hang vpon his necke, and all would

X.6   fay :

say: How o Lord, doſt thou go and leaue vs thus alone, and orphanes in the middeſt of ſo many enemies? What ſhal children do without their Father, diſciples without their Maiſter, ſheep without a Sheepheard, & feeble and weake ſoldiers without their Captaine. But our Lord comforted them, promiſing them the fauour and ayd of the Holy Ghoſt, and his perpetuall aſſiſtance and prouidence, which neuer ſhould faile them.

Gather hence deſires that this Lord, before he depart to heauen, vouchſafe to giue thee his benediction, and taking hold ſpiritually of his hands, caſting thy ſelfe at his feet, & hanging on his necke, thou ſhalt, as an other Iacob, ſay vnto him : I will not let thee go, o Lord, vnles thou bleſſe me : for thereon my whole remedy and euerlaſting bliſſe dependeth.

The 2. Point.

TO conſider how that glorious body of Chriſt our Lord, hauing imparted his benediction to his, in their

presence

presence ascended to heauen, the disciples remayning in suspence and astonished to behold their Elias moūt vp to heauen: and wheras they could not follow their Lord with their bodyes, they followed him with their eyes and harts.

Ponder the great admiration of the Angells and men which were there assembled, seeing that sacred humanity of Christ our Lord to mount aboue all celestiall spirits, towards that Citty, and to be seated at the right hand of the Father, who had been so much debased and humbled: wherefore replenished with excessiue ioy and comfort they would say to ech other: Ascend o Lord, ascend not to mount Caluary to be crucifyed betweene two theeues on a tree, but vnto the holy hill of Sion in the heauenly Hierusalem, to be glorifyed betweene two diuine persons, by the quiers of Angells and blessed soules that inuisibly accōpany thee. Ascend o Lord, ascend to this soueraigne court, not to suffer and dye, but to triumph ouer death it selfe &

sinne

sinne &c.

From hence thou mayst gather how well afflictions endured for the loue of God, are imployed, seeing he can and will reward and recompence them so largely, magnifying and exalting aboue al creatures him, who humbled himselfe and suffered more then all. Beseech him that sith he sayth by S. Iohn: If I be exalted from the earth, I will draw all things to my selfe, it may be fullfilled in thee, that thy mind and affection being separated from earthly vanityes thou mayst ascend with him and his holy company to heauen.

THE 3. POINT.

TO consider how the holy Apostles after they had lost the sight of their God and Lord, They went backe to Hierusalem with great ioy, because the same loue, that caused them so much to lament their losse, enforced them on the otherside to reioyce at his glorious triumph & entrance into that celestiall country, where he shouldbe receaued of those courtiers of heauen with singuler ioy

exulta-

exultation and triumph, some singing others playing on their admirable & melodious instruments.

Ponder how different this thursday in mount Oliuet was from that friday in mount Caluary; there so solitary, heere so well attended; there nayled on a Crosse, heere exalted aboue the cloudes; there crucifyed betweene two theeues, heere attended vpon by quiers of Angells, there blasphemed and scorned, heere honoured and renowned; finally there suffering and dying, heere reioycing and triumphing.

Gather hence great comfort to see this so wonderfull a mutation and change, and reioyce in this day of Chrifts ascension into heauen to be thy aduocate, and feare his comming to be thy Iudge.

THE 4. POINT.

TO consider the ioy of Christ our Lord in this triumph, of whome it is sayd: God is ascended in iubilation, seeing the happy end of his trauels.

Ponder how much the Eternal Father

Father exalted him aboue all, who humbled himselfe more then all, giuing him for the throne of the Crosse a throne of Maiesty, for the crowne of thornes, a crowne of glory, for the company of theeues, companies of Angels, for the ignominies and blasphemies of men, honours and prayses of celestiall spirits. And because he descended fiist into the inferiour parts of the earth, he made him ascend aboue all the heauens. In conclusion, that nature wherto it was sayd: Dust thou art, & into dust thou shalt returne, now is raised from the dust of the earth aboue all the heauens.

Gather hence how requisite it is to humble thy selfe for Christ, so to be exalted with Christ, because if thou wilt not be like vnto him in debasing and humbling thy selfe, in vaine hopest thou to follow him in ascending and raigning.

¶ After the Meditation of the Ascension of Christ our Lord to heauen it were much to the purpose to set down the meditatiõ of his glory, but

in

in regard we haue treated thereof in
the first Booke, togeather with the
last things of man, we remit him that
desireth to read and meditate theron
to that place.

THE X. MEDITATION.
Of the comming of the Holy Ghost.
THE I. POINT.

TO consider how after our Sauiour was ascended into heauen his disciples retyred themselues into an vpper chamber in Hierusalem, where they all perseuered in
continuall prayer expecting the Holy
Ghost.

Ponder that the strongest and
most effectuall meanes that may be
to procure the comming of the Holy
Ghost into thy soule, is a continuall,
inflamed and feruent perseuerance in
prayer: for otherwise, if when others
pray thou sleepest, if when others attend and are carefull of their saluation and spirituall profit, thou remaine carelesse & negligent of thy own,
if

if when others haue their minds and conuersation with God, thou hast thyne with men, although thou be in company of the good and holy, in one house and residence, in one same Religion, this diuine spirit will not come vpon thee.

Gather hence desires to perseuere in prayer, and to be frequent therein, that this diuine fire of the Holy Ghost may come also vpon thee as he came vpon the Apostles, who with so many sighes and longing desires expected his comming.

THE 2. POINT.

TO consider how there came sodenly a wind that filled the whole house where the Apostles were in prayer.

Ponder first how this wind and coole ayre of heauen, did not leaue any chamber, roome, closet or corner of that house, which it did not penetrate, to signify that this quicking spirit is offered and giuen to all men generally in whatsoeuer part or corner of the world they are.

Ponder secondly that when the Holy

Holy Ghoſt entreth into a ſoule, it fil-
leth all her facultyes by his power,
with verityes and celeſtiall vertues,
not leauing any part voyd or vnfur-
niſhed.

From hence thou ſhalt gather
that if thou deſire this ſoueraigne ſpirit ſhould repleniſh the houſe of
thy ſoule with his diuine graces and
gifts, thou muſt not wander out of
it, diſtracting & buſying thy thoughts
about creatures, but remaine ſettled
and quietly repoſed therein, imploying her in good deſires, thoughts &
workes : for doing ſo this diuine ſpirit will fill thee with his aboundant
loue and grace.

The 3. Point.

TO conſider how the Holy Ghoſt
deſcēded in forme of fiery tōgues
vpon all the Apoſtles and diſciples,
that were retyred in that houſe, ve-
rifying that which Chriſt our Lord
ſay.d vnto them : I came to caſt fire
on earth, and what will I, but that it
be kindled, and inflame the harts of
men.

Ponder that the cauſe, why this
Lord

Lord commeth in forme of fire, was that the Apostles might be like vnto burning torches, which should set on fire the whole world, and that they might illuminate & inflame the harts of men with this fire of diuine loue; making them of wolues, to become sheep; of crowes, doues; of lions, lambes; and of brutish people and infernall monsters, spirituall Angells.

Gather hence great desires that this fire would vouchsafe vnto thee one sparke of his heat, that thy lips being purifyed, as were those of the Prophet, thou mayst henceforward neither speake, nor discourse of vaine & base thinges of the world, but of God and his prayses, endeauouring with thy speaches and conuersation to inflame thy selfe and those with whome thou conuersest, with the fire of thy diuine loue.

THE 4. POINT

TO consider that albeit the disciples which were in that chamber, were more then an hundred, and all of so different merits, yet that pure spirit replenished all with his diuine gifts, and

& graces imparted himselfe entierly
to euery one.

Ponder that although all were
full of the Holy Ghoſt, yet ſome receaued greater grace & benefit then
others, that is, the more holy receaued greater plenty of grace. And ſo
the moſt B. Virgin as fulleſt of grace
& vertues, receaued more abundance
therof then all the reſt togeather.

Gather hence a great deſire to
diſpoſe and prepare thy ſelfe to receaue this diuin ſpirit, with the greateſt feruour thou canſt, becauſe he
communicateth himſelfe more abundantly to him that is beſt prepared. &
to make thy ſelfe ſuch, the principal
vertue which thou muſt procure to
haue, is humility, which conſerueth
the reſt, as the Prophet Iſay ſayth :
Vpon whome repoſeth my ſpirit,
ſayth our Lord, but vpon him that is
humble and meeke? Be thou then
ſuch an one, that with like diſpoſition
thou mayſt receaue and preſerue in
thy ſoule this diuine ſpirit, who reſi-
ſteth the proud, and to the humble
giueth his grace.

THE

THE XI. MEDITATION.

Of the death of the most Blessed Virgin our Lady.

THE 1. POINT.

TO consider how the B. Virgin our Lady being now in yeares, & God hauing determined her some tyme in this life (which some beleeue were fifteen, others (more probably) say, that she liued twenty three yeares after the death of Christ and that she departed this life to heauen the 72. yeare of her age) Almighty God hauing preserued her heere al this tyme to giue light to the world, & for the comfort and benefit of the whole Church, & also that she might see the fayth and name of her Blessed Sonne diuulged and spred ouer all parts of the world, she had now most earnest and inflamed desires to go to heauen where she was to find our Lord Iesus Christ her Sonne victorious and triumphant, whome she instantly besought to take her out of this

this exile and banishment, and tempestuous sea, and conduct her to that secure port of happynes, where foreuer she might enioy his glorious sight and company.

Ponder how this most Blessed Sonne approuing the pious desires of his deerest Mother, and acknowledging the aspirations of her hart to be greater then those of Dauid where he sayd: Euen as the Hart desireth after the fountaynes of waters, so doth my soule desire after thee o God; he sent vnto her an Angell (which many holy Fathers imagine, was the Angell S. Gabriel) who came with a palme in his hand in token of the victory that this triumphant Lady had gotte of sinne, of the Diuell, and of death it selfe. And the Blessed Virgin receaued him with great comfort and ioy of spirit, considering what she so much desired was now to be effected.

Gather hence enkindled desires to see and enioy God, that when thy dayes shall end and death arriue, thou mayst receaue it with gust and ioy, hoping by meanes thereof to

parti-

participate in heauen, of the sweet
presence and company of Christ our
Lord, and of his most Blessed Mother.

THE 2. POINT.

TO consider how the Sonne of
God determining to fullfil the desires of his most Blessed Mother, the
Apostles being deuided ouer the
whole world preaching the victories
of their Lord, were miraculously as-
sébled in the house of the B. Virgin,
who reioycing much at their comming, disclosed vnto them the newes
of her death, with a cheerefull and
graue countenance declaring vnto
them her desire to depart this life, &
to goe to heauen, which Almighty
God had graunted vnto her.

Ponder the feeling, teares, and
tendernes of hart wherewith this dolefull relation afflicteth them all, seeing their Mother ready to depart this
life, and that diuine Sunne illuminating the Church, to withdraw it selfe
and go downe.

Ponder secondly how the B.
Virgin without any infirmity or
payne

payne at all (but of meere loue and
desire to see and enioy her Sonne in
heauen) betooke her selfe to her
poore bed, and beholding them all
with a countenance rather diuine,
then humane, willed them to come
neere, and gaue them her blessing,
saying : God be with you my deerly
beloued children, lament not because
I leaue you, but reioyce because I go
to my best beloued Sonne.

Gather hence an exceeding desire to approach in spirit neere vnto
this Blessed Lady, and ioyning thy
selfe to this good company, beseech
her to giue thee her holy blessing also, that therwith thou mayst increase
and go forward in grace and loue of
her God, and thy Lord.

The 3. Point.

TO consider how Christ our Lord,
this happy houre being at hand,
came downe from heauen accompanied with innumerable Angells, by
their sight & presence to reioyce his
most Blessed Mother, and to conduct her to heauen.

Ponder first the gracious and
Y sweet

sweet wordes which the Sonne of
God vsed vnto his sacred Mother the
Blessed Virgin Mary, which might
be the same that the holy Ghost spea-
keth to his Espouse in the Canticles:
Arise, make hast my loue, my doue,
my beautifull, and come : for winter
is now past, the raine is gone and departed: The flowers haue appeared in
our Land : Come from Libanus my
Espouse, come from Libanus : come
thou shalt be crowned , with the
crowne of iustice, which thou hast so
well deserued .

Ponder secondly what & how
great the iubilies and comforts were
that did trauerse the hart of this B.
Lady , what thanks she gaue her Son
and her God , for such benefits bestowed vpon her , and for vouchsa-
fing to cloth himselfe with her flesh
and bloud in her virginall wombe,
and calling to mind the manner of his
death on the Crosse would say: O my
Father, as thou art God, and my Son
as man, into thy hands o Lord I cō-
mend my spirit . And with these
words she yielded her spirit to him,
whome

whome she had inuested within her
selfe.

From hence thou shalt gather
affections to prayse God our Lord,
in whose sight the death of this Lady
was precious, giuing her so copious
and large a recompence for her labours. Trust in like sort to receaue
reward for that thou hast endured for
his seruice & glory, that so thy death
may be precious in his sight, as is that
of his Saints.

The 4. Point.

TO consider how the holy Apostles
and disciples of our Lord, when
they beheld that body without life,
of which our life had taken flesh, they
all prostrated themselues vpon the
ground, kissing it with great tendernes, deuotion and affection: then laying it forthwith vpon a beere, they
tooke it on their shoulders, and carryed it through the Citty of Hierusalem, singing hymnes and deuout
prayers, till they arriued at the sepulcher where it was to be placed.

Ponder how their griefe at such
time as the holy body was put into

the Monument, was renewed, & that they deuoutly kissed, and with great reuerence adored it againe & againe, not being able to withdraw their eyes from thence where they had their harts.

Hence stir vp in thy selfe a tender feeling and sorrow for the absence of this Blessed Lady, & an earnest desire spiritually with thy best endeauour to accompany her holy body, consorting thy selfe with the quiers of Angels and the disciples, to sing with them her prayses : beseeching her to obtaine thee such a death, as thou mayst in her company enioy for euer the presence and glory of her most holy Sonne in heauen.

THE

THE XII. MEDITATION.

Of the Assumption and coronation of our Blessed Lady.

THE 1. POINT.

TO confider how the third day after the death of our Bleſſed Lady, Chriſt Ieſus her Sonne, came downe from heauen, attended on by innumerable Angells, with the ſoule of his moſt B. Mother, & infuſed it into her body, and made it a thouſand tymes more beautiful then the Sunne it ſelfe, and reſtoring it to life, inueſted it with immortality, & with a beauty and grace ſo diuine, as neither can be explicated by wordes, nor comprehended by humane vnderſtanding.

Ponder how glorious the body of this pure Virgin was, rayſed out of the ſepulcher, with thoſe foure dowries of glory, which the glorified bodies haue, of impaſſibility, agility, ſubtility, and clarity. And beholding her ſelfe in this manner, what thanks

Y 3   would

would she render vnto her most B.
Sonne, for hauing dealt so liberally
with her, not permitting her body
(albeit she dyed a naturall death, as
other children of Adam) to be dissol-
ued and turned to dust, conseruing it
with the same integrity and purity,
it had in life.

Gather hence great ioy at the
Resurrection of the B. Virgin, and
the incorruptibility of her body, the
rare and speciall priuiledge graunted
vnto her by her most holy Son, who
fullfilled the desires of her soule. Beseech him to fulfill thyne, which are
to serue him with purity of body and
soule in this life, that thou mayst see
and enioy him in the eternall.

THE 2. POINT.

TO consider how our Lord God
hauing raised the body of the most
Blessed Virgin, the diuine Sunne and
beautifull Moone, would behold ech
other, not now mourning and eclipsed, as vpon good Friday, but most
ioyfull, resplendent and beautifull.
And those two blessed harts of such a
Mother and such a Sonne, exulting
with

with ioy, would giue to ech other
sweet imbracings, and a thousand
wellcomes and congratulations.

Ponder the most solemne procession, which forthwith was made
frō the sepulcher, euen to the highest
heauen, and how that glorious body
of the Blessed Virgin did mount and
ascend on high, carryed with the
wings of the gift of agility, not
standing in need of the Angells to assist or support her. Although they
did all accompany her, some singing,
others playing most sweetly on their
harps and violls, and reioycing and
wondering at so great a nouelty, and
glorious triumph, sayd: Who is this
that commeth vp from the desert of
this life with so great glory, flowing
with delights, leaning vpon her beloued?

Gather hence three things: Let
the first be a most earnest desire, in
spirit to follow the Blessed Virgin in
this iourney, abandoning the world
with thy hart, togeather with all the
sensuall delights thereof. The second
to endeauour to ascend euery day &
Y 4   to

to profit in vertue, not trusting to thy weake forces, nor to thy arme of fiesh but in the potent arme of God. Let the third be to reioyce euer in our Lord, and in whatsoeuer appertaineth to his seruice.

THE 3. POINT.

TO consider the place and seate which the Sonne of God assigned to his beloued Mother in heauen. This was no doubt the best and most eminent (the sacred Humanity of Christ excepted) which was or euer shallbe giuen to pure creature: for she was placed and seated aboue al the nine quires of Angells, at the right hand of God, within his owne curtaine and throne, according to that of the Prophet who sayth: The queen stood on thy right hand in golden rayment, compassed with variety & beauty: for it was most meet that she who stood & was present on his right hand suffering on earth at the foot of Crosse, should possesse the like place reioycing in heauen : & that she who humbled her selfe below all creaturs, should be exalted aboue them all, to

be

be their Miftreffe, and the Queene of
Angells.

Ponder how bright the impe-
rialheauen was with the glittering &
refplendent light of fuch a Sunne and
fuch a Moone, Chrift andhis Mother;
how ioyfull and contented were the
Angells with the fight and prefence of
fuch a Queene, by whofe interceffion
they hoped the feates which their
companions had loft, would be re-
paired; what great ioy did the Bleffed
conceaue at the maiefty and glory of
fuch a Mother, vnto whome all did
reuerence, homage and obedience,
feeing her fo far exalted aboue them
all. O how well fatisfyed and content was that humble Lady, feeing
her felfe raifed from the very loweft
place of the earth, to the fupreme &
higheft heauen.

Wherefore gathering hence affections of ioy for that this Princeffe
of heauen is fo extolled aboue al pure
creatures, thou fhalt congratulate &
contemplate with her, for that God
hath fo much honoured and exalted
her. Hope thou for the fame in hea-
Y 5   uen

uen if thou shalt follow the steps of such a Sonne, and such a Mother.

THE 4. POINT.

TO consider how the most holy Trinity presently crowned the B. Virgin with three crownes. The Eternall Father crowned her with a crowne of Power, giuing her, after Christ, power and dominion ouer all creatures in heauen and earth. The Sonne crowned her with a crown of Wisedome, enduing her with the cleare knowledg of the diuin essence and of all creatures in it. The Holy Ghost crowned her with a crowne of Charity, infusing into her not only the loue of God, but also of her neighbours.

Ponder the admiration and astonishment of those Angelicall Hierarchies, when they beheld the B. Virgin so much esteemed and honoured with such crownes, graces and prerogatiues, and aboue all consider what vnspeakable ioy this soueraigne Queene conceaued, with what affection and deuotion she would renew her Canticle of Magnificat, seeing
how

how great things, he who is Almighty, had wrought in her.

Gather from hence liuely and
inflamed defires to fee and enioy this
Bleffed Lady, who is the daughter of
the Eternall Father, Mother of the
Eternall Sonne, and efpoufe of the
Holy Ghoft. For fhe is crowned with
the diademe of glory, wherewith the
true King Salomon crowned her in
the day of her entrance into heauen,
and in the day of the ioy of her hart.
Befeech her, that feeing fhe is alfo
thy Mother, fhe would alfo vouchfafe to crowne thee in this life with
fuch plenty of her mercyes and vertues, that thou mayft obtaine & enioy the eternal crown of glory, which
God graunt vs. Amen.

*The end of the Meditations of the life
and death of our Sauiour, and his Bleffed
Mother.*

Y 4   *THE*

HEERE
FOLLOW TWO
MEDITATIONS

Seruing for preparation before the sacred Commu-
nion .

AN ADVERTISMENT.

I Haue thought it good to end this
Booke of Meditations with a few
of the most Blessed Sacrament, to
meditate vpon, not only the whole
octaue of Corpus Christi, and other
feasts of the yeare (in regard this most
Holy Lord graciously discouereth
himselfe, and is so often carryed in
publique procession) but also that
seeing it is (through the bounty of
God) receaued so frequently, not of
Religious persons alone, but of secu-
ler also, may haue sufficient matter to
prepare themselues before the sacred
Communion, and to giue due thanks
vnto our Lord after they haue receaued

ued it. For the excellency and soue-
raignty of this diuine Sacrament (in
which is contayned God himselfe)re-
quireth, that the disposition and preparation therto, be made with al care
possible. And therefore one of the
best preparations wherewith all may
come to receaue aboundant grace,
willbe retiring themselues, first to
consider well some one point of the
sixe, which are set downe in the two
ensuyng meditations, which are of
the Feare and Loue of God, because
these two vertues vnite the soulewith
God, and are the two armes wherewith she is to imbrace her spouse, and
which do instruct and teach her what
God is, and what she is. For Feare
causeth in the soule humility and reuerence, Loue, confidence and deuotion. Feare discouereth the greatnes
of God, and thy basenes: Loue, his
goodnes and clemency: Feare his iustice and our sinnes: Loue, the mercy
and confidence we ought to haue of
the pardon of them. If therefore loue
and feare worke so great good in the
soule, thou must endeauour by all
meanes

meanes that these said considerations
may ingender and produce in thyne
these two pearles, But because our
corrupt Nature so much affecteth variety, that though the consideration
be most excellent, yet is it presently
most weary of it: I will put in these
two Meditations six points (as I haue
sayd) which may serue for preparation to six Communions: for new
meate sharpeneth and stirreth vp the
appetite of man, and exciteth in him a
new hunger and desire to vnite himselfe with God: for all these sauces &
seasonings of considerations are necessary to make him eat the bread of
Angels, who hath set his affection on
the delights and food of beasts. After
these shall follow six Meditations,
which contayne eighteen points or
considerations, wherein the seruant
of God may find sufficient matter for
so many communions, to render due
thanks after he hath receaued: out of
which he may reape the fruit & profit he desireth.

THI

THE I. MEDITATION.

Of Feare.

THE 1. POINT.

TO consider the immensity and maiesty of that Lord which really and truly is contained in that most B. Sacrament: for he is the very same who with his only wil hath created, conserueth and gouerneth heauen and earth, and with it alone can anihilate and destroy it all.

Ponder the admiration and astonishment, which it caused to King Salomon to see that the greatnes of God came to liue in that holy Téple which he had built for him, being notwithstanding the most solemne, the most sumptuous, and most magnificent that was in theworld. With how much more reason oughtest thou to maruell, feare, and tremble, being but a poore emmet and silly worme, to go to receaue into thy house of base clay, that immense and diuine maiesty, Creatour, conseruer and gouerner of the world (whome

the

the Apoſtle S. Paul calleth the brightnes of the glory of God) being ſo ill
prepared as thou art , thy breſt alſo
hauing beene, not the Temple of the
Holy Ghoſt (as in reaſon it ought to
be)but rather a denne of dragons , &
receptacle of ſerpents and baſiliſkes.

Gather hence a great feare of
the iuſtice of God, with a deteſtation
of thy manifold ſins: for thou being
ſo vile a creature , and vnworthy to
haue in thee ſo great a good, thou
feareſt not to encloſe, retaine & harbour in thy ſtrait and narrow breſt
this omnipotent Lord & God whom
the heauens cannot comprehend .

THE 2. POINT.

TO cóſider who thou art, and who
he is whom thou goeſt to receaue,
and thou ſhalt find that an abhominable ſinner goeth to receaue his San-
ctifyer; a vile creature, his Creatour;
a wretched ſlaue, his Lord ; finally a
miſerable catiffe the ſupreme & omnipotent God , at whoſe beauty the
Sunne & Moone do meruaile, whoſe
maieſty heauen and earth do reuerence, by whoſe bounty the ſociety
of

of all the Bleſſed is maintayned.

Ponder how , being ſo vile &
baſe as thou art , thou art notwithſtanding admitted to receaue a God
ſo high : how being ſo little, canſt
thou entertaine ſo ſoueraigne a maieſty ? The Creatour of the heauens,
the King of Angels and men ? before
whoſe greatnes the ſtrongeſt pillars
of heauen do tremble , and the moſt
high Seraphims ſhrink in their wings
for very feare and reuerence : and if
all thinges created, be in the ſight of
this great God , as if they were not ,
what I pray thee, wilt thou be in his
diuine preſence to receaue him ? The
Church ſingeth and much admireth,
that this great Lord (vnto whome
heauen and earth is a ſtrait place)
diſdained not to enter into the wóm-
be of a Virgin . Meaſure her purity ,
with thy purity; her grace , with thy
deformity ; her innocency, with thy
malice, and thou ſhalt find far greater
reaſon to wonder at thy boldnes in
harbouring the Sonne of God and of
the moſt B . Virgin, whom ſhe conceaued and conſerued in her breaſt
with

with so great humility .

Gather hence great feare least this soueraigne King and Lord command his seruants to bind thee hand and foot (for that thou commest not with the garment of due innocency, and purity to this holy table and celestiall banquet) & cast thee into the vtter darckenes of hell , there to receaue thy deserued punishment.

The 3. Point.

TO consider the great iustice of our Lord , and how much he abhorreth sinne, & those which full often thou hast committed against his diuine Maiesty , for which thou deseruest many yeares ago to haue beene burning in hell fire : and as if thou wert very iust and holy, with so little feare thou presumest to entertaine into thy house the terrible Iudge and searcher of thy life and manners not remembring the menaces and threats of the Apostle against sinners who vnworthily, as thou, dare eat & drinke the sacred body and bloud of our Lord .

Ponder that if S. Iohn Baptist
so

so pure a creature and sanctifyed in
his mothers wombe sayd, that he was
not worthy to loose the lachet of the
sho of our Lord , how shalt thou be
worthy to receaue him? In like manner if S. Peter, Prince of the Apostles
and head of the Church , being astonished at the power and Maiesty of
Christ, fell downe at his knees saying:
Go forth from me , because I am a
sinnefull man: how darest thou come
to put thy mouth to his diuine side ,
and sustaine thy selfe with that precious wine that breedeth Virgins .

From hence thou mayst gather
a great feare & reuerence before thou
commest & presumest to receaue the
maiesty of this soueraigne God , and
an humble acknowledgement of thy
basenes , and a deep sorrow for thy
sinnes perfectly imitating that sinner
the Publican, to obtaine pardon therof, who knocking his brest , sayd :
God be mercifull to me a sinner .

THE II. MEDITATION.

Of Loue.

THE 1. POINT.

TO confider that as great as God is in Maiefty, in iuftice, and in deteftation of fin (as hath been fayd in the precedent Meditation) fo great he is in goodnes, in mercy, and in loue towards finners, which caufeth him to prefent himfelfe in humane flefh in the moft B. Sacrament, and is the caufe why he permitteth himfelfe to be once, and many times fold, fcorned, crucifyed, and nayled betweene theeues: for fuch are they who receaue him vnworthily.

Ponder how far the goodnes of God reached, and how much the beames of his diuine and inflamed loue extended it felfe : fith it made that generous & magnificent Lyon, who with his roaring terrified the world, to put on fuch meeknes, that he hath couched himfelfe vpon the altar, and is become a meeke lambe

that

that thou mighteſt eat him. And this ſame Lord being he who commaunded that no ſinner ſhould dare to approach vnto him vnder payne of malediction, his loue hath now ſo diſpoſed, and ſo changed him, and he is become ſo deſirous that al men approach vnto him, and to giue himſelf entierly to all; that he doth not only call and inuite them, but alſo eateth with them: yea and his loue doth proceed ſo far, as that he doth not only eat with them, but commandeth them alſo to eate him, giuing them his ſacred body and bloud to eate.

From hence thou mayſt gather feruent deſires to loue him, who hath loued thee ſo much; to haue confidence in him, who hath beene ſo liberall with thee, to haue acceſſe vnto him who is ſo good & ſo communicatiue of himſelfe, ſaying with the holy Prophet: What ſhall I render to our Lord for ſo many fauours and benefits which he hath rendred to me, and eſpecially for this I am to receaue now: but now I know that
it

it is my hart which he defireth, and this will I entierly offer vp vnto him, as his diuine Maiefty willeth and commandeth me.

THE 2. POINT.

TO confider how that Father of mercies who vouchfafedto be chaftized in his owne flefh for thy loue, & to fhed his moft precious bloud & dye vpon a Croffe for thee, this very fame is there glorious, and him thou goeft to receaue. The fame that dyed for thee, is there aliue to giue thee life making himfelfe (as he himfelfe fayd) thy meate, that by vertue of this facred food, thou mayft come to tranfforme thy felfe fpiritually into God, to put on his liuery.

Ponder the great defire this our Lord hath of thy weale and remedy, fith he ftood not vpon his owne coft and charges, nor regarded the loffe of his honour, life and liuing, fo that he might feed and cherifh thee with this diuine food. Giuing it vnto thee, not only to fee, adore, and kiffe, as to the fhepheards and Kinges, but that thou mayft receaue him alfo, & haue

haue him in thy breaſt, as his holy
and chaſt Eſpouſe had.

Gather from hence deſires to
conſecrate thy ſelfe wholy vnto this
Lord, endeauouring to be like vnto
him in life & manners, ſeeing he ſayd,
Be holy becauſe I am holy: & to thee
in particuler he ſayth: I earne of me,
(that is) to be humble as Chriſt, chaſt
and pure as Chriſt, patient and obedient as Chriſt, and by this meanes
thou ſhalt go clad with his garment
and liuery.

The 3. Point.

TO conſider that God loued ſinners
ſo much, as that he was not only
content to take fleſh in ſimilitude of
a ſinner, but vouchſafed alſo, therby
to communicate vnto thee his riches
and treaſures, to remayne in this moſt
Bleſſed Sacrament vnder that ſacred
veile, and in that humble curtaine of
that ſacred hoſt, and this not for a
ſmall tyme, but euen to the conſum-
mation of world.

Ponder how the loue that
brought him into the world, & made
him put himſelfe into the handes of
ſinners

finners, this very fame is that which maketh him to come the fecond and infinite tymes into the world, and to fhew himfelf fo inamoured as it were and fo much in loue with them, that he fayeth, that all his delights, ioyes and affections are to be and conuerfe with finners. And yet he far more affectionatly declareth & fpecifieth his loue, faying that, He who toucheth them, toucheth the apple of his eye, and veines of his hart.

From hence thou mayft gather defires to haue acceffe vnto, and to fet thy loue and affection entierly vpon this Lord. And although thy grieuous finnes on the one fide detaine and terrify thee, notwithftanding let his great loue and clemency on the other fide preuaile and moue thee; imitating that prodigall Sonne who albeit he faw his owne bafenes and mifery, yet the goodnes and loue of his Father encouraged him to go vnto him, and to caft himfelfe at his feet, do thou alfo as he did: & feeing thou haft imitated him that finned, i mitate

imitate him that repented, and thy
heauenly Father wil runne out to receaue thee, and as to a beloued child
will fall vpon thy necke, in token of
his singuler loue vnto thee.

HEERE
FOLLOW SIX
MEDITATIONS
Of the most B. Sacrament,
to giue thankes vnto our
Lord after Communion, &
to meditate vpon the Feasts
and Octaues thereof.

An Advertisment.

THERE is wont to be much negligence and distraction in some
after they haue receaued the
most Blessed Sacrament, & they reap
small fruit and profit thereby, because they are not prepared with
some pious consideration, to render
Z   due

due thankes vnto our Lord, or because they alwayes meditate one and
the selfe same thing. Wherfore to remedy this negligence, and to repaire
this domage, it willbe good that he
who is Priest be prepared before
Masse, and others before Communion, with one or more points of the
six ensuing Meditations, that variety
may take away wearisomnes which
depriueth both of gust & profit. And
heereby they may dresse this diuine
meat in sundry manners, sith it hath
no lesse properties in it, then had
that celestiall Manna, which gaue
such tast as euery appetite desired. So
this diuine Manna is of such vertue
and substance, that euery one may
apply it as he liketh best, and it will
sauour vnto him of whatsoeuer his
hart shall desire: for whatsoeuer is in
it, is profitable to be eaten, and pleasing to the tast, as the diuine Espouse
doth note, and S. Ambrose & other
holy Fathers say: Christ is althings
vnto vs: If thou be sicke of an ague,
he is a Phisitian; if thou feare death,
he is life; if thou fly darknes, he is
light;

light; if thou seeke sustenance, he is
food; if thou be cold, he is fire; if
thou haue want, he is rich. Let the
conclusion be (sayth this holy Do-
ctour) that we proue and taft of this
soueraigne food, because our Lord,
who is in it, is most sweet and pleafing to the palate of the soule. If therfore whatsoeuer may be, and thou
canst defire, thou findest and hast in
Christ, consider him euery time thou
communicatest, according to these or
the like attributes, that thou mayst
reap: the fruit thou desirest, & know
how to render due thankes vnto our
Lord, because that tyme is more fit
for mentall prayer, then to read vocall prayers, or to say beads. Wherfore before thou enter into the Meditation or confideration of any of
enfuing poynts, to illuminate thine
vnderstanding and stir vp thy deuotion, thou mayst first, euery tyme thou
shalt communicate, make briefly t is
compofition of place, with the petitions adioyning.

Z 2   THE

The composition of place.

MAKE account that thou art in the presence of Christ Iesus our Lord true God and Man, seeing with the eyes of consideration how he is really and truly enclosed in thy breast, as in a pix or reliquary, with innumerable Angells there on their knees adoring him.

The Petition.

BESEECH our Lord God to giue thee eyes to see the great good that is entred into thy house, as he gaue to S. Simeon hauing him in his armes, that thou mayst regard & esteeme him as the Sonne of whome he is. And to giue thee grace to bestow that small tyme profitably and fruitfully, as his diuine Maiesty requireth, and thou desirest.

THI

THE I. MEDITATION.

How Chriſt our Lord is a Phiſitian.

THE I. POINT.

TO conſider how that Chriſt our Lord came from heauen into this world, to be the Phiſitian of ſoules, and to cure the ſicke therin, ſeeking them out and offering them health, as he did with that ſicke bed-rid man in the Ghoſpell, whome our Lord himſelfe ſought out at the Piſcina, or Pond of Probatica to cure him.

Ponder the loue and charity of this great Phiſitian, & thy coldnes and negligence, in being thankefull for the good he deſireth to beſtow vpon thee: for wheras he would cure all thy infirmities and ſpirituall diſeaſes, thou like a fooliſh and frantike perſon, wilt not permit thy ſelfe to be cured, but wilt rather perſeuere in thy bad eſtate.

Gather hence a deſire to ſubiect thy ſelfe to the will and pleaſure of

Z 3   ſuch

such a Phisitian , seeing thou art and findest thy self sicke in al thy powers and senses, and in regard he is so excellent an one, that he healeth all of whatsoeuer infirmities: take him by the hand and guide him to al thy diseased parts , saying (as if he knew it not) good Lord , come and see this my memory, vnmindfull of thee, and of the fauours and benefits thou bestowest vpon it , cure it I beseech thee. Behold Lord these infirm eyes of mine, and louers to see that which is not lawful for them to desire, heale and cure them . Behold o Lord this murmuring, talkatiue and vnbridled tongue of mine. Behold o Lord this wretched man poore and miserable on euery side, and haue compassion of him: for if I could touch thee with fayth, thou wouldest heale me, sith as many as touched thee were made whole.

The 2. Point.

TO consider how that the sacred flesh and bloud of this most wise Phisitian ioyned to thyne is an vniuersall medicine to all thy euills ,

which

which is of such vertue, that with his
humility it cureth the swellings of
thy pride, with his sorrowes & pains,
thy vnreasonable pleasures and delightes, with his merits, thy diffiden-
ce and mistrusts, and thy soares ran-
cled and putrifyed by the inueterate
and continuall custome of sinning ,
with the sweet and fragrant balme of
his precious bloud .

Ponder the mercy and bounty
of this benigne Phisitian , which was
such and so great, that not content to
be only the Phisitian (as is manifest
by that which he sayd to the disciples
of S . Iohn , to wit : The blind see ,
the lame walke, the leapers are made
cleane, the deafe heare, the dead rise
againe &c.)he made himselfe also the
medicine, and giueth himselfe vnto
thee to be eaten, thereby perfectly to
cure thee of all thy infirmities .

Gather hence an earnest desire
to haue frequent accesse vnto this
heauenly Phisitian; and beseech him,
that although it be with the cost of
thy affections, honour , life and contentments , to heale and cure thee ,

Z 4   sith

sith thou perceiuest thy selfe to be ful of infirmityes of sinnes and inordinate passions, in regard that there is not any medicine able to cure thee, but only this soueraigne antidote.

THE 3. POINT.

TO consider the worth and price of this medicine, sith it cost this cælestiall Phisitian so many labours and paynes, yea euen his life, to leaue it thee so prepared, tempred and seasoned, that thou mightest take it with gust, sauour and profit in this diuine Sacrament.

Ponder, that the Phisitians of this world most commonly commaund some chicken, or foule to be killed, dressed & giuen to the sicke to eate: but this Phisitian of heauen was not content to ordayne & command alone, but would also, as his Prophet sayth, become sicke to cure thee, be wounded to heale thy soares, & dye vpon the Crosse, that thou mightest liue eternally in heauen.

From hence thou mayst gather a liuely & feruent desire to come neere vnto this heauenly Phisitian : for he
alone

alone can giue thee health and life, &
prostrating thyselfe at his feet say vnto him : Haue mercy on me o Lord ,
because I am weake . Heale me o
Lord, and I shalbe healed . For thou
knowest that from the sole of my
foot, vnto the top of my head, there
is not health in me . And be assured ,
that if thou come with desire of health
and with the fayth and confidence
wherewith the woman which was
troubled with an issue of bloud came
and touched him, thou shalt be freed
of thine infirmity as she was: for if
the garmēt of Christ had this vertue ,
Christ himselfe can do much more ,
whome thou hast within thee.

THE II. MEDITATION.

How Christ our Lord is Fire.

THE 1. POINT.

TO consider that Christ Iesus our
Lord , whome thou hast inclo-
sed in thy breast , is the fire of
diuine loue, whose property and excellency is to consume the humidities

Z 5   of

of vices, and to rayse the soule to heauenly desires, making her despise those that are terrestriall.

Ponder that the vertue & quality of this celestiall fire is, not only to inflame the harts, but to giue light also, and open the eyes of him who receaueth him worthily, as he did to those two discipls that went to Emaus for sitting at the table, in breaking the bread which he gaue them (which as some Holy Fathers say, was his holy body) their eyes were opened, and they knew their God and Lord, and inflamed & burning with this diuine fire which they had in their brests, they returned from Emaus far different & changed from that they were when they came thither, that is, ofdoubtful they became faythfull; of timerous, couragious; of ignorant, learned and well instructed.

Gather hence desires to come from the sacred Communion conuerted and transformed into another man (I meane) from proud to humble; from incontinent, to chast; from angry to patient; and from wicked

and

and sinnefull, to iust and holy : beseeching this Lord, seeing he is a consuming fire, to purify all thy imperfections, and to open and illuminate thyne eyes, that comming often vnto him, thou mayst know him, and know thy selfe, for heerin consisteth thy eternall felicity.

THE 2. POINT.

TO consider that the cause which moued Christ our Lord, to come from heauen to earth, was the desire he had to cast fire into the harts of men, and his will is, that it euer burne.

Ponder the propriety of this soueraigne fire, which is to purify whatsoeuer mettall is cast into it, conuerting it into it selfe, whether it be iron or stone, I meane whatsoeuer sinner, how wicked soeuer he hath beene, though cold as iron, and hard as a stone : for this soueraigne fire (which is God) hath such power & force, that he maketh his ministers a burning fire.

Gather from hence desires that this Lord vouchsafe to do the same to thee, and that, becau'e thou haſt come vnto Him and receaued him into thy breaſt, although thou be iron & ſtone, he will with his diuine heat kindle, melt and inflame thee in his loue, that tryed and tempered in this ouen and diuine fornace, thou mauſt become pure, and without any ruſt at al, of ſinnes and imperfections.

THE 3. POINT.

TO conſider the great deſire which the Apoſtles had of that fire of the Holy Ghoſt, and with what cryes & ſighes, prayers & groanings they craued him of God And after he deſcended vpon them, what manner of men became they? how different, how much changed? and how inflamed in the loue of God.

Ponder what may be the cauſe why, notwithſtanding this diuine fire hath deſcended from heauen and encloſed it ſelfe ſo often in thy breaſt, thou art not inflamed and ſet on fire, Salomon ſaying with admiration: Can a man hide fire in his boſome, that his garments burne not? Wherfore the cauſe of this euil muſt needs proceed

proceed from thy bad disposition &
negligent preparation : for if thou
shouldst dispose & prepare thy selfe,
as the Apostles did themselues, and
desire it as they did it would enligh-
ten and shine vnto thee much more
then it doth, and thou wouldest be
another manner of man then now
thou art.

Gather hence desires to begge
this benefit and diuine fire of God,
saying with his Prophet : Burne my
reines o Lord, and my hart, & leaue
in it some sparke of thy fire, some
token and signe that it hath beene in
my soule, sith thou hast vouchsafed
to come so often vnto her: for where
is fire, there euer remayneth some
heate and signe therof in the ashes.

THE III. MEDITATION.
That Christ our Lord is Food.

THE I. POINT.

TO consider that Christ our Lord
is food of the soule, as he sayd
himselfe; My flesh is meate indeed,

deed, and my bloud is drinke indeed.

Ponder firſt the wonderfull prouidence of this Lord, ſith he had ſuch particuler care, in regard of thy neceſſity and weaknes, to prouide thee this corporall and ſpirituall food of bread and wine, that thy ſpirit might not faint in the way, nor periſh with famine, as the prodigall Sonne did.

Ponder ſecondly, that if the bread which the Prophet Elias did eate had ſuch vertue, that he walked in the ſtrength of that meate fourty dayes and fourty nights through the deſert vnto the mount of God : how much better & greater is the power and ſtrength of this Myſticall bread (whereof that was only a repreſentation) to nouriſh thee in the deſert of this life, till thou arriue at the holy mount of euerlaſting bliſſe, this being the bread that comforteth and conſirmeth the hart of man.

Gather hence a firme purpoſe and reſolution (in regard of the neceſſity thou haſt to nouriſh thy ſelfe and to liue) to come often vnto this
ſoueraigne

foueraigne table to eate this facred
bread, for in it is côtayned thy health
and life, and without it (as Chrift
himfelf fayd) thou fhalt not haue life
in thee.

THE 2. POINT.

TO confider the great louethat God
our Lord hath vnto men, fith he
as one enamoured and poffeffed with
their loue, would that they fhould
eate him facramentally, that he might
eate them fpiritually.

Ponder the great liberality of
this Lord, in inuiting al, though feeble
blind or lame, not reiecting any, be
he rich or poore, great or litile, com-
pelling al to come and fit at his table,
fo that they be not guilty of mortall
finne.

Gather hence a firme purpofe
from this day forward to come vnto
this royall table, feeing God inuiteth
thee to eat him: neither let him be in-
forced to compell thee, & bring thee
in by violence and force: for although thou haft offended him fo often and beene lame of both feet, that
is, of ynderftanding and will, he will
thus

thus much honour thee, that tasting
& seeing how sweet our Lord is, who
giueth himselfe vnto thee in this
meate, thou maist loose thy selfe &
find him, & renounce al things thou
dost pleasingly possesse for this soueraigne foode, wherein is contayned all the good of heauen & earth.

THE 3. POINT.

TO consider the great vertue and
power this diuine food cōtaineth
in it, which is such, that eaten it cha-
geth and conuerteth man into God
by participation: how different an
effect from that which the eating of
that forbidden tree, wrought in the
first man, sith he perswaded himselfe
that eating the fruit therof, he should
be like vnto God, which he did not
only not obtaine, but became also
lesse then man, and made himselfe
like vnto a beast.

Ponder the worth & excellen-
cy of this diuine food, which in such
sort changeth and transformeth him
that receaueth it in state of grace,
that it maketh him like vnto Christ,
as himselfe sayd: He that eateth my
fleth,

flesh, abideth in me, and I in him.

From hence thou mayst gather a great feare of reprobation, that eating so often this soueraigne food, & fed like an infant with the milke of the delights and daintines thereof, thou hast notwithstanding such a languishing appetite, & reapest therby so little fruit and profit, as if thou receauedst him not, persisting in thy wicked life and bad customes.

THE IIII. *MEDITATION.*

That Christ our Lord is most rich.

THE I. POINT.

TO consider that our Lord **God** whome thou hast in thy breast, is most rich and most mighty: In whome (as S. Paul sayth) be all the treasures of wisdome and knowledge hidden, and there thou shalt find them, if with humility & without curiosity thou shalt seeke them, vnder those sacramentall formes of bread and wine.

Ponder that if the goods, which
are

are contayned in this sacred host, that thou hast receaued, be so great and soueraigne (as in very deed they are) why dost thou not rid thy selfe of all the other goods thou hast (which are not such) to possesse and enioy these, as the Apostles did, and Christ himselfe did the same for thy loue, spending liberally all he had for the benefit of harlots and sinners, instructing some, curing others, and shedding his precious bloud for all, and giuing to thee his Blessed flesh to eat that thy spirit might liue.

Gather hence desires to giue thy selfe entierly to him, who gaue himselfe so entierly for thee, and beseech him that seeing he is so rich and thou so poore, and bestoweth his riches so bountifully on such as are so vnworthy therof as thou art, he will vouchsafe to releeue thee, and that, sith he commandeth the rich to fauour the poore, his diuine maiesty being so rich, he will not leaue thy soule deuoyd of his goods, but that he vouchsafe to furnish and enrich her therewith, enduing thee with the graces,

vertues

vertues and gifts of the Holy Ghost,
which thou wantest, and hast need
of.

THE 2. POINT.

TO consider that wheras our Lord
God was rich, he made himselfe
poore (as S. Paul sayth) that by his
pouerty we might be rich.

Ponder how much God loueth
pouerty, being himselfe the chiefest
riches, sith he calleth Blessed the
poore in spirit, promising vnto such
the kingdome of heauen.

Gather hence desires to be
poore in spirit in this world, that thou
mayst be rich in heauen, saying with
the Prophet: Looke vpon me o Lord
and haue mercy on me, because I am
needy and poore. For what King or
Prince is there in the world, that lodging in the house of a poore man,
bringeth not with him his royall furniture for his owne chamber, and at
his departure bestoweth not on him
great graces and fauours. Wherfore
o Lord, seeing thou being the chei-
fest riches hast vouchsafed to lodge
in my poore cottage, adorne it with
                                    the

the hangings of grace and vertue,
which are the furniture of thy royall
house and pallace, doing some fauour to the maister of the place where
thou art entertained.

THE 3. POINT.

TO consider the graces and benefits
which our Lord God did bestow
on Obededom and all his, for hauing
receaued into his house the Arke of
the Testament, which was only a sha-
dow and figure of this most holy
Sacrament, but more and greater benefits are receaued wheresoeuer this
diuine Arke and coffer of the treasure
of God entreth, which is his most sacred body pierced and opened in so
many places discouering his riches.

Ponder how this our Lord,
entring corporally into the house of
S. Peters wiues mother, deliuered her
from her feuer : entring into the
house of the Arch-synagogue, he reuiued his daughter ; In the Pharisees
house he pardoned S. Mary Magdalen her sinnes : finally entring into
S. Elizabeths house he sanctifyed the
infant S. Iohn, and replenished his
Mother

Mother with the holy Ghoſt : for
wh re God entreth, he worketh great
wonders and miracles. Beſeech him,
that ſeeing his diuine maieſty vouch-
ſafeth to enter into thy poore houſe,
and to be lodged therein, and is ſo
rich in mercy , he would make thee
partaker thereof, pardoning thy ſirs
and reſtoring thee to a new life of
grace, to make thee a worthy habitation of his.

THE V. MEDITATION.

That Chriſt our Lord is a good Paſtour.

THE 1. POINT.

TO conſider that Chriſt Ieſus our
Lord to make himſelfe known
to be a good Paſtour, would not
only put on the groſſe ſkin of our humanity, that his ſheep (which are his
elect) might know, follow and loue
him, & not fly from nim ; but would
alſo feed and maintaine them with his
owne moſt precious bloud : Being
parched with heat, & cold with froſt,
ſleeping on the ground, faſting day
and

and night, finally like a good sheepheard being slaine, leaning vnto a tree
to deliuer his sheep from the infernall wolfe.

Ponder the good offices which
this excellent shepheard hath done
for thee an vnprofitable sheep, feeding thee, curing thee, & seeking thee
with the griefe of his hart, teares of
his eyes, and the sweat of his browes,
vndergoing so many afflictions and
toyles to reduce and bring thee back
to the fould vpon his shoulders: and
thou like a lost & vngratfull sheep,
hast strayed and cast thy selfe so often
from him to betake thy selfe to lewd
pastures, which did poison and kill
thy soule.

Gather hence inflamed & effectuall desires to follow the steps of
thy shepheard, walking where he
walketh, and be assured that if thou
permit thy selfe to be ruled and go-
uerned by him, nothing shallbe wanting to thee.

THE

THE 2. POINT.

TO consider how often, in presence of this soueraigne shepheard without feare or shame thou hast grazed and fed in the greene meadowes and forbidden pastures of thy intemperances, not fearing the perill & danger of falling into the gripes & teeth of the infernall wolues which be the Diuells, from whence this good shepheard hath so often deliuered thee that wert their prey.

Ponder how vngratefull thou hast beene to this great and Maister shepheard Christ Iesus, for the fauours and benefits he hath bestowed on thee, in giuing his life for thee, sith not content to be an vnprofitable and erring sheep of his fold, thou art also become a rauenous wolfe, persecuting him with thy sinnes.

From hence thou mayst gather desires to bewayle and lament them, and to call vpon thy Pastour with mournful bleating, that he may seek and find thee, saying as a wandring and lost sheep, vnto him : My Pastour, I knew well to stray & loose

my

my selfe, but how to reclaime and recouer my selfe againe I know not. Seek me O Lord, and fetch me out of the briary bushes of my sinnes, into the fertile pastures of thy fauour and grace.

The 1. Point.

TO consider that this good Pastour sayth : I know my sheep, & they know me, and I loue them so well, that I haue not doubted to giue my life for them . And if this seem much how great an argument of loue may it be to haue offered and giuen himselfe for those wolues which haue mangled and slaine him .

Ponder first how much it importeth thee to treate often with thy Pastour, that thou mayst know him, and vnderstand his pleasure , desire and will , for this is it which he most expecteth of thee .

Secondly how much it auayleth thee to know thy selfe, that if thou haue any thing not beseeming the sheep of such a Pastour, thou correct and amend it, least he expell thee out of his flocke, which were the greatest
disaster

difafter that could befall thee.

Gather hence defires to be the fheep of this fheepheard, giuing him all thou haft, without referuation of any thing to thy felfe, that is, thy foule and body with thy fenes, thy hart, thoughts, meanes, honours, life and contentment, fith he gaue all thefe firft for thee: and now to feale vp the whole he giueth himfelfe to thee as food to eate. And if he haue loued thee fo much, and beftowed fuch fauours on thee being his enemy, what will he giue thee, or what will he deny thee being his friend, & a good and profitable fheep, in regard thou art marked and fealed with his precious bloud.

THE VI. MEDITATION.
That Chrift our Lord is a Spoufe.

THE I. POINT.

TO confider that our Lord is the Spoufe of thy foule, in whom in moft perfect manner is found all that which can be defi-

A a   red

red in a good Spoufe . Beauty, as God and as man, for he was goodly of beauty aboue all the fons of men. Nobility of birth, as well of his Fathers, as of his Mothers fide . Difcretion moft perfeft , for he is wifedome it felfe . Infinite riches, for he is heire of all that God hath in heauen and in earth ; finally he is very louing and of a fweet and peaceable condition .

Ponder that this Spoufe knoweth right well how to honour, adorne and beautify , with his graces and vertues, the foule that is to be his Efpoufe, obferuing towards her the cerimonies of true loue , and taking pleafure to fee and difcourfe with her dayly , and to cherifh her with this precious and foueraigne food of his facred body and bloud , which fhe reteaueth in the moft holy Sacrament that by thefe pledges and tokens of loue, fhe may know that he defireth to be her Maifter and Spoufe alone.

Gather hence defires wholy to yield thy felfe from this day forward as an efpoufe to fuch & fo worthy a
Spoufe,

Spoufe, and for no affliction or tribulation whatfoeuer to abandone his
friendfhip and fweet conuerfation :
and keeping the word thou haft giuen him, befeech him to communicate vnto thee fome of the manifold
graces and vertues which he hath in
himfelfe, that thou mayft be able to
correfpond with loue to that great
loue he beareth ynto thee.

The 2. Point.

TO confider how that Chrift our
Lord only out of his meere goodnes hath fet his affection on thy foule
deformed and poore, thou hauing
beene difloyall and broken thy faith
to him, not once, but an hundred
times: yet the loue neuertheles which
he beareth thee is fuch, that he doth
folicite and intreate thee to open him
the dore of thy foule and hart : for
his defire is to be vnited with thee.

Ponder thy indignity, folly &
want of loue, how vnwife and how
much ouerfeene thou haft beene in
not aknowledging this diuine Spoufe
and as an adulterefse haft been difloyall vnto him, hauing fo often caft try
eyes

eyes and affection on bafe & deformed flaues Yet the boûty of this our
Lord is fuch, that albeit thou defer-
ueſt a thouſand hells, he pardoneth
thee , inuiteth and intreateth thee to
returne as a fugitiue to his houſe , &
falling on thy necke, as on the prodigall ſonne, receaueth louingly, enter-
tayneth, and cheriſheth thee, honouring thee with the garment of his graces and vertues.

Gather from hence deſires to
erter into his houſe, purpoſing rather
to dy a thouſand deaths then to for-
ſake ſuch a Lord, ſuch a Father, and
ſuch a Spouſe. Beſeech him to giue
thee his grace hence forward to keep
thy promiſed fidelity vnto him, com-
mending thy ſoule and al the powers
thereof vnto him, that thou mayſt
be no more thyne, but his, who hath
taken thee for Eſpouſe, ſaying with
her : I haue found him whome my
ſoule loueth : I hold him, neither wil
I let him go.

THE 3. POINT.

TO conſider how great the dignity and honour hath been in which
thy

thy Spouse hath placed thee, sith not
regarding what thou deseruest, nor
thy slender fidelity, he graciously giueth thee his hand & ring of his hart,
that henceforward thou mayst account, receaue & enioy him as thyne
with pledges of so great loue.

    Ponder how great reckoning
thou art to make of thy soule, sith
God esteemeth so much therof, that
he giueth himselfe, and all things els,
to espouse himself with her, notwithstanding her deformity and misery.
And such is his loue and mercy that
he hath full often set his affection and
beene enamoured with foule slaues,
to make the̅ his beautifull daughters
which he hath bought, not with delight and pleasure, but with sorrows
and torments, which is the coine of
the Crosse.

    From hence thou mayst gather
desires to offer vp thy hart and will
to such a Lord, so to be no longer
thyne own, but his who hath bought
thee with his precious bloud, and
taken thee for his espouse. Beseech
him to graunt thee his grace, that

         A a 3   thou

thou mayſt obſerue fidelity and loy-
alty towards him , and that ſeeing
hitherto thou haſt been barren , thou
mayſt from hence forward begin
with his grace to yield fruit of
benediction with holy de-
ſires, words, and deeds.

FINIS.

THE TABLE.

A a 4   The

THE TABLE.

The

THE TABLE.

A a 5

The

THE THIRD BOOKE.

THE TABLE.

Meditations before Communion.

Meditations after Communion.

FINIS.